THE HOME VIDEO HANDBOOK

Second Edition

Charles Bensinger

$8.95

The Home Video Handbook

Second Edition

Revised

by Charles Bensinger

Illustrated by
David McCutchen
and
Susan Salladé

Published by
Video-Info Publications
Santa Barbara, California
1980

Acknowledgements

Written by Charles Bensinger

Copyright© 1979 by Charles Bensinger

Illustrated by David McCutchen and Susan Sallade

Editorial Assistance by Louise Walker and Marc Plitt

Cover by Frederick Bennett Green

Video equipment photographs and associated graphic material courtesy of: Advent Corp., A-Vidd Electronics, Akai America, Comprehensive Video Supply Corp., GBC Closed Circuit Corp., GTE Sylvania, Hitachi, JVC Industries, Kloss Video Corp., Magnavox Video Systems., Nortronics Co., Panasonic Video Systems, Quasar Electronics, RCA Corp., Sanyo Electric Inc., Sears Roebuck and Co., Sony Corp., Toshiba America Inc., Zenith Corp.

Published by:

 publicatiɔns

P.O. Box 1507
Santa Barbara, CA 93102

Printed in the USA

First Printing-June 1978
Second Edition-September 1979
Third Printing-August 1980

LC# 79-54868
ISBN 0-931294-02-9

Foreword

The history of video has always been explosive and marked by rapid technological innovation. Previously, do-it-yourself video enthusiasts had to be either broadcast, educational or industrial users. But now, as the home consumer embraces this exciting technology, dramatic new possibilities exist.

Not only does the home video recorder provide an easy and economical way to record instantly and play back events in and around the home, but it provides a golden opportunity for budding artists, actors, actresses, writers, and producers of all ages to express themselves creatively and communicate their visions and thoughts to anyone willing to listen.

Television has become the Electronic Mother of countless minds — the relentless purveyor of media morality and Hollywood world view. But suddenly, the home video recorder makes many new options available. The television child can now make his or her own personal videotapes or buy, rent or lease a continually expanding range of programming that will bring subject matter of great diversity into the home.

As the television medium now passes into the hands of the people, it becomes a matter of how to use these marvelous new tools successfully. *The Home Video Handbook* is ready to act as your trusty guide on your own personal video adventure.

Table of Contents

How to Read This Book

In order to make this book as easily understood as possible, I have employed several methods of word emphasis. All significant words and terms that refer to video are capitalized when first introduced. For easy reference, a complete listing and definition of these terms can also be found in the Glossary at the end of the book.

Words that are used as labels of functions or input and output connectors on video recorders are always capitalized exactly as they appear on the machine or in the operator's manuals. These words are often partly capitalized as in MICrophone, MIC being the label as it appears on the video recorder.

Italicized words are designed for emphasis of important thoughts, easily overlooked items or for precautionary purposes.

Some word usage in the text may sound grammatically unusual, but certain words and phrases have particular expressions according to video and film nomenclature.

It is probably helpful also to mention the use of the abbreviations VTR and VCR. VTR is generally considered an all inclusive abbreviation for videotape recorder, whereas VCR refers to a more limited category of VTR and specifically to videocassette recorder.

But, since home video recorders are exclusively videocassette recorders, the popular label for them has become VCR, so VCR is the term we will use to refer to all home video recorders.

Without further discussion, we will then proceed on with our journey into video.

1 The Home Video Revolution

The Sun is the cosmic power source for all light and life on this planet. Without light, life could not exist as we know it. Light is the bearer of the images which our eyes perceive, and these images in turn form the visions of our environment.

Through skillful use of tools, early man learned to craft his personal visions of life into forms of his own choosing on stone, clay, wood, fabric, paper and metal. Technological man soon found a way to create images with chemicals, thus magically preserving lifelike forms in black and white and finally in color.

But a far greater image-making discovery waited in the wings that would inexorably and totally alter the thinking pattern, life styles and values of whole future civilizations. A way would be found to harness light itself in the form of electromagnetic energy in such a manner as to actually form a moving life-like color image inside a glass tube! And sound would even accompany it!

This visual and sound image could be transmitted at the speed of light around the world through a chain of artificial satellites in outer space and received in homes anywhere on the planet.

These electronic images of life know no distance nor time in human terms. They fly from source to display instantly. The manipulation of images in time and space affords civilization a mind-boggling potential to communicate on a world wide scale of almost unbelievable magnitude. Here is a tool that if used to its fullest potential could help to reshape the minds and societies of the planet in tremendously positive and evolutionary ways. However, the realization of this potential depends entirely on the imagination and awareness of the people who use this fantastic technology.

> *"Television can teach. It can illuminate.*
> *It can even inspire, but only to the extent*
> *that we are determined to use it. Otherwise*
> *it is merely wires and lights in a box."*

> *Edward R. Murrow 1908-1965*

On The Home Front

Until recently, most people had no control over the electronic images that flowed into their world and minds via the home TV set. Television was a one-way street — programming and time factors were predetermined by the central programmers called TV NETWORKS. What was right for ABC, NBC and CBS was right for America — or so they thought.

Then in 1977, it became possible for anyone with $1,000 to acquire a machine capable of capturing those electronic images permanently, manipulating them, editing them, and recording fresh images at will without regard to predetermined space and time limitations. It became possible to accomplish a "time shift"; images could be recorded at one time and played back instantly or at a later time, with no waiting for processing or matching of sound and picture.   This phenomenon of do-it-yourself television has become known as VIDEO.

In 1978, video was thrust permanently into the minds of the people, and it became a household word in the far corners of America. "The Great Home Video Revolution" had begun, this time for real. But, this was no ordinary revolution. Pulses raced as video cassettes were loaded into video machines, and hearts fluttered as the *Superbowl* or *Charlie's Angels* came into focus on 6-foot wide color video projector screens. A multitude of video games soon began to monopolize untold hours of consciousness as Klingon fighters and Empire death ships dueled daily with the defending forces on the electronic screens of plenty.

Indeed, plenty are the possibilities afforded by the seemingly in-exhaustible stream of new, exotic technology being created to expand the electronic imaging possibilities of the TV set. And just how we use these marvelous new tools to accomplish successful and enjoyable recording and creation of individual programming is what *The Home Video Handbook* is all about.

The Origins Of Video

The term VIDEO has several meanings. Technically, it refers to the picture portion of television and to TV equipment in general. But, it also has a sociological meaning which refers to the phenomenon of do-it-yourself television as a *decentralization of media*. In this context, the term video is used to describe a body ot people, with certain media philosophies and equipment who are engaged in a form of personal, electronic visual/sound expression and communication.

Video recording has been around since 1956 and is continually being improved. The big TV networks use very expensive VIDEOTAPE RECORDERS (VTRs) costing hundreds of thousands of dollars *each*. These big expensive VTRs have been around in various stages of evolution for nearly two decades. Most programming seen on TV originates from these very large and complex machines.

Then in 1967, Sony Corporation of Japan introduced the first portable, low-cost black and white (B&W) videotape recorder and camera to the U.S. Once Sony had placed do-it-yourself TV into the hands of the American natives, there was no halting the inevitable. The idea of personal TV struck deep responsive chords within many an emerging video visionary. The concept of a decentralization of media finally seemed to have become a reality.

Gradually, these small, low-cost and rather primitive video systems began to find more and more uses in schools, Cable TV stations, businesses, hospitals and homes. Over the first 10 years, the variety of video equipment became considerable. The technology itself evolved from heavy, hard to use, b&w recording systems to sophisticated color recording and editing devices that could produce excellent reproductions of all the sights and sounds of real life at a relatively low price.

Evolution Of The VTR

Originally all video machines were the REEL-TO-REEL or OPEN REEL type like early videotape recorders. Two reels are used and the tape must be manually threaded through the machine and onto the empty take-up reel. This process often created problems for many persons who are not mechanically inclined. Then in 1972, Sony introduced the first VIDEOCASSETTE RECORDER (VCR) which was called the U-Matic. The videocassette recorder made operation of a video machine really simple and practical.

Unfortunately, these first videocassette machines were too heavy and too costly for practical home use. A single 1-hour blank tape costs as much as $35. Other manufacturers such as CBS and AVCO tried to market home videocassette machines, but all these early efforts were doomed to failure because of a variety of factors: the technology was not sufficiently developed, tape costs were too high, recording times were limited to 1 hour, the machines were too expensive, and the consumer was not yet ready to make the jump to video.

However, in 1976, Sony Corp., by now the acknowledged "Godfather of Video", decided to make the big home video commitment, and the "dawn of the age" of home video opened with the introduction of the Sony Betamax 1-hour video recording system. Sensing that the doors to home video had, indeed, been thrust aside and that this was not just another false start, other Japanese manufacturers scrambled to ready their own videocassette machines for the consumer market.

The competition between Japanese videocassette manufacturers tends to produce a leapfrog phenomenon as new technology is constantly being introduced by rival manufacturers which is slightly more refined and sophisticated than the previously introduced technology. Thus, the first Sony Betamax 1-hour home VCRs were soon rendered somewhat obsolete in months by the introduction of 2-hour home units such as Motorola's Quasar VX-2000 VCR and JVC's Vidstar VHS (Video Home System) video recorder. Sony's original console model and deck-type systems suddenly became much less desirable to the home user because they were limited to a recording time of only 1-hour in a world of 90 minute to 2-hour programs.

How Video Works

Video is a magnetic and electronic process instead of a chemical process like film. Video is a sophisticated extension of the audiotape recording process and physically bears nothing in common with film, which requires complex, time consuming chemical changes.

Both the video picture and the sound are recorded on a single moving piece of reusable magnetic tape which can be erased and re-recorded like audiotape. To play back a videotape, a videotape machine is required. And of course, a TV set is needed to view the pictures and hear the sound. Once the tape is inserted in the videotape machine and the TV set is connected, the TV set will display the picture and sound from the video machine with comparable quality to a normal TV broadcast TV program.

Most video recorders are able to record TV programs "off-the-air" merely by tuning in a TV station, setting the proper controls and inserting a blank videotape in the VCR.

Do-it-yourself home videotapes can also be created by connecting an optional video camera to the video recorder. A blank tape is inserted into the VCR, the machine is placed in the RECORD MODE and the camera turned on. In this way, a recording can be made immediately. Usually a microphone is attached or built into the camera which records the sound and transfers it to the video recorder.

Once the recording has been finished, the tape can be played back immediately just like an audiotape. No processing is required. If you aren't satisfied with the results, re-record over the tape until you are satisfied. No tape need be wasted by a poor acting performance or technical problems.

Compatibility of Videocassette Recorders

Historically, videotape recorders have multiplied like rabbits, but little or no attention has ever been paid to making them interchangeable or compatible so a tape made on one manufacturer's machine can be played back on another manufacturer's machine. Needless-to-say, this policy has created untold havoc and frustration among many video users over the years. Unfortunately, the home user must also deal with this very serious problem.

Since the advent of the first VCR in 1972, manufacturers have unleashed no fewer than 7 incompatible VCRs originally intended for the home. Each particular type of VCR, or FORMAT, requires its own special videocassette. In other words, a videocassette made on one format VCR could not be played back on another format VCR. So, the particular format of a VCR is something you should consider carefully before buying.

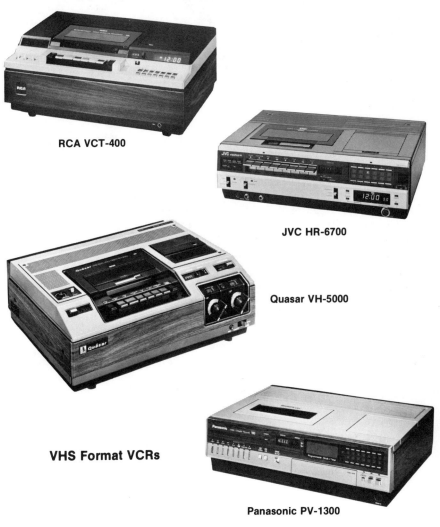

RCA VCT-400

JVC HR-6700

Quasar VH-5000

VHS Format VCRs

Panasonic PV-1300

15

**Sony SL-8600
"Betamax"**

Sony SL-5800

**Sears
BetaVision**

Beta Format VCRs

Toshiba V-8000

By early 1978, the first round of incompatible home videocassette formats had pretty much run its course. The original U-MATIC videocassette, pioneered by Sony, eventually became a master production format for educational, industrial, and broadcast users. Other less sophisticated formats such as the AVCO Cartrivision rode off into the sunset never to be seen again. Emotions still run strong for those who bought the first 1-hour Sony Betamax systems at $1,200 or $2,200 only to find a 2-hour version selling for $895 a year later.

A Primer On Videotape Compatibility

As we discussed, video manufacturers seem to enjoy producing multitudes of videotape recorders that are different enough so that tapes made on one manufacturer's machine cannot be played back on another's machine. This lack of inter-changeability or INCOMPATIBILITY is due to 2 factors:

1. Videotape recorders are designed to use one particular *size* tape. There are 5 different size tapes which are measured in inches of width: 2-inch, 1-inch, 3/4 inch, 1/2-inch and 1/4-inch. For example, a videotape recorder designed to use 2-inch tape definitely cannot use 3/4-inch tape or any other size tape.

2. Even *within* a particular size tape format, there are in-compatible VCRs because different machines may use different mechanical methods of recording on the videotape. Thus, a tape made on one type of 1/2-inch Panasonic VCR may not be able to be played back on certain kinds of 1/2-inch Sony VCRs.

Yet, VCR incompatibility is not as bad as it sounds because all videotape recorders are at least *electronically* compatible. That is, any tape may be electronically TRANSFERRED or copied from one VCR format to another merely by connecting the two incompatible videotape recorders together by means of cables and then re-recording the tape on the second machine. This is the same method used for copying an audiotape. Of course, there will be some quality loss between the original and the copy, but often it is negligible.

Different Reel-to-Reel and Videocassette Formats

In addition to the different tape widths, there exists a difference in tape packaging. As with audiotape, all the super professional VTRs and all the early, low-cost, smaller VTRs used two separate reels of tape which required threading through the machine. Later, the self-contained videocassette was developed and now all home-type and most newer industrial/educational video machines are videocassette-type units.

The 2-inch and 1-inch formats are primarily used by broadcast, institutional, educational and industrial people, and the home user would probably not become involved with these machines. The various videocassette formats that may be of interest to the home video user are as follows:

1. *The 3/4-inch U-MATIC Format.* Developed and introduced by Sony in 1972, the U-MATIC is the only completely standardized videocassette format. All 3/4-inch U-MATIC machines made by any manufacturer are all compatible with each other. A wide variety of U-Matic VCRs are available—from simple player-only units to extremely sophisticated high quality editing machines. Battery-powered portables are also available. Generally, the 3/4-inch format VCRs are considered unnecessarily sophisticated and too expensive for the home video user. Tape costs are prohibitively high—$35 or more for 1 hour of tape. However, 3/4-inch VCRs make excellent machines for editing and duplication. Some home video users may soon have need to rent or lease these machines for these purposes.

2. *The 1/2-inch Sanyo V-Cord II Format.* Around 1977, Sanyo introduced a series of videocassette home recorders called the V-Cord II. These systems featured the first switchable 1-hour standard play ("SP") and 2-hour Long Play ("LP") mode. But this format was not compatible with any other 1/2-inch videocassette machine, and the high cost of blank tapes and machines caused it to become an "industrial product line."

3. *1/2-inch BETAMAX/BETA Format.* In 1977 Sony introduced amidst considerable fanfare, the first really practical home video system called the BETAMAX. Originally designed as a 1-hour recording format, it has since evolved into a series of three different *incompatible* formats: Beta I or X1 for 1 hour, Beta II or

X2 for 2 hours, and Beta III or X3 for 3 hours. The same videotape cassette is used for all three formats. The increase in recording time is gained by slowing the recording speed; by half for the 2-hour X2 format, and down to one third of the original speed in the 3-hour X3 format.

The original single-speed 1-hour X1 Betamax format is now obsolete for home users but is the standard format used for all Sony Betamax industrial VCRs. Several sophisticated 1-hour X1 1/2-inch VCRs are currently available, and the picture quality of these machines is tops in its class. (*See Chapter 11, Industrial VCRs.*)

The 2-hour X2 Beta format was created by Sony in response to the introduction of the 2-hour recording formats of competing manufacturers like Panasonic, JVC and others. Some of the earlier model Beta VCRs are 2-speed and can be switched to record and play on both the X1 (1-hour) and X2 (2-hour) formats. Most, though, record and play in the X2 mode only. Most late model Beta VCRs have also eliminated the X1 format and instead feature X2 and X3 speed capability. The Sony SL-3000 portable VCR records in the X2 mode and plays back both X1 and X2 mode tapes. The three-speed Sony SL-5400 and SL-5600 VCRs can record in both X2 and X3 modes and can play back tapes made in all three Beta modes (X1, X2, X3). Distributers of Beta VCRs include Sony, Sanyo, Sears, Toshiba and Zenith.

Further increases in record and play time can be gained from EXTENDED LENGTH TAPES. Because these tapes are thinner, longer tapes can be packed into the standard Beta format videotape cassette. Using an X3 format, you can get 4 1/2 hours of recording time from an L-750 tape and as long as 5 hours using the Beta L-830 tape.

4. *The 1/2-inch VHS Format.* The Japanese Victor Corporation (JVC) pioneered and developed the *Video Home System* (VHS) format which is now used by fifteen manufacturers and marketers: Akai, Hitachi, JVC, Magnavox, Curtis Mathes, MGA, Montgomery Ward, Panasonic, J.C. Penney, Pioneer, Quasar, RCA, Sharp and Sylvania. The VHS format also has three speeds: the Standard Play (SP) 2-hour mode, the Long Play (LP) 4-hour mode and the Super Long Play (SLP) 6-hour mode. As with the Beta machines, the longer recording time is usually obtained by slowing the recorder speed.

There is only slightly less confusion with VHS VCRs than with all the various models of Beta VCRs. VHS was first introduced with JVC's 2-hour VCR. That was topped shortly thereafter by the other VHS equipment manufacturers with dual-speed 2 and 4-hour mode VCRs.

As if 4 hours wasn't enough, the 6-hour mode was introduced in 1979 by VHS manufacturers, followed by a proliferation of new VCRs. Some, like JVC and Sharp, featured a dual-speed 2-hour/6-hour capability, but other VHS manufacturers such as Panasonic offer all three speeds: 2, 4, and 6-hour modes. With Extended Length tapes, the 6-hour mode can be extended to record up to 9 hours on a single tape. Besides speed differences, there are internal design differences between Beta and VHS machines. We will discuss these later.

5. *Other 1/2-inch Formats.* A series of minor non-competitive special purpose formats exist; some for good purpose such as slow motion, and others, it seems, merely to confuse the buyer or placate the ego of the manufacturer.

Longer Is Better?

It really is as confusing as it seems, but a short history of Beta versus VHS might clarify things. When Sony first introduced its Betamax home system it never occurred to them that Americans would desire anything longer than 1-hour recording time. After all, educational and industrial video users were perfectly satisfied, even with 30-minute VCRs, so Sony's engineers reasoned that 60 minutes was more than enough time for anyone. Herein rests the great miscalculation that may haunt Sony as long as the 1/2-inch VCR home market continues. Unfortunately, the Beta cassette was made too small to allow for significantly increased recording times without reducing the speed of the VCR or resorting to thinner and thus weaker Extended Play tapes. A speed reduction usually results in some loss of picture quality. On the other hand, the smaller Beta cassette, being more compact, is more convenient to use and mail.

VHS manufacturers designed a slightly larger cassette with more tape in it and therefore will always have an advantage over Beta in terms of running times with the same size cassette. Because of this, VHS machines stole a large share of the home video market away from Beta right from the start.

At first, Beta reluctantly fought back with the reduced speed X2 2-hour VCR and added an Extended Length L-750 cassette to squeeze 3 hours out of the X2 mode VCR, but still fell short of the 4-hour range of VHS. The later model X2 mode Beta VCRs did not have an X1 mode capability thereby effectively isolating the 1-hour Beta format and forcing it into oblivion for home users. Thus the X1 1-hour Beta industrial VCRs became a format with limited home VCR interchangeability, as only the Sony SL-3000, SL-5400, SL-5600 and SL-5800 VCRs will play back X1 mode tapes. A partial solution to this probelm was the creation of a cassette changer (AG-200) that will fit early model 1-hour VCRs such as the Sony SL-7200, SL-8200 and SL-8600. The changer allows a second tape to be fed into the machine automatically, thereby increasing the recoding time of 1-hour VCRs to 2 hours with a second L-500 tape. Of course two 1-hour tapes are a very expensive way to record 2 hours of programmed material.

By 1979 it became clear that the VCR horsepower wars were not going to subside. Sony bit the bullet and went for yet another speed reduction. Surely 3.3 hours on an X2 Beta VCR using L-830 tape and 5 hours in the X3 mode would satisfy the most voracious long-playing video fanatic. But no, the VHS forces had already introduced the 6-hour VCR *without* using Extended Play tapes. With Extended Play tapes, a 6-hour VCR could go for an astounding 9 hours on one tape! Sony responded with the introduction of several automatic videocassette changers, the AG-200 and the AG-300 which allow up to 20 hours of continuous recording. (*See Chapter 3, How To Operate Your VCR-Accessories.*)

The Light At The End Of The Tunnel

Although it sounds confusing, all these speeds really break down to two basic formats: the Beta X2 mode VCR and the VHS SP mode VCR. Fortunately, all Beta VCRs that use the X3 mode also have the X2 mode. Only the earlier X1 modes are somewhat isolated. This means that if you record in the X2 mode, the chances are good that the vast majority of Beta VCR owners will be able to play back your tape. Most pre-recorded Beta video cassette programs are made and will continue to be made in the X2 mode. If you record in the X3 mode, only Beta X3 machines can play back your tapes, and you might possibly have problems, as interchangeability becomes marginal beyond the X2 mode. So why the X3 mode? Read on.

Much to the credit of VHS manufacturers, *all* VHS machines have the 2-hour or SP mode, regardless of type or make, and all VHS pre-recorded tapes are made in the 2-hour SP mode. As with Beta, quality and interchangeability drops off somewhat in the 4-hour mode and gets even worse in the 6-hour mode. Since the Beta X2 and the VHS SP modes insure very good picture quality and a high degree of interchangeability, why even bother about the Beta X3 or VHS LP and SLP modes? Read on.

The value of 3, 4, or 6-hour recording and playing times lies in two factors — tape economics and recording for multi-event programmable VCRs.

Tape Economics Chart					
	Cassette Type	Cost	Mode	Time	Cost per Hour
BETA	L-500	$12-$15	X1	1-hr	$12-$15
			X2	2-hr	$ 6-$7.50
			X3	3-hr	$ 4-$5
VHS	T-120	$18-$22	SP	2-hr	$ 9-$11
			LP	4-hr	$ 4.50-$5.50
			SLP	6-hr	$ 3-$3.60

It's obvious how rapidly the cost per/hour drops for tape in the longer play modes. Extended Play tapes will also have the effect of reducing the per/hour tape cost. Of course, the trade-off for the slower speed and lower cost is a slight sacrifice in picture quality and interchangeability. The picture quality differences are subjective to some extent and will vary with the type of tape and VCR used.

Every manufacturer offers PROGRAMMABLE VCRs which can be preset a week or so in advance to turn on and off automatically and record as many as seven "events" or different programs of varying lengths on different channels. Naturally, if you want to record a 1-hour program every night for six nights you would need a 6-hour mode and a 6-hour tape. However, for the best quality recording and maximum interchangeability the 2-hour SP mode is still the most practical. So, for picture quality freaks the 2-hour SP or X2 mode VCRs are quite adequate although tape costs per/hour will be higher.

New Formats

Certainly there is already a wide range of 1/2-inch VCRs. However, there are several other completely different record and play formats that will be on the market soon—the VIDEODISC and the LONGITUDINAL VIDEO RECORDER (LVR). (*See Chapter 15, The Future of Video.*) The videodisc is a *playback only* medium like a record player and uses inexpensive videodiscs instead of videotape. The videodisc, however, suffers from a lack of standardization because several manufacturers are taking different design approaches. Magnavox and Pioneer make one kind of system and RCA, JVC and Panasonic have other kinds of systems. More on this latter.

It should be pointed out at this point that the question of compatibility is only relevant to the VCR because basically all cameras are interchangeable and require only a change of connector to fit any VCR. VCRs, though, are different because of all the possible mechanical variations in the methods used to transport the videotape through the machine and record and playback the pictures on the tape. It seems video manufacturers are always trying to come up with a different way to accomplish this.

Videotape vs. Videodisc

Videotape and videodiscs can work to mutual advantage because they are both electronic mediums. Video programs will always be recorded on either film or tape in the foreseeable future and edited in the film or tape mode. They can easily be copied onto videodiscs at any time. The potential of the videodisc really lies in the low-cost distribution of programming, not in the production of programming, as this is done better by videotape or film.

The videodisc may someday be the long-sought-after pot at the end of the rainbow—the cheap, easy-to-use home audio/visual playback system. Certainly, we have heard these heralds many times before, and I'm sure we'll hear them again. On the horizon we have a 3-D holographic technology, such as Sony's MAVICA magnetic card recording system, and Hitachi's 12-inch holographic disc.

The Advantages Of Incompatibility

There would seem to be no advantage to such a consistent rejection of standardization by video manufacturers. On the other hand, required standardization, especially early standardization of any rapidly evolving technology, will tend to restrict the progression of technical innovation. When manufacturers feel they are totally free to create the best and most advanced configuration of mechanics and electronics, the evolution of such devices is extraordinarily rapid.

Also, the buyer and user of video technology receives the benefit of a much greater range of choice. More machines with special and perhaps better features are made available when manufacturers are free to create whatever they can think up and market. Nevertheless, greater voluntary standardization and co-operation by competing manufacturers would certainly be welcomed by all video users since it would make the job of purchasing equipment and buying and exchanging pre-recorded tape simpler and far more convenient. (A gentle hint to video manufacturers.)

The Future

We know from studies made that TV shapes human behavior. It is therefore obvious that we need alternatives to present media programming. New technology integrated into a receptive social environment on a large scale can bring about considerable change. This change will not necessarily guarantee human progress. Hopefully, the videodisc will not merely proliferate more visual and aural trash but instead will broaden the range of constructive information and communication between people. This is the real media challenge of the future.

2 Purchasing A Home VCR

Who's Into Video?

In 1977 there were 150,000 VCR systems in homes. By 1979 over one million households in the U.S. owned a home VCR. During 1979, VCRs sold at a rate of 30-40,000 per month, with industry experts expecting approximately 500,000 VCRs to be sold during 1979. Meanwhile, over one million pre-recorded family-oriented video cassettes are being sold each year. This all adds up to pretty big business for such a fledgling industry. *Variety* magazine predicts a one billion dollar annual home VCR business by 1985!

Who buys the stuff? According to a recent survey, a typical VCR buyer is a person making $30,000 a year. One half of all users are college graduates and the typical home video purchase totals $2,500. Of home VCR users, 75% buy their equipment for "time shift" purposes, such as recording a TV program at one time and playing it back later. The average user tapes two shows weekly and half of all recordings are played back only once. 12% of the users own a camera and two-thirds of them use their cameras at least once a month. 26% of all VCR users also own quadraphonic sound equipment.

Beginning the Process

As you've seen in the preceding chapter there are a number of formats from which to choose. First you have to decide between having an inexpensive playback-only capability such as the videodisc or going with a current model VCR for recording. If you choose the VCR route, you then have to choose between the Beta or the VHS format.

Let's assume you decide to tackle the Beta versus VHS question and put off your videodisc purchase. If you get hooked on a VCR you will most likely be back for a videodisc machine later, but for now let's consider the basic offerings of Beta and VHS VCRs and then discuss how to define your particular needs and apply these to your VCR purchase.

A Comparison of VHS and Beta VCRs

Sony SL-5800

JVC HR-6700

This is a highly volatile area of discussion—a veritable minefield of emotion, and any sensible writer will carefully avoid taking a position on this issue. It's a little like saying you're a Ford or Chevy person, or more appropriately, a Toyota or Datsun person. Even cranky, disgruntled old X1 format Sony Betamax owners now considering opening antique shops for their VCRs, will discourse for hours on the superior picture quality and legendary dependability of their machines. On the other hand, there are cocky VHS owners that find it inconceivable that anyone would allow a Beta machine into their living room unless it was given to them for free. Any discussion of this touchy issue requires a strict and objective adherence to the facts and features to avoid the treacherous emotional waters that surround the issue. Let's try to examine a variety of factors.

Experience of manufacturer — Sony, which pioneered the basic Beta design, does have more experience (20 years) with video than anyone else, and Sony, the first company to produce a practical home VCR, has always been the leader in the field. Matsushita of Japan, which is by far the largest of the VCR manufacturers and makes most of the VHS VCRs, also has lots of experience. However, the company is not as specialized in video as Sony.

Dependability — Sony is legendary in this department and Sony Beta VCRs have demonstrated an excellent ability to stay out of repair shops.

Costs — All machines are comparably priced within $50 to $100 for the same type model. However, VHS tape economics are slightly better than Beta's because of the longer playing modes.

Warranties — About the same for all models—90 days on labor and one year on parts.

Portable vs. deck VCRs — A large selection of both Beta and VHS portables are available but VHS portables are slightly lighter and more compact. (*See Chapter 6, Portable VCR Systems.*)

Sound — Slight differences in sound fidelity of VCRs exist, but basically they are all about equal.

Record/play times — As we mentioned, this is a highly variable area, depending on model, format, and manufacturer. Maximum Beta playing time is 4-5 hours, and maximum VHS time is 4-9 hours.

VCR Features

It would take an entire book to cover all the variations from model to model, but a listing of the important ones is both feasible and worthwhile.

Record/Play Time—Older Beta VCRs are 1-hour X1 only, 1-hour X1 and 2-hour X2 or 2-hour X2 only. Many newer Beta VCRs are two-speed 2-hour X2 and 3-hour X3 and some are three-speed (X1, X2 and X3). All VHS VCRs have the compatible 2-hour SP mode, while most have a 2 and 4-hour dual speed capability, and many newer VHS units have 2 and 6-hour (JVC, and Sharp) or 2, 4, and 6-hour capabilities (RCA, Panasonic and others). It's important to realize, though, that a single set of video heads can be optimized for *one speed only* so a machine designed to play several speeds will have to compromise picture quality in all modes unless it has a separate set of video heads for each speed mode. One such VCR is the JVC HR-6700 which has 2 sets of heads, one set for the 2-hour mode and 1 set for the 6-hour mode.

Tuner/Timer — Older Beta models such as the Sony SL-7200, SL-8200 and Zenith JR-9000W use awkward external timers. VHS VCRs and newer Beta VCRs utilize built-in LED displays that show current time and tape start and stop time. All programmable VCRs also have quartz-controlled LED displays, some of which simultaneously show current time, the day of the week for which the VCR is programmed, program number, and length of program to be recorded.

Programmable VCRs

Toshiba V-8000

Panasonic PV-1400

Hitachi VT-5000A

Sony SL-5400

Programmability — Both Beta and VHS have programmable models that allow presetting to record a variety of program lengths on different days on different channels. Once the appropriate information is entered into the computer memory system, the VCR will start up at the correct time, switch to the proper channel, make the recording and then shut off and wait for the next pre-selected time. It will repeat the process as many as seven times over seven days (Sharp VC-6700). VHS programmables can generally record four, six, or seven different programs, and Beta programmables, such as Toshiba's V-5420 and V-5425 will record 3 programs. Sony's SL-5600 will record four programs over 2 weeks and the Sanyo VCR-5500 will do five separate programs. **Caution:** Some people may find the programming controls on programmable VCRs too complex and too confusing to operate.

29

Audio Dub — Early Beta VCRs except the Toshiba models lack the Audio Dub feature, which allows you to add sound later to a tape without erasing the picture. All newer Beta and all VHS models have Audio Dub capabilities.

Freeze Fame—Most VCRs provide the ability to stop a tape in the Pause mode and display a still picture. Older VCRs include a noise band in the picture, but newer VCRs have a circuit that removes the noise band. However, the still frame picture is often not really clear and stable. The Sony SL-5800 utilizes a special DOUBLE AZIMUTH playback process which creates a very clear still frame picture.

Special Effects—This category includes a whole variety of variable speed playback capabilities. Most newer model VCRs feature a rapid fast forward mode which is often variable from frame by frame slow motion to at least double normal speed (JVC-6700.) The Sony SL-5800 employs a variable BETASCAN control which allows the user to search at 5 to 20 times normal speed in forward and reverse (Shuttle Search Mode), and Toshiba has a SUPER SCAN which moves the tape at 40 times normal speed in forward and reverse with visible picture. The Panasonic PV-1300, PV-1400 and PV-1750 machines have OMNI-SEARCH which shuttles the tape in forward and reverse at 8 times normal playback speed, but the special effects operate in the SP and SLP modes only. The PV-1750 also has a variable rate remote shuttle search control.

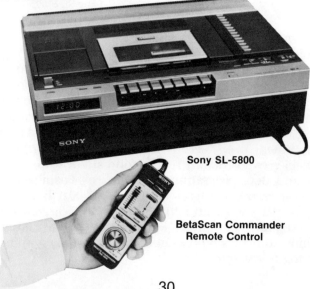

Sony SL-5800

BetaScan Commander
Remote Control

Remote Control Operation—Most older VCRs have remote Pause controls, but newer models now feature multi-function wired remote control units. Examples are the BetaScan Remote Commander used by Sony with the SL-5800 to control all variable speeds, shuttle and frame by frame search and a similar eleven-function device used by JVC with their portable HR-2200U. Other remote control units can change channels and control VCR programming.

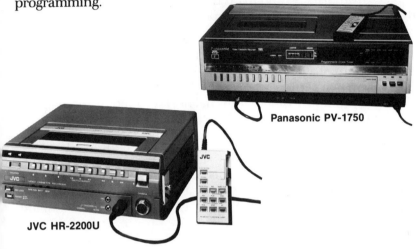

Panasonic PV-1750

JVC HR-2200U

Search mode features — Most VCRs have a Search or Memory button that allows you to return to one spot on the tape by pressing the tape counter to 000 at that spot and rewinding the tape. Programmable VCRs, like the RCA, Quasar, Panasonic, and Toshiba, place electronic signals on the tape which cause the VCR to stop whenever the record mode is activated, thus indicating the start of a new program. This electronic indexing makes it easy to find a particular tape segment.

The Sharp VC-6700 VHS recorder uses an AUTO PROGRAM LOCATE DEVICE (APLD) which automatically advances or rewinds the tape to the desired program. The memory controlled system scans the tape at high speed for special pre-recorded signals which are automatically placed on the tape at the start of recording and then stops the tape when the keyed-in selection is reached. The memory can be programmed for one to ninety-nine selections. The operator must know the program sequence. The RCA VCT-400X also includes a memory backup system.

Electronic Tuners — Like most deluxe 1979 TV sets, most VCRs now incorporate electronic tuners. Such tuners have no moving parts and provide instantaneous error-free tuning at the touch of a button. The tuner receives all 82 VHF and UHF stations and permits the user to select his own particular sequence of stations. Most newer Beta and VHS VCRs utilize these electronic tuning systems.

Sleep Switch — JVC, Sharp and Sanyo have recorders that turn the VCR off at the end of the tape.

DEW Warning Indicator — This light or indicator tells when moisture accumulates on the video head drum. Most VCRs automatically shut off if this happens, otherwise the tape sticks to the head drum, causing damage. Some VCRs, such as the Akai VT-7300, actually have a built-in internal heater which turns on to dry up the moisture.

One Button Recording — A feature of dubious worth. This allows the Record mode to be selected by pushing only one button. Beta VCRs pioneered this idea and some VHS units are adopting it. It's easier to use than the traditional two button method, but valuable recorded tapes could easily be accidentally erased.

Tape Remaining Indicators—This is a nice feature. The Toshiba Beta V-5420 was the first with its TAPE SENTINEL display in the TV picture which tells how much tape remains in the cassette. Sharp's VC-6700 and VC-7400 VCRs use an array of LEDs as indicators so you can plan tape usage.

**Sharp
VC-6700**

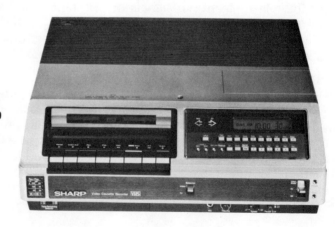

Tape Remaining Indicator

Front Loading Cassette Tape System

Front Loading—The Sharp VC-6700 and VC-7400 both have a unique front loading cassette system which the manufacturer says is more attractive, saves space and keeps the internal workings of the machine cleaner.

Solenoid Controls—Most newer VCRs have feather-touch logic controlled push buttons for all tape functions. Solenoid controls are almost always nicer and better than the mechanical lever types.

Sharp VC-7400

Other Factors

As you can see, there is a vast array of choice available to you in both formats—about 35 different models and 18 manufacturers. Home VCRs have now gone through about three generations of evolution and are quite sophisticated in terms of features. To date, total sales figures show a slight favoring of the VHS format—about 57% VHS to 43% Beta, with Sony getting the lion's share, 26.4% of all home VCR sales and RCA selling 24.3%. In the future this situation could change with the increased features and longer playing times for Beta VCRs. (Media Statistics, Inc. — Feb. 1979)

Pre-recorded tapes referred to as SOFTWARE (as opposed to equipment which is referred to as HARDWARE) is and will be made available in both the 2X Beta mode and SP VHS mode. Because interchangeability is often marginal in the slower speed modes and the pre-recorded tapes cost the same for either format, neither the Beta or VHS VCRs have any advantage in this area.

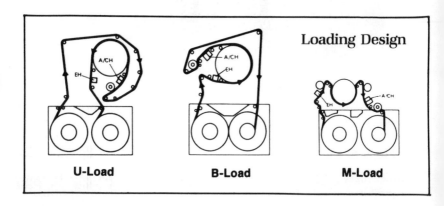

Loading Design

U-Load　　　　**B-Load**　　　　**M-Load**

Internal Differences

Internally, there is a substantial difference between VHS and Beta VCRs. Both formats mechanically draw the tape out of the cassette and wrap the tape around the rotating head drum which contains the video heads. At the same time the tape is also threaded around the audio head. In the Beta system like the U-matic professional VCRs, a single arm wraps the tape around the drum as soon as the cassette is inserted in the VCR. The tape stays threaded until the cassette is ejected. VHS VCRs use two parallel arms that pull the tape forward and swing together, locking the tape around the drum.

Both systems produce good results, but Sony claims greater mechanical stability with its system and less tape wear when doing special effects such as forward and reverse scannng. Also because VHS machines do thread and return the tape into the cassette when you push the Stop button, a slight delay is experienced when switching modes. Hence, on most portable VHS systems you lose your edit capability and actually erase the last part of your previously taped segment which is very annoying. Consequently, most Beta VCRs offer better editing ability than most VHS VCRs.

As to picture quality, there are distinct differences between machines within each format, and this will vary somewhat depending on the type of tape used. If possible, do a side by side machine evaluation using the same picture source and the same model TV set. Ask others who have similar systems how satisfied they are with their equipment.

Hitachi VT-7000

Sanyo VCR5000

Panasonic PV-1400

Defining Your Needs

Now that you have a good conception of the range of features offered by the different VCRs we can arrive at a definition of what's the best VCR for you. Ask yourself these questions:

Will you be recording off the air only?

Do you need portability? Can you get by with moving your deck type model around once in a while or do you want to carry it around frequently? If you desire complete portability, you will need a battery powered VCR. Most manufacturers make a portable version of their VCRs, and these units allow much greater flexibility because you can take them with you and use them for a wide variety of purposes. Portables are usually 30-40% more expensive ($1,400) than deck-type models ($900). When mated with its external tuner-timer system, the portable can do nearly everything the basic deck-type model can do. Also, the portable VCR is much more compact and lightweight and can operate on battery power unlike its desk counterpart.

How important is programmability to you? Perhaps a basic VCR with a 24-hour timer that records one program automatically is adequate for your needs, but if you want to record several programs a day, or several programs on different channels on different days, you will need one of those fancy deluxe programmable VCRs.

Caution: In some areas, your programmable functions may be rendered useless if you have a cable TV system that uses a channel converter box which contains all the tuning functions.

How about a camera? All VCRs will accept a camera (either b&w or color) and you can buy a camera at any time. You may want to try playing with a friend's video camera first to see if it accomplishes what you want. There's no question about the fact that cameras give home video a whole new dimension as this is where the fun really lies, and you can get everyone involved in your video system. Cameras can also be used to transfer your super 8 and film slides and photos to video. Color cameras are changing very rapidly, but they're also getting better and better and more compact and easier to use. Another factor to consider is the potential business use of your equipment. There are many ways to use your video equipment as a writeoff while accomplishing educational and training goals very efficiently within your business. (See Chapter 12, What To Do With Your VCR.)

Once you have some feeling for your general needs, start exploring specific machines and what they have to offer. Your choices will depend strongly on what you can afford, what features you need, and what format your friends and possible co-workers are using. All VCRs are good, and as with many things, you get what you pay for. Plan ahead, but don't pay for what you won't use later.

Factors to Consider

Reading the technical specifications on the back of the VCR brochures can be helpful, but you should try to visually compare the picture quality of your potential purchase. In the playback mode, check such things as picture quality, which includes crispness and sharpness of image and color fidelity; are the reds red and the sky blue? Is the picture noisy or grainy? Is there noticeable jitter or small horizontal or vertical movements in the picture? Is the audio clear and rich without wobble or flutter? Audio imperfections are especially noticeable on high frequencies such as the singing of a female vocalist. Make these observations in the various speed modes and note the differences. Also analyze the quality of the TV tuner's channel reception. How well does it bring in TV stations? This will, of course, depend greatly on the quality of the TV antenna or your cable reception.

How important are specific features to you? Again, consider:

- Playing times — 2 hours/4 hours/6 hours? Tape economics?
- Tuner/Timer — electronic or mechanical?
- Portable or non-portable?
- Programmability — how many events?
- Audio Dub capability
- Freeze Frame
- Variable Speed functions
- Fast Forward and Reverse of tape with picture and/or sound
- Remote Pause control
- Remote Control operation
- Search mode capability
- Sleep switch
- Dew indicator
- One button recording
- Tape remaining indicator
- Front loading cassette
- Solenoid control operation

Other criteria would include local deals and discounts, availability of repair work, and the personal rapport with the video salespeople to whom you will undoubtedly be referring in the future.

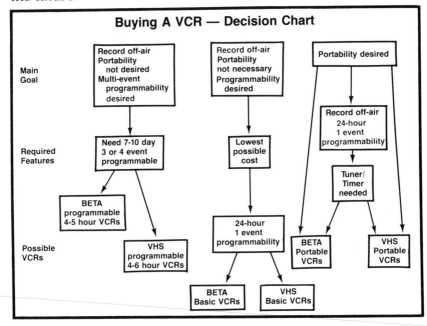

Buying A VCR — Decision Chart

Servicing

VCRs will need servicing at some point in time, especially if they are subjected to heavy use. It's a wise idea to buy a machine that can be *competently* serviced locally because video users tend to get very attached to their video equipment and can't live without them for long periods of time without experiencing severe emotional trauma. If you live in a rural location you may have a problem getting your video equipment fixed locally. Also, it's best to buy video equipment from a video or audio/video specialty store despite the probable increase in cost.

Repair bills are usually expensive. One trip to the repair shop will easily run up a bill of $50-$100. Most video dealers have extended warranty plans, and it's probably a good idea to purchase one of these. You are investing a lot of money, and you will need support from the dealer in terms of tape, repair and accessories, so shop around to find an *honest, reputable* and *competent* dealer.

Dealing with Rapid Obsolescence

It might seem like your machine will be obsolete six months after its purchase. To some extent this is true, but such is the nature of any rapidly evolving technology. The important objective is to select a unit that accomplishes what you want and will serve your needs for some time to come. Innovations are usually in the category of new features or increased compactness.

As video evolves, more and more people will want to own a video system especially as fuel becomes more expensive and people's mobility decreases. Consequently, I think we can look forward to a growing market for used VCRs. But technological evolution isn't about to slow down, so you might as well jump in at any point, unless a specific device such as a videodisc is really what you want. In that case, it might be worth waiting for the "right" model. Otherwise, take the plunge and have a good time with video now.

Good Info

For a really upbeat, refreshing and fun-to-read source of extremely detailed information on home VCRs, **The Videophile Newsletter** is a must. Another good source of equipment evaluation and pre-recorded program information is **Video Magazine**. See the *Video and Television Magazines* section at the end of the book for addresses.

3
How to Operate Your VCR

Now that you put off buying a new car or a trip to Mexico or Florida so you could purchase that nifty video system, how do you get it to do all those fabulous things the ads said it would do?

First, let's examine a typical home videocassette recorder (VCR). Most units have a series of standard features which are the following:

- Extended recording times—VHS 6 hours on a single tape, Beta—5 hours on a single tape.

- 2-Speed Operation—"SP", "LP" and "SLP" or "X1", "X2" and "X3" modes.

- Capstan Servo for improved picture stability.

- Compact and lightweight.

- PAUSE control for deletion of commercials.

- Built-in MEMORY feature which allows convenient rewinding of the tape to a preselected point.

- Ability to watch one channel while recording another.

- Automatic unattended recordings with timer.

- Playback of VCR through any conventional TV set.

- Camera and microphone do-it-yourself recording capabililty.

- AUDIO DUB capability (unavailable on early Beta VCRs).

MAJOR OPERATING COMPONENTS

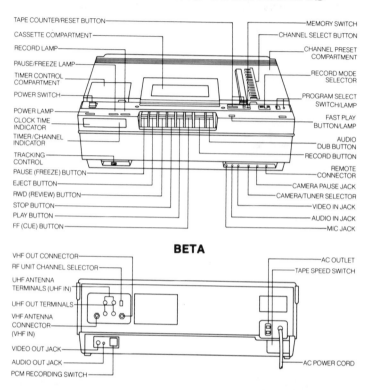

TAPE COUNTER/RESET BUTTON
CASSETTE COMPARTMENT
RECORD LAMP
PAUSE/FREEZE LAMP
TIMER CONTROL COMPARTMENT
POWER SWITCH
POWER LAMP
CLOCK TIME INDICATOR
TIMER/CHANNEL INDICATOR
TRACKING CONTROL
PAUSE (FREEZE) BUTTON
EJECT BUTTON
RWD (REVIEW) BUTTON
STOP BUTTON
PLAY BUTTON
FF (CUE) BUTTON

MEMORY SWITCH
CHANNEL SELECT BUTTON
CHANNEL PRESET COMPARTMENT
RECORD MODE SELECTOR
PROGRAM SELECT SWITCH/LAMP
FAST PLAY BUTTON/LAMP
AUDIO DUB BUTTON
RECORD BUTTON
REMOTE CONNECTOR
CAMERA PAUSE JACK
CAMERA/TUNER SELECTOR
VIDEO IN JACK
AUDIO IN JACK
MIC JACK

BETA

VHF OUT CONNECTOR
RF UNIT CHANNEL SELECTOR
UHF ANTENNA TERMINALS (UHF IN)
UHF OUT TERMINALS
VHF ANTENNA CONNECTOR (VHF IN)
VIDEO OUT JACK
AUDIO OUT JACK
PCM RECORDING SWITCH

AC OUTLET
TAPE SPEED SWITCH
AC POWER CORD

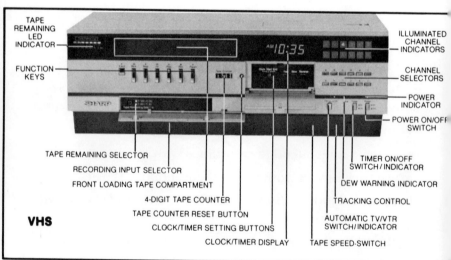

TAPE REMAINING LED INDICATOR
FUNCTION KEYS

ILLUMINATED CHANNEL INDICATORS
CHANNEL SELECTORS
POWER INDICATOR
POWER ON/OFF SWITCH

TAPE REMAINING SELECTOR
RECORDING INPUT SELECTOR
FRONT LOADING TAPE COMPARTMENT
4-DIGIT TAPE COUNTER
TAPE COUNTER RESET BUTTON
CLOCK/TIMER SETTING BUTTONS
CLOCK/TIMER DISPLAY

TIMER ON/OFF SWITCH/INDICATOR
DEW WARNING INDICATOR
TRACKING CONTROL
AUTOMATIC TV/VTR SWITCH/INDICATOR
TAPE SPEED SWITCH

VHS

40

Understanding the VCR

Before trying to hook it up, let's familiarize ourselves with the various controls and indicators on the machine.

Function Controls

The most conspicuous feature of the typical home VCR is a series of function buttons on the front that control the movement and recording of the tape. The functions are similar to any standard audiotape recording machine and include EJECT, REWind, STOP, PLAY, FWD (Forward), FF (Fast Forward), RECORD, AUDIO DUB, and PAUSE. One function that is unique to most video machines is the AUDIO DUB feature which allows you to add new sound without changing the picture. You can use this feature to add music or narration to a previously recorded tape.

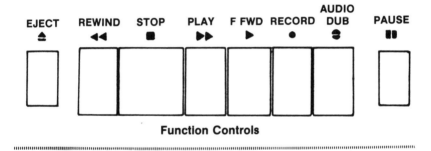

Function Controls

Cassette Compartment

Located behind the function buttons or controls is the tape cassette compartment where the cassette is inserted. Press the EJECT button to release the cassette compartment which then pops up to receive the tape.

TV Tuners

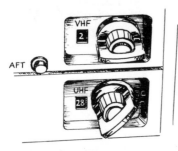 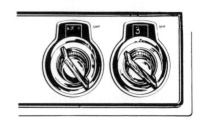

The next big item is the TV tuner system which looks just like the channel tuners on any home TV set. These tuners — VHF (Very High Frequency) and UHF (Ultra High Frequency) allow the VCR to tune in and select a TV program off the air. The VCR tuners do not affect the TV tuners in your home TV set, but rather bypass them and allow both sets of tuners to operate independently of each other. This is how you can record one program on the VCR and watch a different program on your home TV set so when *Wonder Woman* and the *Bionic Woman* are on at the same time, you won't miss a single exciting scene.

VCR Timers

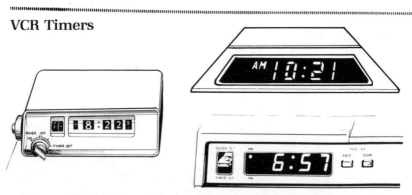

All home video recorders feature automatic timers. The timer allows the user to set the machine for a particular time at which point the VCR will automatically record the designated TV program. However, you must also be sure to set the VCR's VHF or UHF tuner to the corresponding TV station. Be sure to set the VCR tuner, *not* the tuner on your TV set.

On most VCRs, the digital timer is either built into the chassis like the VHS systems or located on top of the unit like the early Beta systems. Controls located near the clock set the timer for the correct recording time.

All Those Switches, Knobs and Buttons

Each VCR has an assortment of switches and knobs scattered throughout the front and top of the VCR that are really not designed to confuse the user but rather to tell the VCR what it is supposed to do.

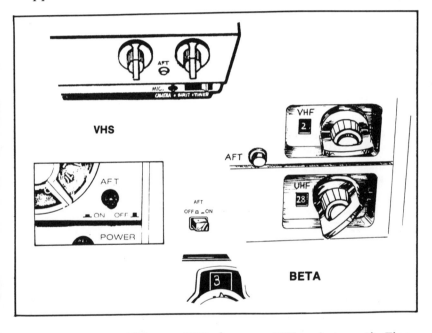

AFT Button — All home VCRs have an AFT or Automatic Fine Tuning button located near the tuner just like most home TV sets. In order to obtain the best quality off-the-air recording, select your channel, disengage the AFT button, and manually turn the fine tuning knobs on the video recorder's VHF or UHF tuner until the picture quality looks best. When you have manually tuned in the best picture and sound, turn the AFT button back on. This will lock in the best picture.

 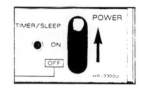

POWER Switch — Obviously, this switch turns the VCR on and off.

DEW Indicator — Some VCRs, such as the Panasonic and RCA VHS machines, have a DEW lamp located next to the ON—OFF light which indicates the machine has been shut off because of an environment that is too damp. If the machine continued to run, the tape would seize up inside the VCR and seriously damage it. When the DEW lamp illuminates, just leave the machine ON and wait for the DEW lamp to go out.

STAND BY Lamp (Beta machines only) — This lamp will illuminate while the tape is being threaded by the machine. When the tape is properly threaded, the light will go out. If improper tape motion is sensed by a built-in tape motion sensor, the STAND BY light will go on and the VCR will revert to the STOP mode. If this happens, try to fast forward or rewind the tape in the cassette and try playing the tape again.

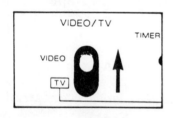 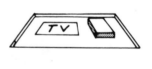 

TV/VTR(VCR) SELECTor or PROGRAM SELECTor/ANTENNA Switch — This switch selects the output from the VCR to the TV set. Basically, this switch either sends the signal from the TV antenna or the Cable TV connection directly to your TV set (TV mode) thus bypassing the VCR, or it sends a signal from the VCR to the TV set (VTR or CASSETTE mode). The off-the-air or Cable TV signal is blocked out in the VCR or CASSETTE mode. Different VCRs have different switches.

Input Signal Selector — Found primarily on all VHS and Beta-2 hr. only machines, this switch sets the VCR for the proper recording input and is generally a 2 or 3-position switch which selects CAMERA/VTR/AUXilliary (LINE) or TV TUNER. On the Sony SL-8200 and Zenith JR-9000W Beta VCRs, the input is selected automatically, and no switch is needed.

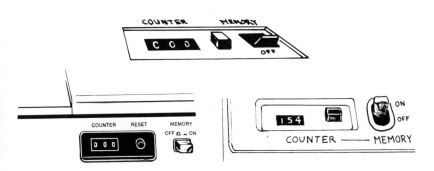

COUNTER/MEMORY/SEARCH Control — The tape counter on a video machine operates like the counter on any audio recorder. Press the counter reset button to "000" at the start of the tape, and you can then reference to any part of the tape later. Most VCRs also have a MEMORY feature which allows you to automatically stop the rewinding of the tape at a preselected point. Turn on the MEMORY ON switch, set the counter to "000" at the point you want to return to, and when you place the VCR in REWIND mode, it will return to "999" and stop. You can now play your scene right from the beginning.

The only problem with this system is that once you reset the counter to "000", you are unable to locate any other point in the tape because the counter is no longer counting chronologically from the start of the tape. It's best to shut off the MEMORY switch during normal operation, otherwise, the tape will always stop at "999".

SPEED Selector or RECording TIME Selector—Many home VCRs are 2-speed. Most VHS machines can record and play in a Standard Play (SP) mode of 2 hours and a Long Play (LP) mode of 4 hours. Some newer VHS VCRs have a SP mode of 2 hours and an LP mode of 6 hours, and some have 3-speed modes—2/4 and 6-hour (SLP) modes. Early Beta VCRs have a 1-hour (X1) and 2-hour (X2) mode and some only an X2 mode. Newer Beta VCRs have dual-speed X2 and X3 (3-hour) modes. Some Sony models play back in all three speeds (X1, X2 and X3).

On playback, the VCR senses the proper tape speed and sets the correct speed automatically. Generally, there is a slight loss of picture quality in the longer playing modes such as the Beta X3 and VHS SLP modes. Since there are so many speed variations on different manufacturer's machines, be sure you understand what speed the machine you want to buy will play.

———

TRACKING Control — Generally, this knob shouldn't need attention and should remain in the FIX position. It may, however, need to be adjusted if a tape was made on a different *same format* (compatible) VCR.

Normal

Adjust TRACKING

If the picture shows distortion or a jagged horizontal band running through the picture during playback, turn the TRACKING control until the picture clears up. This control should be operated in the *playback mode only.* It compensates for slight mechanical and electronic differences between machines and tapes.

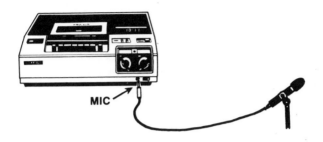

MIC

MICROPHONE or MIC Input — The MICrophone plug is not used for off-the-air recording but rather for sound dubbing or live recording with a camera and a microphone.

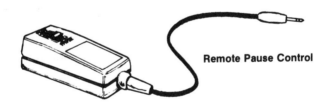

Remote Pause Control

REMOTE PAUSE Plug — This switch, generally found on VHS machines and newer Beta VCRs allows you to momentarily stop the VCR by placing it in the PAUSE mode. This feature is great for shutting off the machine during those annoying commercials between TV programs, thereby preventing them from being recorded. Very unfortunately, there is no way to do this when the machine is automatically recording programs with the timer. CAUTION: Do not hold the PAUSE mode for more than 5 minutes, as this may cause damage to the tape.

How to Connect Your Home VCR

Plugs and Wires — Before you begin to connect your home VCR, you will notice that one of two types of cables is used to connect your TV set to your antenna or cable TV system. If you have an antenna hooked up to your TV set, you probably have a flat wire with 2 prongs on the end of it which connects to the VHF and UHF terminals of your TV set. This flat wire is called a 300 OHM CABLE.

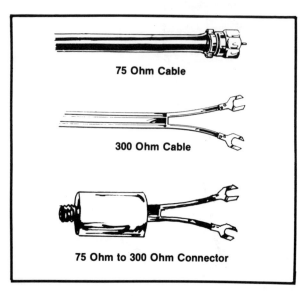

The other kind of cable in use is a round kind that has a screw-in, drum-like metal connector on the end with a small pin protruding from the middle of the connector. This round cable is called a 75 OHM COAXIAL CABLE and is used if you have a cable TV connection.

Quite often an adaptor or MATCHING TRANSFORMER is used to convert the 75 ohm connector and cable to the 300 ohm VHF terminals on most older TV sets. Newer TV sets can accept the 75 ohm screw-in connectors directly.

The round metal connector on the 75-ohm coaxial cable is known as a TYPE "F" or "F" TYPE CONNECTOR and is used in all home VCR systems.

You may need to attach "F" type connectors to your cables. It's really very simple, and no soldering is required.

Step   **1**   Strip the cable and expose the center wire.

Step   **2**   Insert the connector.

Step   **3**   Crimp the ring with a pair of pliers.

"F" Connector

Connecting The VCR

Before you start, *read the instruction manual thoroughly.*

Step   **1**   Disconnect the Cable TV cable (coaxial cable with "F" connector) or the antenna cable (300 ohm cable) from the VHF and/or UHF terminals on the back of your TV set.

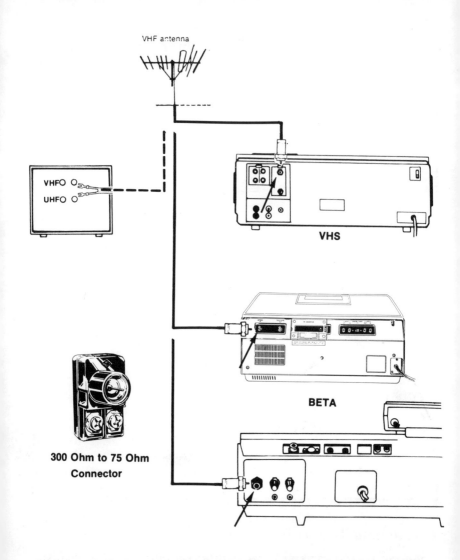

VHF antenna

VHFO
UHFO

VHS

BETA

300 Ohm to 75 Ohm Connector

Step 2 Connect the coaxial cable or 300 ohm cable to the VHF IN and UHF IN terminals on the back of your VCR. You may need to use a 300-ohm to 75-ohm adaptor for the connection to the VHF terminal input on your VCR which will be labeled VHF IN or ANTENNA. The adaptor should be included in the box with the VCR. If not, you should be able to buy one from your video/TV dealer.

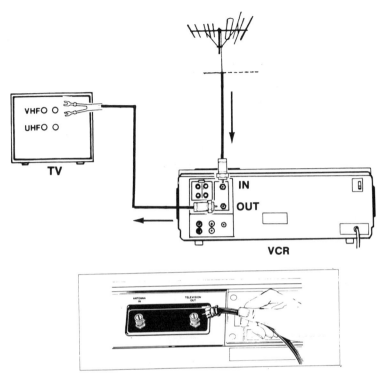

Step 3 Connect your TV set to the output of the VCR using the enclosed coaxial cable with "F" connectors.

NOTE: Be sure to connect the *output* of the VCR (VHF OUT, RF OUT, and/or UHF OUT) to the VHF terminals to your TV set. Longer cables can be made up by buying additional cable and connectors. Be sure to ask for 75-ohm RG-59U coaxial type cable. *Do not* use 50-ohm CB coaxial cable which looks very similar. Sony supplies an optional extension cable called the RFC-8 (8 meters long).

Since the TV set is now operating through the VCR, many people find it more convenient to locate the VCR near the couch or sitting area instead of near the TV set so they can change channels on the VCR or stop the recorder momentarily during commercials without having to move.

Step 4 Plug the VCR into any standard wall socket.

Step 5 Turn on your TV set, and tune it to correspond to the pre-selected VCR output channel, usually channel 3 or channel 4. Use the channel which is *inoperative* in your area if possible. Also, check to see which channel produces the best picture and sound quality. Be sure to fine tune the TV set to the channel for best results. Check the back of the VCR for a switch which should be labeled RF CONVERTER — CH 3 or CH 4. The TV set must be set to the channel that you select on the VCR.

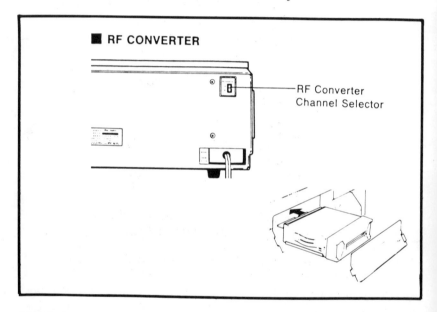

RF CONVERTER

RF Converter
Channel Selector

RF Converters

All video machines require an RF CONVERTER or RF ADAPTER in order to play back a video signal on a conventional TV set. All home VCRs have built-in RF Converters. If your VCR does not have a built-in RF Converter and you did not purchase one, you will not be able to play your VCR on your home TV set. You would instead need to purchase a more expensive VIDEO MONITOR. So, you must buy an RF Converter if you want to use your TV set for VCR playback. Video monitors cost about $300 more than a standard TV set, so it's much cheaper to buy the RF Converter which is usually less than $100.

Normal TV Viewing

Step 1   Turn on the TV set. Make sure the VCR timer is turned *off.*

Step 2   Place the Beta VCR PROGRAM SELECTor or ANTENNA switch in the TV mode and the VHS VTR/TV SELECTor is in the TV mode. The VCR *does not* have to be turned on.

Step 3   Select the desired TV channel on your TV set. The VCR is now completely bypassed, and your TV set will operate as it normally does.

Recording TV Programs Off-the-Air.

Step 1   Connect the VCR to the TV set as shown.

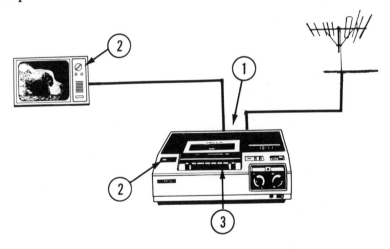

Step 2   Turn on the VCR and TV set, and set the TV to the proper RF channel (3 or 4).

Step 3   Load the cassette into the VCR by pushing the EJECT button on the front of the VCR. The cassette compartment will pop up. Insert the blank cassette, and press down the cassette compartment until it clicks and locks in place. Make sure you have the proper length tape for the desired recording time.

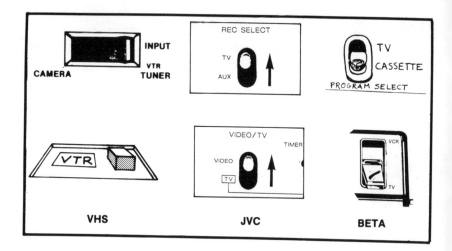

Step 4 Place the INPUT SELECTor on VHS machines in the VTR/TUNER position and the TV/VTR SELECTor in the VTR mode. The timer should be turned *OFF*. JVC VCR's REC SELECT should be in TV mode and the VIDEO/TV switch should be in the VIDEO mode. Beta machine's PROGRAM SELECTor or ANTENNA switch should be placed in the CASSETTE or VTR mode, and the automatic timer should be turned *ON*.

Step 5 Set the SPEED switch for the proper recording time— 1, 2, 3, 4 or 6 hours.

Step 6 Turn the VHF or UHF tuner on the video recorder, and select the channel that is playing the program you want to tape. Disengage the AFT button, and fine tune the TV program by adjusting the VHF or UHF fine tuning controls on the VCR.

NOTE: The tuning of the TV set *will not* affect the recording of the VCR, but the TV set must first be perfectly tuned so you can properly adjust the VCR tuner.

Step 7 Press the tape counter reset button to "000".

Step 8 If the picture on the TV set looks okay, press the PLAY and RECORD button together on the front of the VCR and the recording will begin. Most Beta VCRs require only the RECORD button to be pushed.

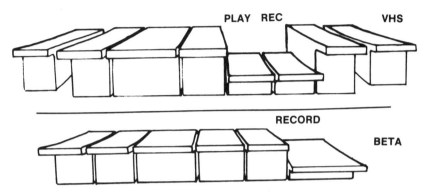

NOTE: You may want to make a test recording first! Often it's a good idea to record 20 or 30 seconds of the program just to see if everything is working properly. Rewind the tape, and prepare it for recording again.

Step 9 While the VCR is recording, sit back, relax and enjoy the program, or do some jogging or Yoga to compensate for all those sedentary hours spent watching TV. You could maybe even help your husband or wife fix dinner.

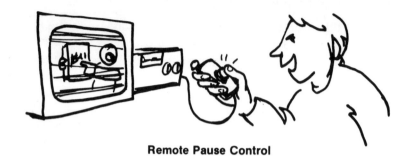

Remote Pause Control

Step 10 You can stop the recording by pushing the STOP button or the PAUSE button. The PAUSE button will stop the VCR momentarily while recording. This is a good way to avoid recording commercials. Push the switch or button once again to restart the tape.

Step 11 Rewind the tape by pressing the REWIND button. When the tape stops, press PLAY and replay the program if desired.

NOTE: Any interference or distortion that occurs during the recording will be permanently recorded onto the tape. The quality of the recording depends on the quality of your reception, but generally you shouldn't be able to tell the difference between the original broadcast picture and your tape playback.

The Videocassette Safety Tab

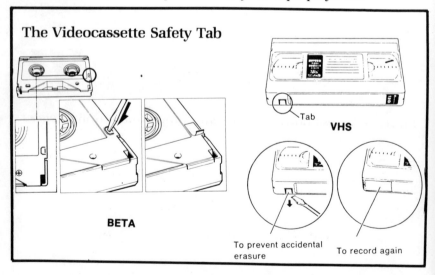

Tab

VHS

BETA

To prevent accidental erasure

To record again

All videocassettes have either a plastic tab or removable red plastic button on the bottom of the cassette to prevent accidental erasure. If the tab or button has been removed, you will *not* be able to record on the tape or engage the VCR in the RECORD mode. If you do not want a tape erased, simply remove the red button by hand or the tab by using a screwdriver. If you want to record on a tape after the tab has been removed, cover the hole with a piece of cellophane or vinyl tape.

Playing Back Tapes

Step   1   Turn on the TV set and the VCR.

Step   2   Push the EJECT button on the VCR, and the cassette compartment should pop up.

Step   3   Insert the pre-recorded cassette into the VCR.

NOTE: Since the full width of the tape is used for recording, it *cannot* be turned over. It will record in one direction only.

Step   4   Press down the cassette compartment until it clicks and locks into place.

Step   5   Make sure the TV set is tuned to correspond to the pre-selected VCR channel, usually channel 3 or channel 4.

Step   6   Press the REWIND button to rewind the tape, if necessary.

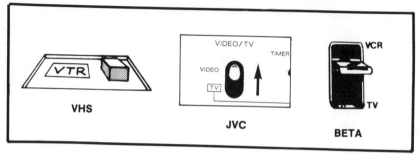

VIDEO/TV

TIMER

VIDEO

TV

VHS

JVC

VCR

TV

BETA

Step 7 Make sure all switches are in the CASSETTE, VTR, VCR, or VIDEO mode.

Step 8 Push the PLAY or FORWARD (FWD) button on the VCR.

PLAY

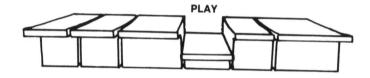

Step 9 Adjust the volume and color on the TV set for the best quality.

Possible Playback Problems

No picture on the TV set — Check the connections between the VCR and the TV set. The cable should go from VHF OUT, RF OUT, or TELEVISION OUT on the VCR to the VHF terminals on the back of the TV set. Also, check to see if the TV set is fine tuned and adjusted to the proper RF channel. The tape may need rewinding. If so, rewind the tape and try again.

Recording One Program While Viewing Another

Step 1 Insert a cassette into the VCR.

Step 2 Turn on the VCR and the TV set. (Beta SL-8200 or Zenith JR-9000W VCR's timer must be turned ON).

Step 3 Make sure the TV set is set to the correct VCR channel, usually channel 3 or 4.

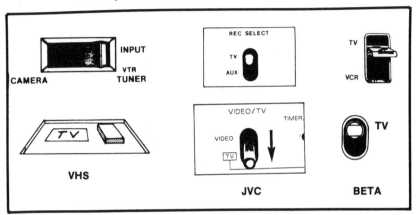

Step 4 Set the VHS VTR/TV SELECTor to VCR or VTR and the INPUT SELECTor to TUNER. Set the JVC REC SELECT switch to TV and the VIDEO/TV switch to TV. Set the Beta VCR's PROGRAM SELECTor or ANTENNA switch to TV.

Step 5 Select the channel to be recorded on the VCR's VHF or UHF tuner, and fine tune the desired TV program. Check it on your TV screen for best picture and sound quality.

Step 6 Press RECORD and PLAY on VHS machines and RECORD on most Beta machines to begin recording. Reset the tape counter to "000".

Step 7 Select whatever channel you want on the TV set. The VCR's recording will not be affected. To view the recorder's output, switch the TV back to the VCR's RF channel, and switch the PROGRAM SELECTor to VTR/ VCR or CASSETTE.

Recording With the Automatic Timer

All home VCRs feature some kind of automatic timer system. All VHS machines and newer Beta machines have digital LED clocks built into the unit while most older Beta systems have external timers that sit on top of the VCR. Check your particular instruction manual for proper timer operation. Basically, this is how they work:

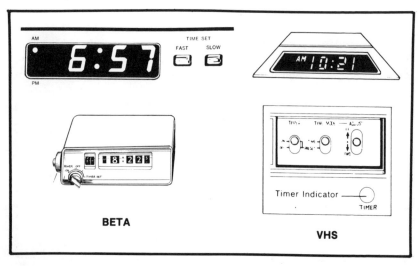

BETA

VHS

Step 1 Make sure the timer is properly connected to Beta VCRs that have a separate timer.

Step 2 Place a cassette of the proper length into the VCR.

Step 3 Select the proper channel to be recorded on the VCR's VHF or UHF tuners.

Step 4 Set the SPEED control switch to the desired mode.

Step 5 Set the VHS INPUT SELECTor to TUNER and the JVC REC SELECT to TV.

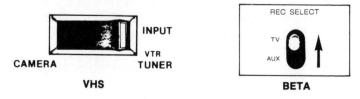

VHS

BETA

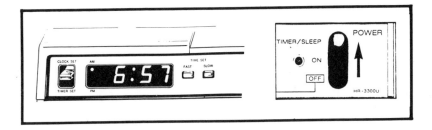

Step 6 Set the timer turn-on time and turn the timer *ON*. Make sure the VCR is also turned on. On most VCRs the timer should be placed in the TIMER SET or AUTO SET position. On JVC machines, set the POWER switch to TIMER/SLEEP.

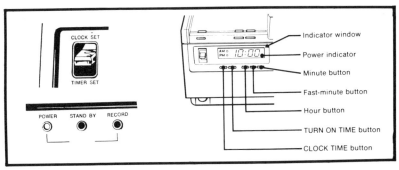

NOTE: It is normal for the LED clock/timer on most VCRs to start flashing on and off when the power to the VCR has been interrupted. Simply reset the clock to the correct time and the flashing will stop.

Step 7 Place the VCR in the RECORD mode, and turn the TV set off. The RECORD indicator lamp should light.

Step 8 Set the SLEEP switch on certain VCRs if you want the VCR to turn off by itself when the tape is finished. All VCRs will stop the tape when the end is reached.

Step 9 The VCR should now turn itself on at the preset time and automatically record the program.

Possible Problems

Most problems are due to human error such as a switch in the wrong position or an improper connection. When something doesn't work as expected, refer to the convenient TROUBLE SHOOTING CHART in the *Maintenance and Troubleshooting* chapter near the end of the book..

NOTE: Some Cable TV systems require a channel preselector box which overrides your TV set tuner. If this is the case, your VCR will *not* be able to record one program while you view another unless you obtain several additional switching devices at extra cost. Check your VCR operator's manual and consult with your Cable TV company.

VCR Accessories and Tapes

A wide variety of VCR accessories are available through a number of suppliers. The VCR manufacturer generally has a listing of specific optional accessories printed on the back of the appropriate VCR brochure and also in the VCR operator's manual. Your dealer usually stocks a few of these accessories, but there are a lot of general accessories that aren't listed in the brochures on which you can also spend your money. The largest and most complete selection of video support items can be found in the Comprehensive Video Supply catalog. Although this is a professionally oriented catalog, it lists plugs, adapters, lights, cables, microphones, cases, tripods — just about anything practical for video. Serious videophiles should send for their catalog.

There are two other smaller video accessories supply catalog companies that also list useful video items. Send for their catalogs as well.

Total Video Supply Co.	WIDL
9060 Claremont Mesa Blvd.	5245 West Diversey
San Diego, CA 93123	Chicago, IL 60639
Tel. (714) 560-5616	Tel. (312) 622-9606

●REMOTE PAUSE CONTROL — Available for use with newer Beta and most VHS system recorders, these devices allow the VCR to be stopped and started during recording and playback. They are included on most systems.

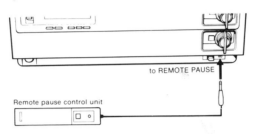

●CAMERAS — Optional b&w and color cameras are available for use with all home VCR systems. Costs run from $250 for simple b&w cameras to $600-$1,300 for a color camera. *(See Chapter 5, The Video Camera.)*

●MICROPHONE — An optional microphone allows sound to be added to a video recording. Most microphones will work with most video recorders.

●EXTENSION CABLES — Available for both microphones and cameras.

●CASES — There are a variety of rugged, hard-shell carrying and shipping cases available for just about any VCR camera or system combination. Comprehensive Video has a wide range of carrying cases in their catalog. Also companies like ANVIL and THERMODYNE make super cases that rock groups and broadcasters use to transport their equipment. They're expensive ($200–$300) but offer the ultimate protection for your equipment.

Addresses:

ANVIL Cases Inc.
4128 Temple City Blvd.
Rosemead, CA 91770

THERMODYNE International Inc.
1260 Yukon Ave.
Hawthorne, CA 90250

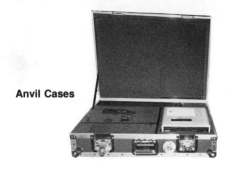

Anvil Cases

•COVERS — A selection of leather-grain vinyl VCR case covers with protective cloth backing and convenient glass windows for reading the VCR timers is available from the Total Video Supply Company catalog.

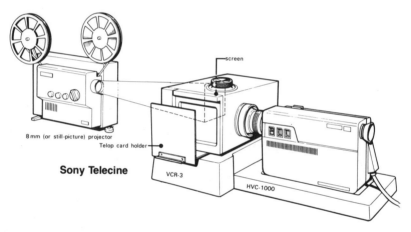

8 mm (or still-picture) projector

screen

Telop card holder

Sony Telecine

VCR-3

HVC-1000

•TELECINE CONVERTOR — Several manufacturers (Sony, JVC, Panasonic, Quasar) offer TELECINE CONVERTERS ($130) which are basically just a small box with a lens, a mirror and ground glass for converting super 8 or 16mm film and slides to video. Of course, you also need a slide projector, a film projector, a color video camera (for color) and a VCR to do this. It works quite well, although films transferred to video will have a noticeable flicker in the picture because of the difference in frame rate (film speed). Super 8 moves at 16 or 20 frames a second and video moves at 30 frames a second. These differences in speed cause the flicker in the picture. Professional film transfer services like Fotomat eliminate the flicker.

•VIDEO SWITCHING DEVICES — When you get to the point where you have several VCRs or a VCR, a videodisc unit, an audio amplifying system and Cable TV and Pay TV boxes, you will go crazy constantly connecting and disconnecting cables from everything. But, cheer up, there is a company which makes several handy video switching systems. One is a simple black box model called the "Home Video Patch Bay," and the other is a more sophisticated pushbutton switcher called the "Distrivid." Both these units allow you to interconnect two TVs and two VCRs or a single VCR with an auxiliary source such as a videodisc player or a video game. Write to them for information.

KAPPA VIDEO
9626 Lurline St. Unit J
Chatsworth, CA 91311

**Sony AG-300
AutoChanger**

•SONY AUTOCHANGER — Sony has two automatic videocassette changers. One is called the AG-200 which is used with the older model VCRs such as the LV-1901, SL-7200, SL-8200 and SL-8600 and changes 3 tapes. The newer programmable BetaStack Autochanger Model AG-300 can be programmed to record, playback and rewind up to four Beta videocassettes when used with the Sony models SL-5400, SL-5600 and SL-5800.

•VIDEOTAPE — Tapes come in a variety of different lengths. The standard tapes are 30, 60 and 120 minutes. Extended length thinner tapes are available also. Costs vary widely, depending on manufacturers, local discounts, and whether the tape is Beta or VHS. Generally the tape cost ranges from approximately $12-$15 for a 1-hour Beta tape to $22-28 for a 2/4/6-hour VHS tape. (See Chapter 4, Videotape.)

Be Kind To Your VCR

The trouble-free life and usefulness of your home VCR will depend on how well you take care of it. Also, proper care and storage of videotape will help to prevent problems and servicing. A list of helpful suggestions and precautions follows to assist you in keeping those repair bills to a minimum or eliminating them altogether.

A home VCR should normally provide many hours of trouble-free home viewing. Generally, home video recorders are well-made but must, like people, be treated with care and love if you desire the optimum relationship.

There is much you can do with your home VCR, and the potential for personal expression and group creativity is unlimited. In the next few chapters, we will begin to explore ways of fulfilling this exciting potential.

VCR Precautions

- On Beta VCRs, always wait for the STAND BY lamp to go out before pressing any function button.

- On VHS machines, make sure the timer switch is OFF when operating the VCR.

- Do not insert your fingers into the VCR.

- Do not operate the VCR near magnetic fields or intense heat sources.

- Do not block the ventilation slots on top of the machine.

- Operate the VCR in a *horizontal* position only.

- Before recording, check to see if the safety tab has been removed.

- Avoid moving the VCR from a cold to a warm place. Allow some time for the machine to return to room temperature before operating.

- Avoid damp environments.

- Always keep a dust cover on the machine when not in use.

- Do not operate the machine with dust cover in place.

- Do not leave a cassette inside the VCR when not in use.

- If liquid is spilled inside the VCR, unplug the unit and take it to a repair facility.

- Do not disassemble the VCR.

- Do not keep the VCR in PAUSE mode longer than 5 minutes.

NOTICE: The unauthorized recording of television programs and other materials may infringe the rights of others.

4

Videotape

Perhaps the most critical element in the video recording process is the recording medium itself, the videotape. The quality of the camera and VCR are very important determinants of picture and sound quality, but are completely dependent on the condition and quality of the videotape used. Poor quality videotape will definitely detract from your eventual picture and sound reproduction, and good videotape will noticeably improve your picture image. Faulty storage or a prolonged exposure of tape to temperatures above 50°C (124°F) can destroy the videotape and all the material on it. So, tape represents a big variable in the videotape recording process. Consequently, some understanding of videotape and its strong points and shortcomings will prove invaluable to the success of your recording endeavors.

Videocassette Size Comparison

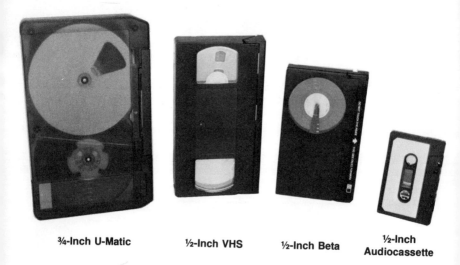

¾-Inch U-Matic   ½-Inch VHS   ½-Inch Beta   ½-Inch Audiocassette

What Is Videotape?

Video is an electronic recording process like audio recording. It is very different from film, which is a chemical recording process. Since video is electronic it requires a magnetically senstive material on which to store the images and sound. Videotape must be able to capture and reproduce more than 200 times as much information as audio tape. Audio frequencies range from 20–20,000 cycles, but video frequencies range from 0–4,000,000 cycles. Also, the eye is much more critical than the ear. The practical way of accurately recording such information is to place a very thin magnetically sensitive material on a sheet of plastic film. The total tape thickness of the combined material and film is only .79 MIL (20 microns).

The video and audio heads on the video recorder produce a tiny magnetic field, and the magnetically sensitive material on the videotape responds to this magnetic field in such a way as to record and store the picture and sound information generated by the camera and the microphone. The VCR can then "read back" the magnetic information stored on the tape and reproduce the information on a TV set. Truly amazing!

Unlike film, any piece of videotape will record both b&w and color pictures. However, color is *not* a function of the videotape. Rather, it depends on whether or not the camera, VCR or TV set is b&w or color. Also, unlike film, videotape can be erased and reused many times.

Like film, videotape is an image storage medium. Both film and videotape record individual pictures or frames of information. Unlike most film, though, videotape contains the capacity to store *both* picture and sound. While 16mm motion picture film records 24 individual frames every second, video records 30 frames a second. On film, these frames are visible and located next to the sprocket holes which control the rate at which the images are run through the camera or projector. The sound track is then placed next to the picture images and synchronized to match. Sound-to-film sync often requires additional equipment and a variety of added steps.

With videotape, the frames are not visible to the eye, but they are present in a series of diagonal lines formed by magnetic particles on the tape.

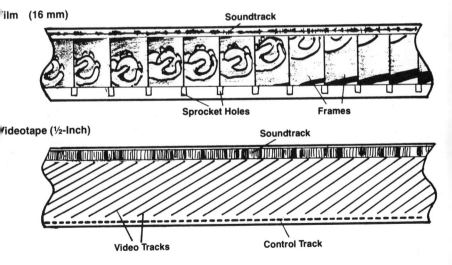

Film (16 mm)
Soundtrack
Sprocket Holes   Frames

Videotape (½-Inch)
Soundtrack
Video Tracks   Control Track

How Tape Is Made

You may take that little videotape cassette that you so routinely shove into your VCR very much for granted. However, the manufacture and quality control of that tape requires incredibly complex, expensive and sophisticated technology. Exotic formulations of magnetically sensitive materials, usually a type of ferrous magnetic oxide, are used, which have the ability to store a great amount of electronic information in a very small space. This is accomplished by packing a high density of fine magnetic particles of extremely uniform size on a piece of thin plastic tape. Very close tolerances of particle distribution and spacing are required, and the particle distribution, orientation and packing density all contribute to the quality of the recorded image. Different manufacturers have various secret tape formulations. Fuji, for example, uses a proprietary formulation called BERTHOLLIDE IRON OXIDE which produces very good image quality and tape durability.

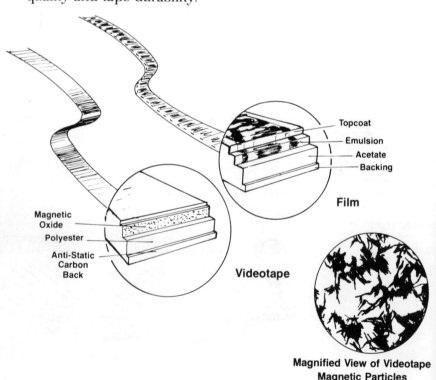

Topcoat
Emulsion
Acetate
Backing

Film

Magnetic Oxide
Polyester
Anti-Static Carbon Back

Videotape

Magnified View of Videotape Magnetic Particles

The trick is to produce a tape that has the highest amount of magnetic energy. The result will be a picture that is strong and bright with brilliant natural colors, very little noise or grain, and with colors that won't bleed or shift.

But the process doesn't stop here. This magnetically sensitive material must be attached or bound to the tape in such a manner that it remains stable, doesn't chip or flake off, and is free of bumps, dips or scratches. The tape must be able to adhere closely to the tape head drum so that it can precisely align with the video head and yet withstand the repeated pounding of the sharp ferrite metal video head, which contacts it 30 times a second. Such wear is tough enough when the tape rapidly passes the head at a fast speed, but the tape receives even greater wear when it is slowed down in long playing modes or subjected to special effects, such as rapid forward or reverse scanning. Still frame playing of the tape in the Pause mode creates very rapid wear on the tape and should be minimized. Extended Play tapes, being thinner, will have even less ability to hold up to such demanding use.

In creating tapes that can handle such demands, the binding process of adhering the magnetically sensitive material to the plastic tape and the choice of binding and tape materials are crucial factors. Generally, an acetate or mylar backing material with good flex characteristics is used, and the surface of the tape is polished to a mirror-smooth state. The smooth surface allows the tape to travel through the VCR and pass the video heads with a minimum of friction, abrasiveness, and wear. This contributes to longer video head and tape life and a minimum of tape deterioration and DROPOUTS.

Dropouts

Tape Dropouts

Tape DROPOUTS are tiny pieces of the oxide which fall off the videotape. These dropouts create a "hole," at which point the videotape can no longer store any information. As a result, you will see a small black or white streak or line of missing information displayed during playback of your tape. All VCRs have DROPOUT COMPENSATORS to try to cover up the missing lines of information, but some dropouts still get through. Dropouts are particuarly annoying to the video perfectionist.

There are a number of factors that contribute to tape dropout, but the most important is poor quality control during tape manufacturing. Absolutely no dust must get into the tape while it is being made or loaded into the video cassettes. Even the cardboard cassette cases can produce debris that can get into the cassette, producing problems. Some tape manufacturers, like Fuji, use plastic cases and plastic-based labels to minimize such problems.

It is normal to expect some dropouts near the beginning and end of each videotape because of increased wear on the tape. In the middle of the tape, though, dropouts should not really be noticeable. If you are experiencing constant dropouts in your picture on the first play—perhaps 20 or 30 a minute or more—you have bad tape and should return it to the manufacturer.

When a tape is played repeatedly it will develop more dropouts. Some brands of tape will begin shedding oxide particles after 10 or 20 passes. Good tape with a good binder and good quality control should be able to make 100 plays (passes) or more without significantly noticeable deterioration. Unfortunately, tape quality control seems to vary widely with some manufacturers; one batch may be good, the next batch may be unacceptable. Of course, if you're just taping programs off-the-air, you're generally not as critically concerned about image quality as a person who wants to make a master of an important production for editing or copying, or someone interested in the large scale duplication of important tapes which will be played frequently.

Since the special effects modes and slower speeds of newer VCRs subject the videotape to much greater wear, several manufacturers have introduced HIGH GRADE (HG) improved formula videotapes. The new formulations will provide more durability and better picture quality at all speeds due to the smaller size and greater number of magnetic particles on the tape. Tape costs are about 10% higher. Examples are TDK's Super Avilyn HG series and Maxell's Epitaxial HG tapes.

Opinions vary as to who makes the best tapes, but generally videophiles speak very highly of TDK, Fuji, Sony, Maxell and RCA tape. Sony makes most of the Beta tapes and with its extensive involvement in tape manufacturing has always maintained good quality control. The major videotape brands are: Sony, Panasonic, JVC, 3-M (Scotch), TDK, Fuji, Maxell, RCA, Memorex, and Ampex.

Kinds of Videotape

A variety of tape lengths are manufactured for both Beta and VHS machines. Also available are so-called EXTENDED LENGTH tapes, which provide longer play times without changing the speed of the VCR. As we mentioned, the tradeoff here is that the Extended Length tape must be made thinner, hence it is a less durable tape.

If you time your tapes, you will also notice that some brands advertised as a certain length will have extra tape on the cassette, resulting in longer playing times than specified. This is particularly true of RCA VHS tape, which may run an extra 10 or 20 minutes in a 2-hour mode. Beta tapes have an extra 5 or so minutes but even a small difference will be doubled or tripled in longer play modes.

Tape Comparison Chart

Cassette Model	Time SP (2-hr)	LP (4-hr)	SLP (6-hr)	Tape Length
VHS				
T-30	30 min	60 min	90 min	68 m (223.1 ft.)
T-60	60 min	120 min (2-hr)	180 min (3-hr)	128 m (419.9 ft.)
T-120	120 min (2-hr)	240 min (4-hr)	360 min (6-hr)	248 m (813.6 ft.)
Extended Length T-180	180 min (3-hr)	360 min (6-hr)	540 min (9-hr)	384 m (1259 ft.)

Cassette Model	Beta I (1-hr)	Beta II (2-hr)	Beta III (3-hr)	Tape Length
BETA				
L-125	15 min	30 min	45 min	42 m (125 ft.)
L-250	30 min	60 min	90 min	78 m (250 ft.)
L-370	45 min	90 min	135 min	114 m (370 ft.)
L-500	60 min	120 min (2-hr)	180 min (3-hr)	150 m (500 ft.)
L-750	90 min	180 min (3-hr)	270 min (4.5-hr)	225 m (750 ft.)
Extended Length L-830	100 min (1.6-hr)	200 min (3.3-hr)	300 min (5-hr)	250 m (830 ft.)

Tape Speed Chart

	Mode	Speed of Tape
VHS	SP	1.31 ips/33.35 mms
	LP	.656 ips/16/67 mms
	SLP	.437 ips/11 mms
BETA	Beta I	1.57 ips/39.97 mms
	Beta II	.787 ips/20.03 mms
	Beta III	.523 ips/13.31 mms

Care And Storage Of Tape

The life of your videotape and your precious recorded images depends greatly on how you handle and store your tape. Unfortunately videotape, as it now exists, has a somewhat limited tolerance to environmental conditions. The oxide doesn't lose its magnetic potency with time, but the base materials in the tape may become brittle, distorted, and lose their intrinsic properties if not stored correctly. Binder material which adheres the magnetic material to the tape may also degenerate which could result in a complete loss of stored data.

What happens is that tape warps and shrinks when exposed to very high and low temperatures, and consequently will not track or play back correctly on the VCR again. Also, stray magnetic fields from electric motors will affect the recording, and dust particles will create dropouts.

The ideal temperature range for archiving is very limited — around 50% humidity and 20°C (70°F) or less temperature. As temperature and humidity vary up or down, tape degeneration occurs at an increasing or decreasing rate. Tape manufacturers recommend that tape not be subjected to temperatures below –40°C (–40°F) or above +80°C (176°F). However, binder degradation begins above 55°C (130°F) and permanent shrinkage of polyester based tapes commences at 60°C (140°F). A car trunk on a hot day can easily exceed 55°C (130°F). More temperature resistant tapes are presently being researched by tape manufacturers.

In the meantime, you can safeguard your valuable recordings for years to come; heat, moisture and dust are the enemies of tape and if avoided, you will minimize or eliminate future problems. One should store tape in a way as to slow down whatever intrinsic deterioration may occur, and certainly tape should be stored in such a way as to prevent contact with moisture or stray magnetic fields. Wrap your tape in plastic bags with tapes stacked vertically in a controlled temperature room, especially during hot summer months.

Use a *dry* basement room that will not produce mildew. As we mentioned, the most devastating opportunity for tape heat damage is the transport of tape by car or by common carrier. Try to safeguard your tape in hot weather by using cooled, insulated boxes, and never leave the tape in an area exposed to direct sunlight. Make copies of valuable material and store them somewhere else. Until more durable tape is developed, it is wise for the video user to anticipate these critical situations and avoid them. Many years of enjoyment from tape can thus be assured.

CARE OF VIDEOTAPE

- Store in a cool dry place.
- Avoid leaving tapes inside cars on hot days.
- Avoid any kind of heating unit.
- Avoid direct sunlight and high humidity.
- Avoid dust, dirt and moisture.
- Never touch the tape.
- Avoid magnetic fields (motors, transformers, magnets, etc.)
- Avoid physical shock.
- Never store tapes only partially wound. It's best to "tight wind" your tapes by allowing the VCR to continue in PLAY mode until reaching the end of the tape. The tape will then be uniformly wound on the reel.
- Store cassettes in their cases, standing upright.
- Remove erase prevention tabs on cassette.
- Do not smoke in rooms with videotape or video equipment.
- Allow tapes to reach room temperature before playing.

5
The
Video Camera

Most home video systems can also be used for recording with an optional camera and microphone. This feature allows you to make your own program for instant replay without having to take your film down to Fotomat or send it off to Kodak for processing. And what's really nice is the *cost!* One hour of super-8 film would require 20 rolls and cost at least $160! And this includes only the picture and not the sound. Further, film can only be used once, and playback usually requires you to thread a projector and tolerate all that chattering noise. With videotape, however, you get instant sound and picture; up to six hours of reusable tape, and no expensive processing is required — all for $4 to $15.

But video has its high initial purchase cost, especially for a color camera. It also has more wires and boxes to deal with and a definite lack of portability as compared to super-8, although this may change soon. Both Sony and RCA have announced plans to introduce a low-cost CCD (CHARGE COUPLED DEVICE) portable color camera which would reduce the weight and size of the video camera considerably. A CCD camera uses a tiny solid state chip with hundreds of thousands of circuits on it to produce a picture image. This tiny chip replaces the bulky camera tube and performs the same function of converting light into electrical information. The CCD camera should also be less temperamental, more rugged and dependable than the camera tube and could be mass produced very cheaply.

Both film and video have their considerable advantages and disadvantages. It's not really a question of video replacing film, at least not immediately, so both will co-exist in the home in the foreseeable future, each doing what it can do best. Overall, film is best for cheap color and portability and large screen projection, and video is best for off-the-air recordings and the taping of long dialog-type events in the home and in the community. Plays, speeches, sports events, birthday parties, award events, etc. are ideal subjects for video.

How The Video Camera Works

The first big shocking realization about doing your own recording with video is the fact that unlike the film camera, the video camera *does not store the picture* inside it. You don't put the tape inside the video camera. Rather, the tape goes on the separate videotape recorder where the pictures and sound are recorded simultaneously. This means that the camera must always be connected to the video recorder. Consequently, you won't be able to take your deck-type video equipment out on a picnic very easily like you can your super-8 camera. Practically speaking, then, you are generally limited to the inside of your house and always limited to the length of your camera cable, unless you have a *portable* videotape recorder.

Since the video camera contains no tape or film and does not store the image, its main purpose is to change the light emitted or reflected from an object into an electronic signal. The process is accomplished by a light sensitive device called a CAMERA TUBE which is located inside the video camera.

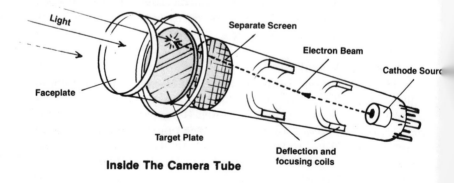

Inside The Camera Tube

Camera Tubes

Low cost cameras use a type of camera tube called a VIDICON tube containing a COLOR STRIPE FILTER which produces the color. Vidicon tubes are inexpensive to make, but can be burned easily by bright lights and produce a characteristic "image lag" or streaking effect at low light levels. The first round of home cameras used a 1-inch diameter tube, but the second generation cameras are using smaller 2/3-inch diameter tubes which makes possible smaller, less expensive, and more energy efficient cameras.

After the camera tube changes the physical light from the object into an electronic signal, this signal is relayed to the VCR where it is stored and recorded on the videotape. Most portable video cameras contain a built-in microphone which picks up the sound and sends the sound to the VCR for recording along with the picture from the camera. Some cameras require an EXTERNAL MICROPHONE. Since both the sound and picture are recorded on the same piece of tape together, they will be in SYNCHRONIZATION (SYNC) with each other at all times. This is accomplished by recording the video and the audio in separate TRACKS on the videotape.

Tracks On Tape

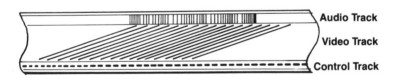

½-Inch Videotape

Color vs. Black And White

As we mentioned in the videotape chapter, the videotape, unlike film, does not determine whether the picture is reproduced in b&w or color. Rather, it is the camera and the VCR that determines whether the picture is color or b&w. Since all home VCRs record both color and b&w, the camera then becomes the primary determining factor. Up until 1979, there was a significant difference in cost between color and b&w video cameras. Prior to 1973, color cameras cost at least $10,000. They then came down to $3,000-$5,000, and finally, 1978 introduced the year of the under $1,000 color camera. Now, basic color cameras for home use cost as little as $650 retail price. It's doubtful that the price will be reduced significantly further without going to radical new technology such as CCD camera tubes. Unless new optical technologies are also forthcoming, limiting camera costs will then be the lenses and electronic viewfinder systems. Some camera systems allow you to add the "bells and whistles" later, like an electronic viewfinder and zoom lens, both very useful, but then you're up to $1,000-$1,300.

Since b&w cameras cost from $200–$500, it makes sense to dig deep for the extra bucks and go for the color camera at $650. The new color cameras are quite lightweight, 4 to 10 pounds, come in a variety of styles with different lenses and viewfinders, and have built-in electret-condenser microphones to record the sound. They also have VCR remote start/stop switches located in the hand grip on the camera body. Color cameras are more complex than b&w cameras, usually need slightly more light than the b&w cameras to produce a good picture, and must be adjusted specifically for the type of lighting under which you are shooting. Color is especially exciting when shooting colorful scenes outdoors with children, or of fairs and parades. Those red, green and blue toys around the Christmas tree will look great and so will your special friend's sexy blue eyes. Color is, of course, a *necessity* if you're shooting color art work, selling products for a business, or intending to make a tape for large scale distribution.

AC/DC Operation

All home video cameras are 12-volt DC-type cameras so they can be easily operated on battery power. When used with a portable VCR, only a single multi-pin cable from the VCR to the camera provides all functions: of power, video, sound and remote start/stop. When the camera is used with the deck-type AC operated VCR, use the CAMERA CONTROL UNIT (CCU) which is always provided by the manufacturer. This allows the camera to interface with the AC-type VCR. The CCU, often called an AC ADAPTER, operates the DC camera off the AC power, and on some models, separates the audio and video outputs from the multi-pin camera cable so they can be plugged into the deck-type VCR.

80

System Connection For Camera
and Microphone

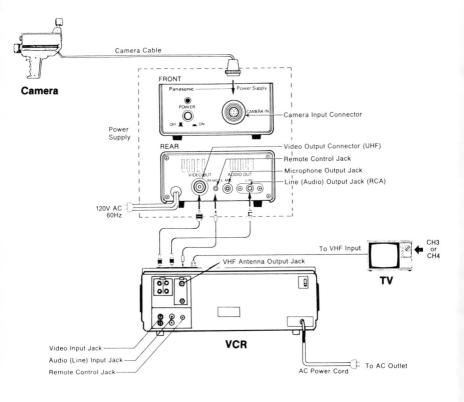

Camera Cable

Camera

FRONT

Panasonic

POWER

OFF ◼ ON

Power Supply

CAMERA IN — Camera Input Connector

Power Supply

REAR

VIDEO OUT   AUDIO OUT

REMOTE   MIC   LINE

Video Output Connector (UHF)
Remote Control Jack
Microphone Output Jack
Line (Audio) Output Jack (RCA)

120V AC
60Hz

To VHF Input

CH3
or
CH4

VHF Antenna Output Jack

TV

Video Input Jack
Audio (Line) Input Jack
Remote Control Jack

VCR

AC Power Cord   To AC Outlet

Connection Procedure

Step 1 Connect the VCR to the TV set.

Step 2 Connect the camera power unit to an AC plug.

Step 3 Connect the camera power unit VIDEO OUT plug or video cable to the VIDEO IN or CAMERA plug on the back of the VCR.

Step 4 Connect the camera power unit AUDIO OUT plug or audio cable to the AUDIO IN plug on the back of the VCR or connect the MIC OUT or microphone cable to the MIC or MICROPHONE input on the front of the VCR.

81

NOTE: The Sony b&w camera (AVC-1420) does not have a built-in microphone so you will need to connect a separate microphone to the MIC input plug on the front of the VCR.

Step 5 Turn everything on and fine tune the TV set to the correct VCR channel, usually 3 or 4.

To monitor the scene while you are shooting, plug the camera into the video recorder, set the proper controls for camera recording, turn on the TV set, and adjust it to Channel 3 or 4, whichever looks better. When you turn the camera on, its picture should appear on your TV set.

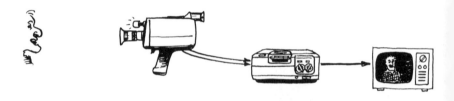

Step 6 Load a tape into the VCR.

Step 7 Make sure the VCR INPUT SELECTOR is in the CAMERA mode and set the *PROGRAM SELECTor* to VCR or VTR.

Step 8 Place the VCR in RECORD mode and use the TV set to monitor the scene you are shooting. The camera's picture should now appear on the TV set. You should hear the sound if the TV volume is turned up. If you don't get any picture or sound, check your connections and repeat steps 1-6.

NOTE: It's best to turn down the sound on the TV while you are shooting in order to avoid audio feedback.

Step 9 If the sound and the picture are okay, set the tape counter to "000" and begin recording.

Step 10 Rewind the tape when finished and playback the program.

C-Mount

Most home video cameras use a standard C-mount type lens mount. This means many other C-mount type lenses can be used with the camera. C-mount adapters can also be purchased in photo stores to allow use of 35mm camera lenses. Sometimes, though, the color may not be as good due to the less than optimum position of a different lens relative to the placement of the camera tube inside the camera.

Camera Design

Most home video cameras now look exactly like super 8 cameras. They are lightweight and are generally held in the hand. Unfortunately, this design makes them difficult to hold smoothly. Broadcast TV manufacturers found that cameras under 14 lbs. became impossible to hold smoothly and had to have weight added to them. The ideal camera for the more serious home video person is the kind that rests partly over one shoulder, has a good hand grip, and weighs in the range of 8–10 lbs. Most top-of-the-line color home cameras are of this type, but are more lightweight.

There are three basic camera designs to choose from. Both b&w and color cameras are available in all three of these categories.

B&W Camera

Color Camera

Basic Model — The least expensive models generally cost about $650 in color, $200 in b&w. These are just a camera body with a simple top-mounted optical viewfinder and fixed focus non-zoom lens. Even the basic models, though, include built-in microphones.

B&W Camera

Color Camera

TTL Models — The TTL or THROUGH-THE-LENS viewfinder camera works just like a 35mm single-lens reflex camera. You can see what you are shooting in color. The problem with this system is that it is often hard to focus accurately, although the diopter eyepiece allows adjustment for individuals with different eyesight. However, it is cheaper and simpler than the electronic viewfinder system. Costs for color cameras are about $800 or $350 for b&w cameras. Also added are 4:1 power zooms and automatic iris lenses used in cameras like the Panasonic PK-500 or RCA CC003. Useful extendable directional microphones are mounted on the camera for improved quality sound. Wind screens on the microphone are a necessity for outdoor shooting.

Color Camera

Deluxe Models — The top-of-the-line models generally include all the "bells and whistles" such as shoulder mounts, electronic viewfinders, in-the-field VCR playback, 6:1 auto-iris power zoom lens, and, in some cases, a macro close-up ability (JVC cameras), auto and normal Color Temperature, White Balance controls, and extendable microphone. The weight of these cameras is about 6-10 lbs. Costs are around $960-$1,300 for color, and $500 for b&w.

Choosing A Camera

What camera is right for you? Nearly all these cameras produce really amazing color pictures under good lighting conditions. You will be happy to hear the oohs and ahs when you play back your first outdoor pictures of the family on your TV set. Certainly it's nice to have the 6:1 power zoom lens deluxe model, but it really doesn't take any better pictures than the basic model. But in the hands of a creative camera person the deluxe model will definitely provide a much greater range of shooting options and therefore a more professional looking and interesting tape.

If you don't intend to use your camera very much, it may make more sense to stick to the basic models. On the other hand, if you really intend to try and tape events for money, such as weddings and sports events, the 6:1 zoom lens and electronic viewfinder are a must, as a fixed focus lens is almost useless in these kinds of situations. Of course money is a factor too, and that may determine what you can afford. Try out the various cameras before you buy and get a feel for how easy or difficult the various models are to work with. If you do purchase a basic model you will find that it helps to use your TV set as a monitor to see what you are shooting, although this is not a very portable situation.

Camera Features

VIEWFINDERS — Electronic viewfinder cameras use a 1.5 inch miniature TV set to monitor what you are shooting. Unfortunately, electronic viewfinders are b&w only because the cost and complexity of a color viewfinder would make the camera prohibitively expensive. It is definitely difficult to photograph certain things like flowers when you can only see in b&w. You often can't distinguish the flowers from the weeds. However, the pictures sure look impressive and surprising when you watch the playback in color later on your TV set. The TTL viewfinder has an advantage here because you can see the picture in color. Many cameras also provide instant playback (monitoring) of the picture from the VCR through the cameras' electronic viewfinder. Some cameras will also playback sound through built-in sound monitors like the Hitachi VK/C 500R or Toshiba IK-1610 cameras. It's a nifty idea — otherwise you must use the earphone to hear the sound from the VCR. The in-field playback ability comes in very handy sometimes to locate a starting point on the tape, to check to see if you brought the right tape, or if your VCR is recording properly.

Electronic
Viewfinder

Light Level
Indicator

Electronic viewfinders usually contain a number of handy LED indicators that show under-exposure, over-exposure, and proper exposure to light, low battery charge, and whether or not the VCR is running. Also displayed on some cameras is the proper Color Balance adjustment. TTL cameras also have some display indicators.

ZOOM LENS — A zoom lens is several lenses in one and usually has a three-to-one (3:1), 4:1, or 6:1 range. This means the object can be made three times (3x), four times (4x), or six times (6x) closer or larger at full telephoto relative to the full wide angle position. Some cameras like the JVC G-71USJ and GX-77U also have a macro closeup position on the lens which allows you to actually place the lens against the object and focus on it. New zoom lenses are also very "fast." They have very wide apertures and are able to admit a lot of light, thus enabling the camera to shoot under low light conditions. Lens speeds are generally F2.8, F1.8 or F1.4. Zoom lenses are really useful and if you use your camera frequently, you will probably want a 6:1 zoom lens.

POWER ZOOM — Most newer deluxe cameras now feature power zooms which help give your camera work a professional look. The drawbacks are increased power drain and complexity, and usually the zoom speed is not variable. However, you can also manually zoom.

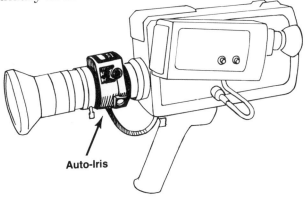

Auto-Iris

AUTOMATIC IRIS — A very useful lens feature is an AUTOMATIC IRIS. The auto-iris automatically adjusts the lens opening or aperture to admit the proper amount of light for the camera. It also helps prevent accidental burn of the camera tube. Since video cameras do not have the ability to deal with a wide range of contrast (ratio of brightest area of picture to darkest area) in the shooting scene, the aperture setting is very critical to obtaining good color. Film is much more tolerant of high contrast ratios in scenes than video. The auto-iris lens works quite well and can deal with most lighting situations except strongly back-lighted scenes where the subject might be standing in front of a bright doorway or sky. Most newer cameras have a special

BACKLIGHT CONTROL which lets you compensate for this problem. Also, most better auto-iris lenses allow you to manually override the control and set the lens iris for unusual lighting circumstances. Cameras with backlight control switches accomplish this also. Most electronic viewfinders also have exposure indicators to signal proper exposure. TTL cameras also have some built-in exposure indicators.

AUTOMATIC FADE — Some cameras such as the Sony HVC-2000 and the JVC GX-68U have an electronic fade-in and fade-out mechanism like some super-8 cameras. Merely press the fade button on the camera to automatically activate a 5-second fade-in or fade-out.

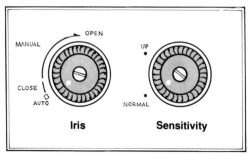

LOW LIGHT LEVEL SWITCHES — Some cameras, such as the JVC cameras, have a LOW LIGHT LEVEL SWITCH which boosts the camera sensitivity in low light situations. This technique is similar to "pushing" film. As with films, some "noise" or graininess is usually evident in the picture when the sensitivity is increased. Generally speaking, most cameras recommend a minimum practical light level of 100 LUX or 9 foot-candles (ft-c) in the increased sensitivity low light level mode. 9 ft-c is about the average illumination in the moderately lighted house. Optimum recommended lighting is 1000-2000 LUX or 90-180 ft-c.

TRIPOD MOUNTING — All cameras should have a standard tripod mount under the camera body. Some, such as the JVC cameras, have one tripod mount under the handgrip and another under the camera body. It's better to be able to mount the camera body directly on the tripod without the handgrip in between. This allows much better stability and permits mounting on accessory shoulder mount devices, graphic stands and wall mounts.

OTHER CAMERA FEATURES — Some cameras like the JVC GX-33U and GX-66U have a RUN-LOCK-START/STOP TRIGGER SWITCH on the camera so that accidental switch operation can be eliminated. Most cameras have a bracket mounted on top of the camera for mounting an external microphone or an auxiliary light.

Color Temperature Control

All color cameras must be properly adjusted for the specific lighting circumstances. Otherwise, your pictures will have a green, blue, or yellow tint in them. This is because different types of light have different COLOR TEMPERATURES.

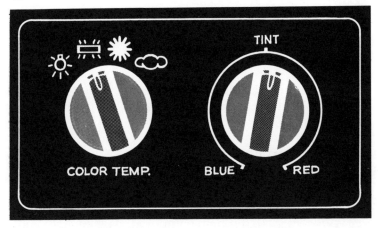

Color Temperature and White Balance Controls

Color Temperature is the measure of the temperature of light expressed in DEGREES KELVIN (°K). Daylight contains a full spectrum of color, but flourescent and incandescent lights lack certain color components. Sunsets, sunrises and shade also lack certain colors. The eye is able to adjust to these variations, but color video cameras cannot, so every color camera must have some kind of color control ability. Generally, a camera has a two, three, or four-position switch located on the side or back of the camera, or in some cases such as the JVC G-31/G-71/USJ camera, you merely place an orange filter in front of the lens for outdoor shooting. Most other cameras use either filters or electronic Color Temperature conversion systems to properly set the camera.

At least two positions of Color Temperature settings are needed for basic outdoor or indoor settings. Three positions are better, but four positions are better still. The primary color environments are:

Color Temperature Chart		
Symbol	Situation	Color Temperature
⌒⌒	Cloudy Bright or Shade	7000° K
✹	Daylight or Bright Sun	6000° K
💡	Fluorescent lighting	3200° K
💡	Incandescent lighting	3000° K

White Balance

But for really precise color adjustment, an additional control is required. Usually called a WHITE BALANCE control, this consists of one or two knobs labeled RED and BLUE. The White Balance enables the camera to reference to how white should look under the prevailing lighting conditions. Once this condition is established then the camera can easily get all the other colors correct because white contains all colors. The White Balance control is used along with or instead of the preset Color Temperature settings on the camera.

To manually set the White Balance, merely point the camera at a large white object that is being illuminated by the light you will be shooting under and adjust the RED and BLUE controls until the meter (usually inside the camera viewfinder) registers the correct position as indicated by the camera's operating manual. Under most circumstances, the three or four preset color temperature settings are adequate, but it's nice to have a White Balance control as well. Remember: the White Balance or Color Temperature must be *reset every time* you change from one lighting environment to another.

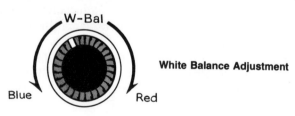

White Balance Adjustment

A Look At Color Cameras

Hitachi

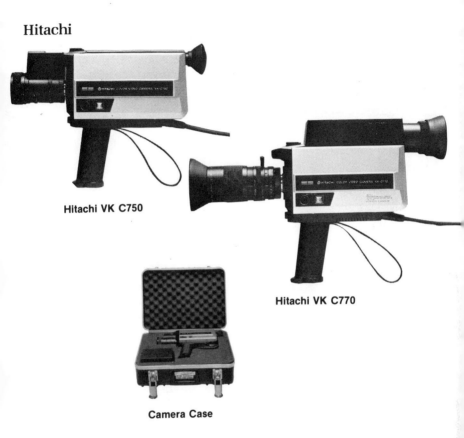

Hitachi VK C750

Hitachi VK C770

Camera Case

Hitachi has two cameras, the VK C750 and the VK C770. The VK C750 is a TTL optical viewfinder model with a 2.8 to 1 zoom lens, built in uni-directional mic, and single knob color Temperature control with meter. It's quite lightweight at 4 lbs.

The deluxe model VK C770 also includes the single knob Color Temperature control with meter but adds the electronic viewfinder, a 6:1 zoom lens and a Macro close-up capability. Weight is only 4.8 lbs. Both cameras use a 2/3-inch TRI-ELECTRODE Vidicon tube. Hitachi also has a nice camera carrying case.

Panasonic/RCA/Quasar

PK-800   PK-750   PK-700   PK-530

Panasonic makes a whole series of cameras which several other manufacturers such as RCA, Quasar and others also distribute. The newer series of cameras include the PK-530, a basic 3:1 zoom TTL camera, the PK-700 with electronic viewfinder, 6:1 zoom lens and extendable microphone, the PK-750 with rotatable electronic viewfinder, 6:1 zoom and extendable mic and the PK-800 which includes all the features of the PK-700 and PK-750 but uses a more sophisticated 2/3-inch SATICON tube instead of the usual 2/3-inch Vidicon tube.

The Saticon tube resists permanent burning created by bright lights and minimizes ghosting or image lag which often appears when the camera pans in low light conditions. All these cameras weigh from 4 to 5 lbs. and include Color Temperature controls.

JVC

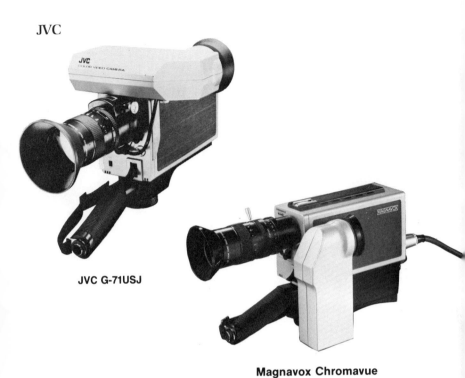

JVC G-71USJ

Magnavox Chromavue

The older JVC G-71 USJ camera has now been retired in favor of more feature-laden lightweight cameras. Nevertheless, it remains a real trendsetter with its great picture quality, shoulder mount design, auto-iris lens and macro-focus ability. However, it lacked adequate White Balance adjustments.

JVC's newer cameras include the GX-68U and GX-77U cameras. Both use 2/3-inch Vidicon tubes, have a COUNTERLIGHT COMPENSATION Switch (GX-68U) or a BACKLIGHT CONTROL Switch (GX-77U) to deal with strong backlight situations. The electronic light sensing system in the GX-68U uses a center-weighted automatic control to give optimum exposure to the main subject at the center of the scene being shot. The GX-68U's automatic iris allows shooting in as little as 7 footcandles (very low light) and has a 3-position Color Compensation Switch and Manual Tint Control.

JVC GX-68U

JVC GX-77U

A really nice feature of the GX-68U is its automatic fade-in and fade-out control which gives professional looking fades. Another good feature is a practical power saving Standby Switch which conserves battery power. Although the camera is a TTL optical viewfinder camera, an optional electronic viewfinder may be mounted on top, giving you a choice of either viewfinder simultaneously. Optional accessories include a nice camera carrying case and screw-on wide angle and telephoto lenses. Camera weight is only 3.3 lbs. with lens and handgrip.

The JVC GX-77U camera is only slightly heavier at 3.7 lbs. but feels much more rugged, has 5:1 power zoom and one of the sharpest (270 horizontal lines pictures) of any other camera in its class. Only the Sony HVC-2000 exceeds this at 300 lines. The lens is a fast f1.4, and it offers a Macro close-up function and has a microphone mounted in the base of the handgrip. The camera is a TTL viewfinder design and has very low power consumption.

Sony

Sony HVC-1000

Sony's first entry into the home color camera field was the HVC-1000, a TTL type lightweight camera with a 3:1 non-removable lens. It used a 2/3-inch MIXED FIELD TRINICON tube which is a type of proprietary tube that has been used in nearly all Sony non-broadcast cameras for years. Although the HVC-1000 produced a good color picture, it suffered from a lack of optional electronic viewfinder, a short range non-interchangeable zoom lens and the use of a non-standard 14-Pin camera connector. Most portable VCRs use 10-Pin camera connectors.

The HVC-1000 was followed by 2 more sophisticated cameras, the HVC-2010 and the HVC-2000. Both these newer cameras also utilize a 2/3-inch Trinicon tube and produce good color pictures down to only 70 lux or 7 footcandles. These cameras seem rugged, easy to carry, are well designed and have lots of useful features.

The HVC-2010 is an optical viewfinder camera and has a unique 2 posiiton f 1.8 zoom lens that switches from normal to telephoto instantly without need of focusing. It has an automatic or manual aperture control, 4-position White Balance Selector with Color Temperature Conversion Filter, tally, battery level, low light and white balance indicators.

Sony HVC-2010

Sony HVC-2000

Now here's a camera with all the bells and whistles. The deluxe model HVC-2000 just may be the best consumer video color camera available. Like the HVC-2010, the HVC-2000 also has a picture resultion of 300 horizontal lines, the best of the home cameras. It also has many useful features such as a quality f 1.8 Canon 6:1 power zoom lens, automatic or manual iris control, and a rotatable electronic viewfinder with tally, battery level, low light, white balance, iris and video level indicators.

The camera's really unique features include a 3-position Sensitivity Selector for low light level, automatic operation in normal light or high light level, a 3-position Sharpness Selector (high, normal, and soft), an automatic fade-in and fade-out control, waveform (video level) monitoring in the camera's viewfinder and a Peaking Switch for the viewfinder that provides easier focusing and fatigue-free viewing. The weight of the camera is about 6½ lbs., the power draw is 8.3 watts, and the camera seems quite rugged and durable. Cost is about $1,250.

Sony HVC-2000

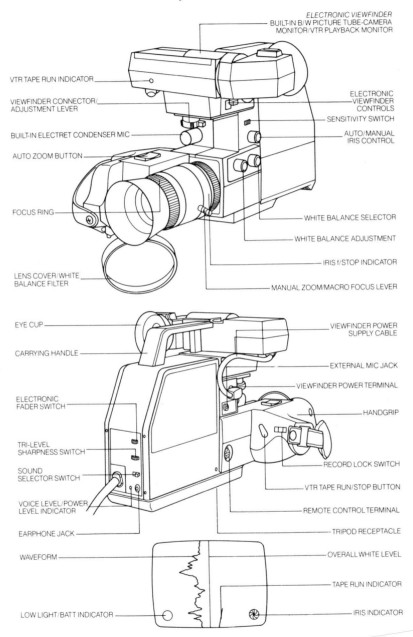

ELECTRONIC VIEWFINDER
BUILT-IN B/W PICTURE TUBE-CAMERA
MONITOR/VTR PLAYBACK MONITOR

VTR TAPE RUN INDICATOR

VIEWFINDER CONNECTOR/
ADJUSTMENT LEVER

BUILT-IN ELECTRET CONDENSER MIC

AUTO ZOOM BUTTON

FOCUS RING

LENS COVER/WHITE
BALANCE FILTER

ELECTRONIC
VIEWFINDER
CONTROLS

SENSITIVITY SWITCH

AUTO/MANUAL
IRIS CONTROL

WHITE BALANCE SELECTOR

WHITE BALANCE ADJUSTMENT

IRIS f/STOP INDICATOR

MANUAL ZOOM/MACRO FOCUS LEVER

EYE CUP

CARRYING HANDLE

ELECTRONIC
FADER SWITCH

TRI-LEVEL
SHARPNESS SWITCH

SOUND
SELECTOR SWITCH

VOICE LEVEL/POWER
LEVEL INDICATOR

EARPHONE JACK

WAVEFORM

LOW LIGHT/BATT INDICATOR

VIEWFINDER POWER
SUPPLY CABLE

EXTERNAL MIC JACK

VIEWFINDER POWER TERMINAL

HANDGRIP

RECORD LOCK SWITCH

VTR TAPE RUN/STOP BUTTON

REMOTE CONTROL TERMINAL

TRIPOD RECEPTACLE

OVERALL WHITE LEVEL

TAPE RUN INDICATOR

IRIS INDICATOR

97

A number of accessories are available including a rechargeable battery pack (HVD-200), a telecine adaptor (VCR-4), camera titler (HVT-2100) and a 20-foot camera extension cable (VFC-6CB). Unfortunately, though, all the Sony cameras use a non-standard 14-Pin camera connector. Therefore, the cable connector will have to be specially adapted to work with other portable VCRs (all VHS VCRs use a 10-Pin connector).

Toshiba

Toshiba IK-1850

Toshiba's first camera was the model IK-1650 which has now been improved and become the model IK-1850. It's features include a side-mounted rotatable electronic viewfinder and an auto-iris C-mount 10:1 zoom lens. The camera weighs only 3.7 lbs. Toshiba also has a revolutionary AUTO-FOCUS model, the IK-1850AF which continually focuses the lens automatically. The IK-1850AF has a 6:1 auto-iris zoom lens and requires only half as much light for pictures as other similar cameras. The minimum light is 50 lux or only 5 footcandles!

This amazing sensitivity is accomplished by using a newly developed highly sensitive 2/3-inch UNIVICON-2 Vidicon pickup tube which improves resolution and color characteristics. The auto-focus ability is made possible by using a CHARGE COUPLED DEVICE (CCD) solid state spectrum sensing system in the camera. Toshiba has also added a Vidicon auto-shutoff device to prevent damage to the camera tube. The IK-1850AF is priced at around $1,400 and uses the 14-Pin Sony/Beta camera connector.

Other Cameras

Sharp has one home camera model, the QC-35, a 1-inch Tri-Electrode Vidicon model with a rotatable electronic viewfinder, incident light level indicator, and C-mount 6:1 f1.8 auto-iris zoom lens. Color temperature controls are included, and the camera is a practical shoulder-mount design with a convenient carrying handle and weighs 7.7 lbs. The price is about $1,000.

Akai has 2 models, the VC-30, an optical viewfinder. TTL camera with 3:1 zoom lens, auto-iris and the usual basic features and the electronic viewfinder model, the VC-65 with a 6:1 auto-iris zoom lens with macro-focus and Color Temperature controls. The weight of the VC-65 is 4.8 lbs.

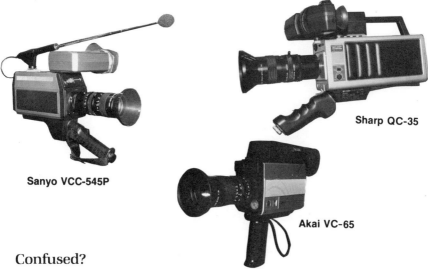

Sharp QC-35

Sanyo VCC-545P

Akai VC-65

Confused?

Obviously, in the camera department, there is lots to choose from too. Most of these cameras perform comparably for their price range, so you have to make your choice based on camera features and your particular needs. Try out a camera in low light and daylight and check the color and listen to sound quality. Is it easy to focus and adjust for correct color balance? As we mentioned earlier, color cameras are the most rapidly evolving video technology and are likely to become obsolete more rapidly than other components in the video system. However, all of the cameras will work well in most situations and can produce considerable enjoyment.

6

Portable Video Systems

Portable video recorders add an exciting new dimension to home video. Now you can take your VCR almost anywhere and record several hours of good color picture and sound on location. Portable video can bring the spontaneity and life of the outside world into your living room with an ease that invites investigation.

A wide variety of systems are available. A portable video system includes a battery powered recorder that weighs from 14 to 22 pounds and a battery powered camera that weighs from 4 to 12 pounds. The cost is approximately $2,500 retail for the VCR and a color camera, and systems are available both in the Beta and VHS format. All portable home VCRs have at least a 2-hour X2 or SP mode and some two-speed VCRs have a 4-hour or 6-hour LP mode (Panasonic PV-2300).

All VCR systems have a particular color camera that is recommended by the manufacturer for the system, but generally any camera can be used with the proper plug adapters. All portable VCRs include an RF Adapter which allows you to play back your tape immediately on any TV set, on either channel 3 or channel 4. If you have a camera with an electronic viewfinder, the tape can be played back in the camera viewfinder and the sound can be monitored with an earphone or a headset from the VCR. Certain cameras such as the Hitachi VKC-500R and the Toshiba IK-1610 have a built-in speaker for sound monitoring. Internal batteries inside the VCR generally provide from ½ hour to 2 hours of VCR and camera operation, depending on the power draw of a particular camera and VCR and the type of battery used.

All batteries are rechargeable, generally overnight, and extra batteries can be carried for longer shooting times. All portable combinations come with an AC Adapter/Battery Charger. Optional items include an external Tuner/Timer for recording off the air, and an assortment of lenses, carrying cases, car battery cords, microphones and other useful items.

The total portable VCR and camera system represents a considerably larger investment than the stay-at-home deck-type model system. The cost is considerably greater for the portable VCR alone ($1,400 versus $800), but the portable system affords much greater flexibility. With the Tuner/Timer, the portable system can do nearly everything the deck-type models can do. Some portables have the two or three-speed capabilities and the only feature most lack is the three or four event programmable function. However, if you really plan to be active with your VCR, the portable system is the only way to go. There are an incredible number of applications for fun, profit and education with the portable VCR. (*See Chapter 12, What To Do With Your VCR.*)
System

The Basic System

First we start with the portable VCR. You have to decide whether you want a Beta or VHS type. (*See Chapter 2, Purchasing a Home VCR.*) Also check out the portable VCR systems comparison section at the end of this chapter.

Next, select your color camera. There isn't much choice with some systems like the Sony SL-3000. You have to use the camera specified (HVC-1000). If you do have a choice, however, the electronic viewfinder camera with an auto-iris lens with 6:1 zoom lens is almost essential for serious shooting. You may find that the optical viewfinder cameras can be difficult to focus. However, they are less expensive, more lightweight and do display the picture in color.

Included with most systems is a rechargeable battery which is supposed to provide 30 minutes of battery operation of the camera and the VCR with the older Panasonic/Quasar/Magnavox portable VCR and large portable camera and up to 1 hour or more on many of the newer systems which use the smaller more energy efficient cameras. However, the effective battery operating time with some batteries seems to decrease fairly rapidly with use, so you're soon down to only 20 or 30 minutes on a charge. You will need from 3 to 8 hours (depending on battery type) to recharge the battery which fits inside the VCR.

The battery can be recharged inside the VCR when the AC Adapter/Battery Charger (included in the system) is plugged into the VCR. A second battery can also be recharged simultaneously by the adapter.

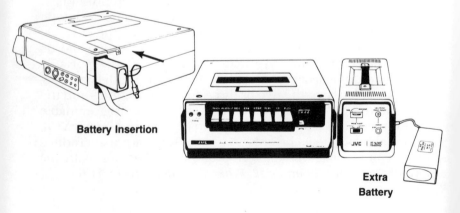

Battery Insertion

Extra Battery

102

Battery Care—Power for the People

The type of battery used by most home VCRs is a lead-acid gel battery. Unfortunately, they are tricky and can be ruined easily. They should not be stored near heat or for a long time without charging; the battery should be recharged immediately after each use. You should never run them down completely otherwise they may not recover. Battery capacity may be reduced by half in temperatures below 5°C (41°F). They are delicate and shouldn't be dropped and they should never be charged with anything other than the manufacturer's specified charger. The correct charger automatically reduces the charge rate as the battery nears full capacity so as to prevent damage from overcharging.

Also, when some batteries are new, they have a habit of remembering only the duration of their last usage. Thus, if you use it for 15 minutes and charge it back up, it might only run for 15 minutes again before showing a discharged battery and soon after may die. When starting with a new battery first charge it all the way up, then place the VCR in the Play mode and let it run until the battery charge meter shows discharge. Then charge it up again and repeat a second time. This should restore it to full charge. Eventually, in normal use after 100 charges or so, the battery life is shortened and you will need to get a new battery. They're expensive—$45 or so and often hard to locate.

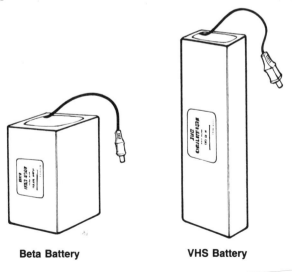

Beta Battery   **VHS Battery**

Fortunately, most home VCR batteries within the VHS or Beta format are interchangeable, since Panasonic makes the VHS batteries for Quasar, JVC, and RCA portables, and Sony batteries fit all Beta portables. An extra battery is an essential accessory for extensive shooting.

Caution: Do not short out the battery plug as it will explode and could cause severe injury to people!

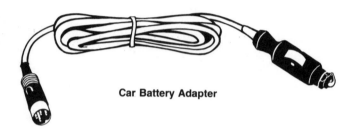

Car Battery Adapter

Since all portable VCRs are 12 volts DC and use a standard 4-pin power plug, a variety of 12 volt DC power sources can be used if wired correctly. A car cigarette lighter/adapter is available for about $20 from each manufacturer, and while it will not recharge your battery, it will prevent it from running down while it is plugged into the car's electrical system. Also, motorcycle batteries can be used if they are hooked up correctly and there is a wide variety of professional power belts used for video and film equipment that will run your equipment for 4 to 8 hours. These however are very expensive ($200 to $400).

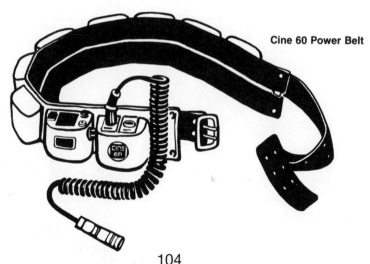

Cine 60 Power Belt

Vital Accessories

There are certain accessories that you will absolutely need and others that are really nice to have.

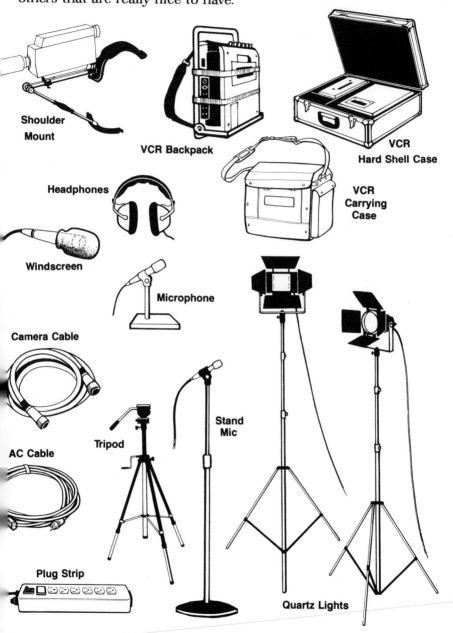

Shoulder Mount

VCR Backpack

VCR Hard Shell Case

Headphones

VCR Carrying Case

Windscreen

Microphone

Camera Cable

AC Cable

Tripod

Stand Mic

Plug Strip

Quartz Lights

105

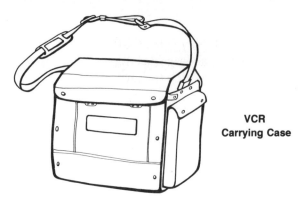

**VCR
Carrying Case**

VCR Carrying Case

The first accessory that you should buy is the protective carrying case for your VCR. Each manufacturer has a special case for each VCR. The case has nice cutouts for the controls, often an auxiliary pouch for extra batteries and a shoulder strap that immediately requires some good foam padding where it contacts the shoulder. Twenty-two pounds of VCR can really be hard on your shoulder after 10 minutes or so.

The carrying case is necessary as the VCR tends to be bounced around a lot; you will be setting it down on pavement, rocks and behind car seats, and it can get damaged fast. Forty dollars or so for a carrying case is a small investment to protect your $1,400 VCR. You might also consider getting an inexpensive pack frame. A VCR is a lot easier to carry around when the weight is distributed on both shoulders rather than concentrated on the strap over one shoulder. These pack frames can be purchased in many backpacking and hardware stores. Make sure you fasten the VCR securely to the pack frame so it doesn't fall off.

VCR Backpack

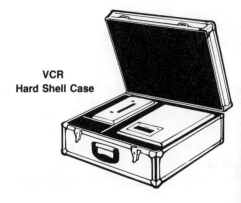

**VCR
Hard Shell Case**

Camera
Hard Shell Case

The camera also needs some kind of carrying case to protect it from damage. A medium-sized luggage bag might suffice for those of you on a minimum budget, or you might get one of those really nice, but expensive, foam padded photographic cases. Other options are the deluxe fiberglass carrying cases or reinforced metal equipment shipping cases from manufacturers like Anvil or accessory supply houses such as Comprehensive Video. The big cases run $150 to $300 but offer extremely effective protection.

Battery

The next essential item is an extra battery. If you intend to use your VCR for long period of time (2 to 4 hours without recharging) you'd better bring one along. As we said, they may be hard to find, but keep at it. It is better for the battery (longer life and shorter recharge time) to use two batteries for 30 minutes each than one battery for 60 minutes.

Tripod

If you intend to videotape people speaking at lectures, class plays and the like, and you want a steady professional look to your tape, you should definitely consider the purchase of a good tripod. Unfortunately, most inexpensive photographic tripods ($20 to $80) are of the friction-head type and don't provide smooth panning and tilting for film or video cameras. Friction-head tripods are usually designed for still cameras. What really works nicely is a FLUID-HEAD tripod. All professional film and video crews use this type of tripod, but they are expensive, even the small ones ($200 to $800). Look for deals on used ones and check film supply stores in big cities for bargains.

Fluid Head Tripod

Lighting

If shooting primarily outdoors lighting is not a problem as there is usually plenty of it from the sun. Color cameras are sufficiently sensitive to be able to shoot until well after sunset.

Indoors though, you will need an extra light or two for good picture quality. The least expensive option is to purchase one or two photographic lights and stands from a photo store and just aim them in the general direction of the subject. If the walls are white you can bounce the light off the wall to get a less harsh effect. Even just one extra lamp 10 to 20 feet from the subject will make a big difference in the quality of your picture (*See Chapter 8, Production Aesthetics—Lighting.*)

Vital Cables

Nothing works without the correct cables. Your first purchase will be an AC plug strip, one or two 25-foot AC extension cables and, as mentioned before, long microphone extension cables. Another long cable that will prove very useful is the RF Cable which connects the VCR to the TV set for playback. If you show tapes to large groups you will want three cables and a two-way RF SPLITTER (available at any electronics store) so you can run two TV sets at once with sound and picture. You could run 3 or 4 TV sets with more cables and a four-way RF SPLITTER, but you shouldn't add any more TV sets without using an RF AMPLIFIER.

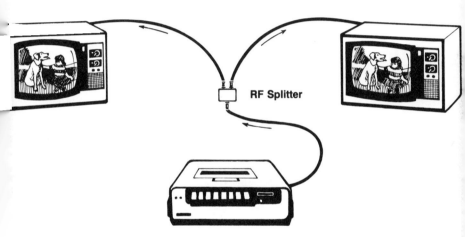

Vital Audio Accessories

If shooting lectures, plays, interviews and concerts where the camera will be more than 10 feet from a critical sound source you will definitely need an external microphone and extension cables. The microphone in the camera is adequate for picking up sounds within 5 to 10 feet, but it is omnidirectional in most cases and thus not very selective of sounds. You should buy a good hand-held low impedence (250-800 ohms) cardioid, electret condenser microphone in the $40 to $80 price range. Also purchase or make up two 30-foot microphone extension cables with metal plugs on them. A mike stand, desk and/or floor model, is also necessary. Finally, a good set of high impedance headphones is required to accurately hear what you are recording. Eight-ohms home-type headsets will not work. The Sennheiser model 414X works really well. They are often on sale at $40 or so. They come with a stereo PHONE plug which must be adapted down to a mono-MINI plug. Most hi-fi stores have such an adapter.

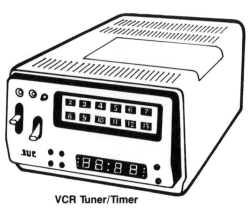

VCR Tuner/Timer

Other Accessories

External Tuner/Timers are available for most portable VCRs which allow recording off-the-air TV programs. Some systems, such as the Panasonic PV-2100/PV-2200, include the Tuner/Timer AC Adapter in the VCR package. With JVC and Sony, it is a separate option. Price is $250 to $500 depending on the manufacturer. CAUTION: In most cases the Tuner/Timer is **also** the Battery Charger and AC Adapter, so if you don't have one you can't charge your batteries.

Preparation for Shooting

So now you've got your basic system and you're ready to set it up. As soon as you get it home from the video dealer you'll probably want to try it even if it's 3 AM. Immediately, you'll be amazed at how carefully, and elaborately, it's packaged. Each component is individually wrapped and fitted into the box. You may despair of ever repacking it so neatly, but be sure to keep the various boxes and plastic bags for shipping or transport. Be careful when unpacking: tiny screws, adapters, plates, cable filters and straps can easily be lost in the pile of boxes.

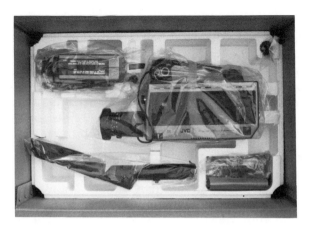

Before you assemble the camera, read the assembly directions included in the enclosed book. You will have to place the lens on the camera, and assemble the electronic viewfinder and handgrip. Be extremely careful with the plugs on the cable that connect the auto-iris zoom lens and electronic viewfinder to the camera. On certain cameras, particularly the JVC G series cameras, the pins on these plugs are very fine and delicate and can be bent and broken quite easily. They are very difficult to replace. Extreme caution must be taken to correctly align the plugs to the socket so that the plug pins are not bent.

After you get everything assembled, read all the directions in the operating manual first before turning anything on. Once you have a good basic understanding of how the camera operates, set it up and turn it on. Make sure you aren't aiming it at any bright lights, you have the right filter and the INDOOR/OUTDOOR switch in the correct position. At this point we should mention again, that you should never point the camera at any bright lights even if it's turned off. Always be aware of where the sun is if you're shooting outdoors or where bright lights or bright reflectors might be inside.

Camera Adjustments

With b&w cameras, no adjustments other than lens focus, zoom and aperture settings are necessary. Color cameras though must also have their Color Temperature settings adjusted for specific indoor and outdoor environments. (*See Chapter 5, Cameras* for Color Temperature adjustment and White Balance setting.)

111

Some cameras like the JVC G-series have a low-light level switch that boosts the camera's sensitivity at low light levels. JVC calls it an Automatic Gain Control (AGC) or sensitivity switch. The trade-off for using the switch is a slghtly noisier or grainier picture. If possible, shoot in a room that admits a lot of daylight (set filter for OUTDOORS) or have strong indoor light (set filter for INDOORS). Some cameras do better in low light than others.

It will take a little practice to understand the switch and lens adjustment that are necessary to produce the optimum color picture for a particular situation. Naturally, shooting indoors is more difficult than shooting outdoors because of the lighting problem, but don't despair if you forget to take the filter off or adjust the switch for proper White Balance control. At least you haven't wasted costly "film."

Another difficulty that presents frustrations is the fact that with electronic viewfinder cameras, you have no way of knowing from the b&w picture in the viewfinder whether the Color Temperature filters and switches are correctly set. There is of course no change in color that you can see, so you just have to check the camera physically for the correct settings or plug your VCR into your color TV set and monitor the color as you shoot.

Most newer cameras have an auto-iris lens that automatically adjusts the lens opening for the correct exposure. It works quite well under a variety of lighting circumstances. However, it averages all the light together and thus has difficulty with high contrast or back lit scenes. Fortunately, many have a manual override control or a special Back Light Control switch which allows you to precisely set the exposure for the subject you are shooting, even if you are shooting toward a bright back lit window. With a little practice, the light level indicators inside the camera will help you to adjust the lens opening perfectly for most situations.

Some cameras such as the Hitachi VK/C 500R and the Panasonic PK-200 and PK-300 are not as versatile in various lighting situations. The Sony HVC-1000 has a good auto-iris system, but no manual override, and the older Panasonic/Quasar and RCA cameras have light level indicators but no auto-iris system. The Hitachi VK/C 500R only lets you know when the light level is too low.

Once you feel comfortable with the camera and have the filter situation under control, you have conquered the hardest part. Charge up your batteries, connect the camera cable from the camera to the VCR, load up a tape and you are almost ready to begin shooting.

Power and Battery Control

The length of time a battery will provide on one charge depends on many factors. The power draw of the VCR and camera is the most significant factor, and the camera's power consumption will be increased if it has an electronic viewfinder and power zoom lens. If just the VCR is turned on, it may run for two or three hours, but if both the camera and VCR are on, the battery may run down in an hour or much less.

						Camera/VCR recording time on one battery charge
Manu– facturer	**Format**	**VCR**	**Watts**	**Camera**	**Watts**	
Sony	Beta	SL-3000	16	HVC-2000	8.3	45-60 min.
Toshiba	Beta	V-5530	13	IK-1850	11.2	45-60 min.
JVC	VHS	HR-4100	10	G-71USJ	12.0	40-60 min.
JVC	VHS	HR-2200U	10	GX-68U	5.8	45-60 min.
Panasonic	VHS	PV-2200	11	PK-300	29.0	15-30 min.
Panasonic	VHS	PV-3200	9	PK-700	7.2	45-60 min.
Quasar	VHS	VH-5300	9	VK730SE	7.2	45-60 min.
Hitachi	VHS	VT-7500A	8	VK/C770	8.3	45-90 min.
RCA	VHS	VEP150	8	CC004	8.9	45-90 min.
Akai	VHS	VPS-7350	18	VC-30	12.0	45-60 min.

Relative Power Consumption Chart

The JVC G series cameras have a convenient on/off switch located on the camera so you can keep the VCR going in the Pause mode and turn off the camera and conserve power. You should always STOP the VCR when you are not about to shoot to conserve battery power. NOTE: *A VCR in the PAUSE mode will draw battery power!* Minimize any Fast/Forward or Rewinding which also rapidly draws power. Since the Beta recorders don't have to retract the tape when placed in the Stop mode, they use less power than the VHS M-load VCRs which unload the tape every time you use the Stop button. This unloading and reloading drains the batteries. All these things should be kept in mind while shooting to get the maximum time out of your battery.

In The Field

As you begin taping outdoors you will find certain kinds of events most conducive to videorecording. Circuses, fairs, school and social gatherings are good because people are prepared to be seen and photographed. However, at resorts, camp grounds and parks, people seem more intent on privacy and anonymity. Consequently, they take a dim view of being photographed. Keep in mind that a portable VCR and camera is very conspicuous and seems quite threatening to some people. Your photographic manners are important. If you would like to tape someone, it always helps if you ask them first. You may avoid having to unexpectedly eat your camera.

Shooting outdoors is great fun. A colorful event with lots of interesting people and action can present a gold mine of visual and sound opportunities. Try to get a wide variety of interesting angles and people's faces and things that move and make strange noises. Let the camera stay with things for a while. It doesn't cost like Super 8. Perhaps even do a commentary as you go along. Be sure to experiment with your microphone so you know how close you have to be to the sound source to record properly.

Creating a Professional Tape

Gracefully flowing action-packed constantly interesting tapes take practice like everything else. Some people are naturally better at this than others. However, we will discuss some helpful guidelines to follow.

1. Think ahead in full sequences. Try to make each shooting sequence a unit in itself. Consider what each shot will contribute to the whole. Where is your program going? As you create sequences one after the other, try to feel the cumulative impact that each additional sequence will have as you continually build your program. Random unrelated "grab shots" sometimes tend to confuse the viewer, although these quick shots can create a tapestry effect—giving select and interesting pieces of the whole picture.

2. Shoot as if you are telling a story. Stories usually have beginnings and endings. The viewer needs to have the location established and needs to know what is going on and who the main characters are. Then anything can happen to the characters. The more surprises the better. As soon as the viewer knows what's going to happen next, you lose him. Try to keep the unexpected happening on the screen.

3. Keep your camera movement smooth and intentional.
Try not to appear indecisive. Don't pan one way and suddenly
reverse, or zoom out at one speed and halfway through the
shot, zoom out again at a different speed. This appears very
amateurish unless the action warrants it, i.e., taping a man
wrestling a crocodile. A general rule of thumb is to pan and
zoom much slower than you think you should.

4. Don't overuse the full zoom. The best part of having a
zoom lens is that it is several lenses in one (wide angle,
telephoto and in between). A certain shot may have a stronger
feel with just a short, slow zoom at the right moment. Also,
when one zooms or pans to something, he is taking the viewer
to that place. Give him a moment there before cutting,
panning or zooming away.

5. Try to get an interesting variety of camera shots. Use
wide angle shots, medium closeups and closeups. Try high
and low angle shots. Shots that are from a higher or lower
point of view than we experience while sitting or standing
often seem to have an interesting appeal to the viewer.
Closeups always look better than long shots on TV because
they have more detail, emotion, and impact on the small TV
frame. Don't be afraid to get up close to your subject—unless,
of course, it's a live crocodile.

6. Be creative with sound. Perhaps 8mm film buffs will be
well prepared for dealing with visualization in camera work,
but sound presents a whole new dimension, even for them.

A Few Words About Sound

If you're taping spontaneously occurring events, there's not
much you can do with the sound except record it randomly as
you shoot. However, creative sound recording technique could
still result in a good tape. If you're dealing with people speaking
to you or others, you need to think of shooting not only in terms
of cohesive visual units but in complete cohesive sound units as
well. In fact, the length of time the camera must be on will often
be *dictated by the length of time the speaker is talking.* You will
find the visual will often have to be keyed to the sound in order for
the sequence to make sense to the viewer.

If you're taping a woman explaining a technique for natural childbirth, you can't cut her off in the middle of a sentence if you want the tape to be understandable. Wait until she finishes before moving to your next shot. Situate yourself so that you can move the camera around, getting different angles and zooming in and out, without having to shut off the camera until there is a natural pause in the sound.

Obtaining good sound is often more difficult than obtaining a good picture because the microphone, unlike the camera, must be close to the sound source. Any serious documentary videophile will need both a good directional hand-held microphone and a lavalier microphone, as well as several microphone extension cables and a good headset. Portable VCRs are capable of recording sound quality equal to that of a fairly good audio cassette recorder, so don't underestimate the sound capabilities of your VCR. You may also be surprised at how well music will be reproduced, especially music that is not too loud. If you are taping loud rock bands, place your microphone about 50 to 100 feet away from the music source. Even then it still may distort. Accoustic guitars and singers should have the microphones placed in front of them.

You will find that the camera's built-in microphone works very well indoors in quiet environments where the ambient noise level is low. However, the mic will pick up the cameraperson's heavy breathing and even the sound of one's hands on the camera's grip and the sound of the camera's on/off switch. Outside, strong wind noise will be picked up by the camera mic. An external microphone with a wind filter avoids these problems; your sound quality, especially in noisy environments, will be excellent with a good hand held microphone placed correctly. But this requires a wire to the camera or the VCR, and the handling of the external mic and 30 feet of cable can reduce your mobility while the extra equipment can become a nuisance to others.

A shotgun mic attempts to gain the best of both worlds—mobility and good remote pickup. Many portable cameras can have a telescoping or shotgun type microphone mounted on top of their frames, thereby avoiding the extra wire. It won't work quite as well as an external hand held microphone placed near the sound source, but it's better than using the camera's built-in mic.

Audio Dub

If you're taping in an environment that's too hostile to use a hand-held microphone or too noisy or quiet to get good sound with the camera's built-in mic, you can always fall back on your VCR Audio Dub feature. Just plug in your external mic to your portable VCR, play back your tape and dub new sound over your pictures. You can do a narration, add humor and other sound effects, or use live or pre-recorded music. (*See Chapter 8, Production Aesthetics-Audio*). Of course you will erase the live sound you previously recorded. You can either dub over selected segments of your tape or over the full tape. Dubbing continuous sound (music and/or narration) over a series of separate shots have a way of pulling them together into a single unit.

Editing

All portable home VCRs do an effective job of starting and stopping *from the PAUSE mode* so each sequence exactly follows the previously taped one without interruptions or "glitches". This is definitely not true of the deck-type VCRs. On portable VCRs, shooting sequences can then be consecutively shot to look like a professional edited tape when played back. This is called IN THE CAMERA EDITING and is really the most practical way to edit ½-inch video cassette programs. It's certainly the fastest. You could also use your portable VCR as a second editing deck and ASSEMBLE EDIT from another playback VCR using the Pause control to start and stop the recorder at the various edit points, but this is, of course, very time consuming. (*See Chapter 9— Editing and Dubbing.*)

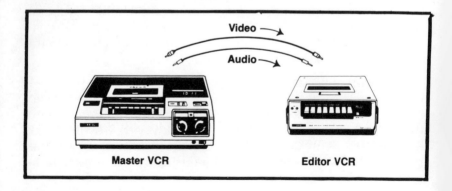

Master VCR   Editor VCR

There is one problem, though, with in-camera editing in certain portable VCR's. With some VHS VCRs such as the JVC HR-4100 recorder, the tape retracts back into the cassette when you turn the VCR off. Unfortunately, the tape backs up too far so when you place the VCR in Play mode again, it will erase the last part of the last scene and place a big glitch or noisy interruption in your picture. Obviously, you will need to occasionally turn off your VCR to conserve power, and at that point you will always lose the nice clean scene transitions.

Beta portables like the Sony SL-3000, though, keep the tape threaded even when you turn off the VCR: you can conserve power, go to your next location, start shooting again and maintain clean scene transitions. You will, however, lose your spot if you remove the cassette from the VCR as it will then retract into the cassette. So if you want a clean unbroken sequence of scenes you must assemble each sequence as you go in a continuous manner. You can not go back and insert a scene into a previous place on the tape without risking some interruption or glitches in the tape.

Visual and Sound Esthetics

It's really true that a good picture is worth a thousand words. A person speaking can only say 100-200 words a minute, but in a minute you could show many different images all evoking powerful emotions in the audience. Sight remains our most informative sensory perception, and it is the *visual* with which video is primarily conceived. People talking is not what TV can do best. This kind of information might better be accomplished with audio cassettes. Nevertheless, there are exceptions such as powerful speakers whose words and personality create extremely strong images.

Start with the goal of creating as strong a visual image as possible. Then use the sound as an enhancement of the visual image. You can also try the reverse; start with a particular sound track and create visuals to compliment it. Ideally, there can be a good balance between your audio and your video image. Try and have them work in support of each other.

As you begin taping and isolating scenes from the environment (which is what a camera lens does), you will become aware of the immense chorus of light, sound, color and vibratory elements that are present around you at any given moment. A camera and microphone enable you to pick and choose from these various offerings. With these tools you can express your particular way of seeing and hearing this cosmic concert the cornucopia of life, and share it with others via the videotape and TV screen.

Evaluation Of Specific Portable VCR Systems

Introduction

Although portable VCRs, like all other video equipment, are experiencing rapid evolution, they share many of the same basic features:

- Lightweight—14-21 lbs.
- Full function controls including AUDIO-DUB and PAUSE MODE.
- Built in RF Adapters for playback on any TV set
- Somewhat standard camera connectors
- Inputs for external microphones
- Earphone/headphone output for sound monitoring
- SEARCH or MEMORY controls
- Rechargeable batteries
- AC Adaptor/Battery charger
- Tape counter
- Operation from car battery

Features that vary with models:

- Dual speed
- Variable Speed playback
- Still Frame
- Programmable tuners
- Remote PAUSE control
- Dew Control shutoff switch

Prices range from $1,200-$1,600 for complete VCR and tuner/timer systems.

VHS SYSTEMS

JVC HR-4100 AU/G-71USJ System

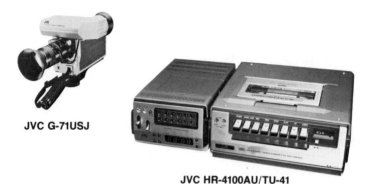

JVC G-71USJ

JVC HR-4100AU/TU-41

The JVC HR-4100AU/G-71USJ was one of the first portable home VCR systems. It still remains one of the most popular and best quality VHS systems on the market. The HR-4100AU VCR is easy to operate, and being a single speed 2-hour only machine, it produces a very clean sharp picture.

Drawbacks of the HR-4100AU are its weight (20 lbs.), and the VHS Stop mode dethreading problem. When the VCR is placed in the Stop mode and then returned to the Play mode, a small portion of the previous scene is erased. Also, valuable battery energy is used up threading and dethreading the tape. Other problems include an Auto Gain Control of the sound which allows an annoying roar to be heard on the sound track when sound levels are low or non-existent. This is a typical problem with most non-professional VCRs. Also, the 10-Pin camera connector is fastened directly to an internal circuit board instead of flexible wires. If the cable connector is pulled or pushed excessively it will break the connection with the board.

The HR-4100AU is a very popular VCR and receives high marks from most users. Its flexibility and quality sets a standard for ½-inch VCRs. It has all the necessary inputs, outputs and features necessary for serious portable recording. JVC also has a playback-only version, the HP-4000AU, which is intended for industrial use.

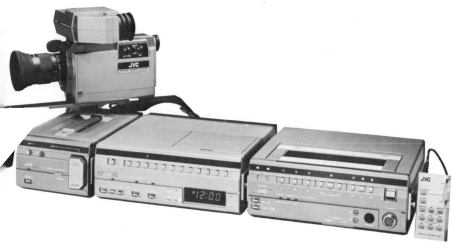

JVC HR- 2200U Portable VCR System

The newly designed HR-2200U/GX-68U system offers a wide range of state-of-the-art features. At only 11.4 lbs, the HR-2200U is one of the lightest and most compact VCRs available. Features of the 2-hour mode VCR include a four-motor drive system, logic-controlled solenoid pushbuttons and an eleven-function remote control unit. Other features include a unique power economy switch that keeps the tape engaged even when the power is turned off, thereby insuring a clean assemble edit when the unit is turned back on. The VCR also has an Edit Start Control (ESC) which creates a clean edit most of the time when the camera is turned on and off and a shuttle-search mode that provides a visible picture in forward and reverse.

A slow motion mode with variable speed is also provided when the remote control unit is used. Nickel Cadmium (Ni-Cad) batteries are used instead of the usual lead acid batteries found in most other VCRs. The advantages of the Ni-Cad batteries are longer running time (1 hour with camera), faster recharging time (only 90 minutes), and less weight. The HR-2200U has an electronic Liquid Crystal Display (LCD) tape counter and a series of LED indicators to warn of battery time, tape operation and moisture condensation.

OPTIONAL ACCESSORIES

❶ **CB-P22BU** Carrying bag for the recorder. (Brown type) ❷ **CB-P22SU** Carrying bag for the recorder. (Silver type) ❸ **CB-P50U** Carrying bag for the camera. ❹ **HD-P22U** Carrying handle for the HR-2200U. ❺ **SC-P2U** Shoulder cart for the recorder. ❻ **VF-P30U** 1.5" CRT electronic viewfinder. ❼ **NB-P1** Ni-Cd rechargeable battery pack for the HR-2200U. ❽ **GL-P06U** Wide conversion lens. ❾ **GL-P15U** Teleconversion lens. ❿ **VC-234-10U** Camera extension cable. ⓫ **AP-P2U** Car battery cord.

An electronic Tuner/Timer, the TU-22U also functions as an AC Adapter and Battery Charger, and its design allows the VCR and Tuner to be stacked on top of each other. The Tuner is programmable, allowing a program to be taped anytime over a 10 day period. A basic AC Adapter (AA-P22U) is available that powers the HR-2200U and allows the charging of 2 batteries at once.

The VCR system is designed for use with the GX-68U camera, and a wide range of accessories are available such as carrying cases, handles, a clever shoulder cart, extension cables and wide angle and telephoto lenses.

Panasonic PV-3100/PV-3200
Quasar VH5300SE
Magnavox 8371

Quasar VH5300SE

Panasonic PV-3200 System

124

Magnavox Model 8371

The lightweight (13.2 lbs.) and very compact Panasonic PV-3200 VCR is a 2/4/6 hour mode VHS system that is simple to operate, features solenoid controls, can be powered by several power sources and can be stacked. It also has a still frame and frame by frame advance with the remote control. Being a single-set-of-heads multiple-speed VCR, the unit must make some picture compromises because the heads cannot be optimized for any single mode in a multiple mode VCR. Nevertheless, for a 3-speed VCR, this model makes pretty good pictures. One very annoying drawback of the VCR is its lack of an AUDIO IN Line Level input plug for dubbing sound or copying tapes. Instead, a transformer must be used with the MIC input to get prerecorded sound into the VCR. The VCR has a good backspacing editing system which works well except for a rainbow effect that frequently appears following the edit.

Two Tuner/Timers are offered, the PV-A32E, and 24-hour unit, and the optional PV-A35P 8 event/4-day programmable unit. The PV-A30 basic AC Adapter unit is also available. Panasonic has a line of several camera models that would work well with this VCR system. The running time of the VCR and camera on one battery charge is about 80 minutes.

Hitachi VT-7500A
RCA VEP150

RCA VEP150

Hitachi VT-7500A

A popular, compact and lightweight (14.5 lb.) system is the Hitachi-made VHS VT 7500A/VT TU75A VCR system. The system uses five direct-drive motors which enable it to produce a good stable picture in all modes. The VT-7500A is a 3-speed 2/4/6-hour mode machine and, like the JVC portables, has a full compliment of standard audio and video inputs. It is also a good rugged machine that edits well.

Matching electronic programmable Tuner/Timers, a VT TU70A 1 program/24 hour system and a VT TU75A 5 program/7 days system, are available. Also, a compact AC Adapter/Battery Charger can be purchased as well as a wide assortment of camera connecting cables, auxiliary battery pack and carrying cases.

The VCR uses four solenoid push button controls with built in logic control. LED indicators signal selected modes. A special automatic control signal circuit enables clean camera editing between scene transitions, and the VHS cassette rethread erase problem has been minimized. A damped cassette mechanism allows smoother cassette insertion and removal, and a clever removable carrying handle folds out of the way when not in use. A full complement of input and output plugs is provided on the side of the VCR and one hour recording time is possible with the built in rechargeable battery. An illuminated battery indicator shows battery condition.

Akai

Akai VPS-7350

Always one of the more innovative companies in video, Akai has again demonstrated a novel video recording system. Taking the approach that VCR systems don't appear very attractive next to well designed stereo equipment, Akai set out to create a home video system that wouldn't feel inferior next to a $1000 stereo receiver or a tape deck. Instead of having to buy two VCRs, one to program off-the-air recording and one to take to the school picnic, why not create a modular system that does both, thus increasing its flexibility and economy. So goes the Akai marketing philosophy.

The Akai "ActiVideo" VHS system is a high quality, reasonably lightweight (14 lbs.) VCR/Tuner/Timer system that when originally designed as the Model VP-7300, recorded in the 2-hour SP mode only. Thus, its picture quality is one of the best of any VHS system. The later model VPS-7350 is a multi-mode 2/6-hour system and sacrifices picture quality for the dual modes. Both the VP-7300 and the VPS-7350 use Ni-Cad batteries for a full 1-hour recording time, and the battery can be recharged in less than 3 hours.

Other features of the Akai VCR include excellent assemble editing, variable speed playback with picture and single frame advance. The VPS-7350 offers two channels of sound with Dolby noise reduction for stereo or bilingual programs, an instant program locating (IPLS) system which searches the tape for blank spaces between programs, a 4-digit tape counter, a key activated VCR locking system and a 6-event/7-day programmable Tuner/Timer. The VPS-7350 offers a remote control to operate the variable speeds of the VCR, although the variable speeds function in the 6-hour mode only. Drawbacks of the Akai is its lack of standard video and audio inputs and camera connector. Adapters are needed.

127

BETA PORTABLE SYSTEMS

Sony

Sony HVC-2000

Sony HVC-1000

Sony SL-3000

The SL-3000/HVC-1000 was the first home Beta portable system. Like its VHS counterparts, it offers playback on any TV set, an automatic Tuner/Timer (TT-3000), and 3-way power operation on batteries, AC power or car battery with optional car battery cord. The VCR is capable of recording up to 3 hours on a L-750 tape.

Unique features of the SL-3000 VCR are a Timing Phase (TP) circuit which produces near perfect editing between scenes each time the camera is started or stopped during recording. The system also provides a two-speed playback ability that automatically selects the X1 or X2 mode and a Cue feature that lets you skip over undesired portions of the tape quickly and easily without rethreading the tape.

Since the Beta system threads the tape around the video head and keeps it that way during all control functions until the tape is ejected, the tape can be easily and quickly cued and reviewed without requiring dethreading as in the VHS system. This gives the Beta portable an advantage because the VCR can be paused and stopped without requiring valuable battery power to dethread the tape. The VCR can be started up again and the tape remains in the same position and the edit point is not lost.

Another unique and very nice feature of the Beta VCR system is its logic function in the Pause mode. It senses whether or not the camera or VCR has accidentally been placed in the ON position. If that is the case the circuitry figures out what the right mode is and automatically places the VCR in the correct mode. With VHS portables it's all too easy to have the VCR running accidently.

The disadvantages of the Sony SL-3000 VCR are its large size and weight (20 lbs.), lack of standard audio and video inputs (an adapter cable is needed), the 14-Pin camera connector is not compatible with many cameras, and the VCR has no special effect modes and is limited to a single 2-hour speed only. However, the SL-3000 has a good reputation for durability and high picture quality. When used with the newer HVC-2000 or HVC-2010 cameras, it just may be the best quality ½-inch portable system available.

A wide range of accessories accompany the system, such as the TT-3000 Tuner/Timer, the VCR-3 Telecine Adapter for film and photo transfer, a two camera switcher, and various cables, a tripod, and a unidirectional extendable microphone for mounting on the camera.

Sony SL-3000/TU-3000

Toshiba 5530

Toshiba IK-1850

Toshiba V-5530/TU-530

The only other Beta portable system is the Toshiba 5530. It's slightly smaller than the Sony SL-3000 and appears to be a more practical design. At 17.5 lbs. it's reasonably lightweight, and can record up to 2 hours in the Beta II mode with an L-750 tape cassette. Relying only on battery power, however, it can record 1 hours worth of tape before needing to be recharged. It has a built in rechargeable battery, Audio Dub, Memory Tape Counter, and Remote Pause for instant editing. A videotape Review feature, and an optional manual Tuner/Timer give it good versatility. Like the Sony SL-3000, the Toshiba also uses the 14-Pin camera plug, so the Sony and Toshiba cameras could be used with either VCR.

In This Next Section

So far we have dealt mainly with the specific equipment —
VCRs, cameras and microphones — how to hook them up and get
them to function properly. We will now proceed to the creative
aspects of video such as how to organize a video production,
write scripts and develop good camera technique. And finally,
we will cover sound, lighting and editing, also very important
aspects of the video taping process.

7 Organizing Your Production

Think Ahead — Plan Your Program

Now that you're ready to make your own videotapes, it's time to explore ways of accomplishing this most successfully. Since broadcast television has exerted such a profound influence in everyone's life, it tends to set the standard by which all TV programs will be judged. Obviously, there is little chance an inexperienced home video producer with one b&w video camera and minimal technical equipment is going to create a tape that will look like an NBC or CBS TV program. However, don't despair, for the home video producer has other advantages which can make his programming very effective.

Your major advantage is your *people.* The viewing audience is always excited about seeing themselves or someone they know appear on the TV set. Great technical difficulties will be excused when Johnny, Mother, Spot the dog or Rodney the household hamster miraculously come to life and cavort across the face of the living room tube. When the shrieks of delight start, you'll know your audience is right in the palm of your hand. Home videotapes are the definitive grandmother pleaser.

Another factor which NBC can't match is your ability to create tapes that are local in nature and feature neighborhood or home settings and issues and subject matter which are personally significant to people. Your local talent is guaranteed to draw an audience for these tapes. For instance, you could do a tape on the third grade's annual play, or perhaps the Boy Scouts' fund raising frog jumping contest. Playback of such tapes is sure to win the enthusiastic attendance and support of all those involved and their parents, relatives and friends.

The list of sample programming possibilities is limited only by the imagination. So, given the powerful advantages of your local talent and local settings and events, how do you create the best possible tape?

THE PRODUCTION PROCESS

Step 1   Planning

The secret to creating a successful film or tape is *Planning*. Planning requires you to sit down in a quiet place and try to crystallize in your mind what you want your program to look like and do. Ask yourself:

What will it cover?

What events will happen?

What sequence of events might take place?

Who will be in the program?

What will the location be?

How should it affect the audience?

Who will the audience be?

Take out a piece of paper and write down these questions and your possible answers. If you're not too clear on all this, find others who might help you brainstorm the project. Often the insight of others can offer valuable aid on an undertaking such as this.

Step 2   The Approach

There are basically two different approaches to the making of video programs:

1. The DOCUMENTARY or "shoot it as it happens and see what we get" approach. This refers to the birthday parties, home happenings, and/or events such as the Lions Club athletic competition. You can't really do much preliminary planning, so just shoot what looks interesting. Since videotape is erasable and reusable, you won't be out huge quantities of costly "film."

2. The DRAMATIC or structured program approach which could require a considerable amount of preparation. Perhaps you might need to write a script and select people to be actors and actresses.

In a dramatic type of production the timing and continuity of scenes may require some preliminary consideration. This type of production can be very ambitious and time consuming. It may take many weekends of preparing and shooting to produce a 15-minute finished tape. This kind of program is just like creating a play except you have the added complications of sound recording and camera placement. However, the results can be very satisfying, and who knows what budding genius directors, producers, actors, actresses, audio or camerapersons may suddenly experience their life's inspiration during these humble home-made media beginnings.

Most tapes will be of the documentary type because that's by far the easiest, and you can't really do much practical editing of the tapes with a home recorder. But again, even though you may be limited technically in what you want to do, much can be done with a single camera and VCR if you use creativity and have some awareness of what your machinery can or can not do.

Step 3 Organization of Ideas and People

Since many home video systems are not really very portable, and the camera and microphone cables limit you to 25 feet or so from the recorder, you will be doing most of your shooting in and around the living room. You can increase your flexibility by purchasing or building a TV/VCR cart with rollers on it so you can move everything into different rooms or outside by the pool or patio. A good cart can be purchased from Comprehensive Video Supply Corp. for about $40.

Given the physical flexibility of your equipment, you can begin to organize for your taping. If you intend to shoot Grandmother's 50th anniversary in the dining room, not much is required except to move your equipment into the room beforehand, find the best position for your camera and microphone, load tape into the recorder and begin shooting. *(See Chapter 8, Production Aesthetics.)*

If you are planning something more elaborate like a dramatic program, you might find it helpful to write a small script for the production. The script is, of course, always used by the big time TV and film people for their productions because it's the best way of explaining exactly what is to take place, in what sequence and for how long. Scripts let everyone know just what is supposed to happen and when.

Scripts come in many forms and can be just a simple outline explaining the sequence of events that will take place in the program. Or, they can be very elaborate and detail every nuance of expression, and every sound and camera angle.

DETAILED SCRIPT

23. EXTERIOR   Mountain Cabin- NIGHT ESTABLISHING SHOT.
    LONG SHOT- LOOKING THROUGH frantically waving pine
    tree limbs at mountain cabin about 100 feet away.
    Thunder clashes and lightning momentarily illuminates
    rustic cabin. Rain falls heavily.
                                            CUT TO:

24. MEDIUM SHOT- HIGH ANGLE through rain splattered window.
    Roberts is crouched down and desperately trying to
    get a fire going in the fireplace while Susan is next
    to him holding a few pieces of kindling wood and trying
    to assist. Room is dimly lit with 2 kerosene lamps.

                                            CUT TO:

25. EXTREME CLOSE UP- ROBERT'S HAND with match trying to
    ignite wet kindling wood. His hand trembles and match
    goes out again. The wood smokes weakly.

                                            CUT TO:

26. MEDIUM CLOSE UP- LOW ANGLE from point of view of the
    fireplace.

                         ROBERTS
                         (angry)

        "Damn, what the hell is wrong with this wood.
        It can't be that wet! Ouch!

                                            CUT TO:

27. CLOSE UP- FIREPLACE- He drops match into fireplace
    alongside a dozen other burned out matches.

                                            CUT TO:

28. CLOSE UP- OVER ROBERT'S SHOULDER- to Susan's face.
    Her hair is messed and stringy, she is obviously
    terrified, tired and is staring intensely at Roberts.
    The scrabbling noise on the side of the cabin starts
    again.

29. 2-SHOT FROM BEHIND THEM- Susan tenses up and grabs
    Robert's arm. He drops a new match.

                    SUSAN
                  (desperate)

    "There it is again. We've got to get out
    of here or get help. I- I can't take this
    much longer!!!"
                                        CUT TO:

30. CLOSE UP from ROBERT'S POINT OF VIEW- She stares
    out front picture window, her mind afraid to recognize
    whatever her eyes might see.

                                        CUT TO:

31. Camera HIGH ANGLE over the couple's shoulder.
    They both turn toward the window. Camera ZOOMS
    SLOWLY toward large darkened picture window. The
    wind is blowing harder and the tree limbs are
    moving violently outside. As the camera ZOOMS
    CLOSER toward the window, thunder crashes and
    lightning briefly illuminates a strange metallic
    object situated in the dense grove of pines- just
    beyond the cabin. Dark shapes appear to be moving
    through the woods.

    Darkness once again obscures the forest.

                    FADE TO BLACK
                        and
                    FADE OUT

So, do whatever you think is necessary, given the complexity of
your own program production. You can get feedback and a
critique from others, if you like, and in that way work the bugs out
before you shoot.

Have meetings with the actors and actresses in your tape and
also the persons who will be helping operate the equipment if
you intend only to direct. Make sure everyone understands what
they are supposed to do and give everyone a chance to provide
input into the discussion. When people feel their personal
contribution is desired and appreciated, they will be much more
willing to put out a greater creative effort. The skillful director is
aware of these human dynamics and utilizes them constructively
and creatively.

Step 4   Organize Your Technical Resources

This may mean merely connecting the camera to the VCR and turning everything on. Or, it could mean transporting the whole system and accessories across town to the county park for the afternoon. If this is the case, it's a good idea to make up an EQUIP-MENT LIST so you can buy whatever you think you will need beforehand, take everything with you to the taping location and finally bring it all back again. It's really incredibly easy to forget just one crucial item, such as tape, especially when you are traveling more than 25 miles from your home base.

Step 5   Check Out The Scene First

If traveling to a remote location such as a park, an auditorium, theatre or meeting hall, you can avoid untold delays and confusion if you check out the place beforehand.

Important considerations are:

1. **Placement and availability of wall plugs.** Are they conveniently located or will you need to buy long extension cables? Do the wall plugs have three prongs or two prongs on them, and will they match your plugs or will you need adapters?

2. **Lighting.** Is there sufficient lighting on stage or in the area to be photographed? Maybe you will need to bring extra lights and extra extension plugs. Flood lights in homes may blow fuses, so be sure to distribute the load by plugging the lights into plugs in different rooms.

3. **Camera-to-subject distance.** Is there enough room to place your camera far enough away to shoot the whole scene, but close enough to be able to distinguish the people? Remember the TV set is a very small display screen.

4. **Sound.** Can you get your camera and/or microphone close enough to adequately pick up the sound and get a good picture? Will you need microphone extension cables, and do you need to cover the mic cables so people won't trip over them?

5. **Location of VCR, camera and TV set.** Is there a good place to locate the equipment so it's convenient to use, that is near a wall plug and not in the way of other people? Can the camera be placed so other people will not block its view?

6. **Access.** Is there an entrance where it's easiest to load and unload the equipment with the least amount of hassle?

Step 6   Assembly Of People And Equipment

Have everyone meet at a designated point early enough so that equipment can be set up and ready to go in time to tape the big event without inconveniencing people or causing embarrassing delays.

Step 7   Shooting and Directing

Set up your equipment first. Generally the video recorder and TV set should be placed on a sturdy table off to the right or left side of the scene to be shot. The camera should be placed on a tripod or hand held in front of the action if no tripod is available.

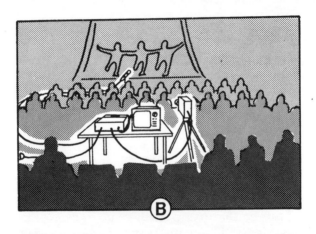

Situation A and B give good camera coverage but require running cables around people and possibly blocking their view. Situation C places all the equipment on the side, but the sound won't be very good unless you place a microphone near the speakers. Also, the camera's point of view will be slightly offset and the speaker will appear to be talking to empty space rather than the camera.

Situation B is the most convenient technically, especially if the TV set is located slightly in front of the camera operator so he or she can monitor the camera's picture. This setup may block the view of others, but some trade-offs are usually required. Try to minimize the impact of your equipment and activity on others but consider also the importance of a good camera angle, proper microphone placement and the limitations of your cables.

Make sure you have enough extension cords for the camera and microphone and AC power extension cords for the VCR and TV set. A multiple plug box with four or five plugs is a big help.

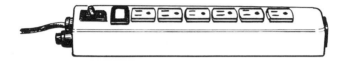

Test out your microphone and camera, and run a test recording to make sure everything works. Is the picture bright enough and is the camera properly focused and adjusted? Does the cameraperson know how to focus the camera? You may want to tape a title graphic naming the show, speaker or date. If you haven't already taped your graphics, do so at this point so you will be ready to begin when the show starts.

If everything looks go, rewind your tape if necessary and prepare for shooting.

At this point the equipment is all set up and the action is about to begin. It's usually necessary or helpful for someone to direct the events happening in front of the camera, so a short discourse on good directing may be helpful.

Good directing is a fine art which requires a person to be both patient and understanding with people, yet forceful enough to plow through the many technical impediments and personality difficulties that might be involved in the production. The director should also know the abilities and limitations of his people and equipment. He or she must possess the clearheadedness and organizational ability to deal with many fine details and simultaneous events. Emotional, intimidating and repressive personality types may get tapes made, but will command little or no respect from their co-workers and will only create destructive and negative morale. Videotaping can be and should be a fun and enjoyable experience.

"A leader is best
When people barely know that he exists,
Not so good when people obey and acclaim him,
Worst when they despise him.
Fail to honor people,
They fail to honor you.
But of a good leader, who talks little,
When his work is done, his aim fulfilled,
They will all say, 'We did this ourselves.' "
　　　　　The Way Of Life by Lao Tzu

Step 8　Complete the Tape

Rewind the tape, relax and watch the playback. If it's not what you want, you can redo it if possible and desirable.

Taping Should Be Fun

It makes no sense at all to get all anxiety-ridden and frustrated if everything doesn't happen exactly like you want, or your production isn't comparable to *Star Wars, One Flew Over the Cuckoo's Nest* or *Jaws*. Hollywood has millions of dollars to work with and the best technicians, personnel and equipment in the world. However, even the most basic film or video equipment can be used cleverly to reveal imaginative and new ways of perceiving a very common or local event, and can surely bring out the charm, humor and beauty of people. Warmth, love, sadness and happiness can just as easily be conveyed by skillful use of a $250 b&w camera as with a $150,000 movie or TV camera. Be careful not to use the lack of equipment as an excuse. Try to capitalize on your own unique visions, scenes, environment and the people around you. Much can really be done with the most basic equipment, and you may really surprise yourself.

8

Production Aesthetics

The Camera is the Eye

The video camera is the eye through which we interpret our shooting environment or scene. The camera sees only what we want it to see. The video camera then, is a very important link in the video system. The camera's picture quality and the operator's creative and technical skills determine what will be recorded on the VCR.

Creative Camera Technique

Camera technique can be a very personal matter. Different individuals will soon develop their own style of perceiving or interpreting a scene. Like anything else, good camera work comes with practice. Try different lenses and angles, and experiment with camera motion. If the subject can not move, move the camera around him.

Generally, camera movement looks much more professional if it is steady and smooth. It should appear planned, deliberate and fluid. If possible, use a good fluid-head tripod.

A variety of shots is much more interesting than one single point of view. A zoom lens, which is several lenses in one, makes it possible to have a variety of shots without moving the camera. On the other hand, the WIDE ANGLE LENS which takes in much more picture area, can produce a very dramatic angle if used properly but requires the camera person to get in close to the subject in order to produce a good picture.

If you are hand-holding your camera, it is best to rotate your whole body at the hips, rather than move the camera with your hand. This will make your camera work look more professional. Try to move *smoothly* from one location to another while shooting but watch out for sleeping dogs and cats or other hazards such as children, chairs and skate boards.

In film and TV there are actual designations for particular camera shots. They are:

LONG SHOT

MEDIUM SHOT

CLOSE UP

EXTREME CLOSE UP

A typical program sequence might open with an ESTABLISHING SHOT, also called a LONG SHOT (LS), so the viewer can get his bearings. It may be followed by a MEDIUM SHOT (MS) as the action begins. Next might come a series of CLOSE UPS (CU) and Medium Shots (MS) to convey a sense of close action and excitement. Finally, the scene might end with a slow zoom out or a Long Shot (LS).

LS

MS

CU

LS

Camera Composition

Composition or placement of the images and their relative sizes is important to the impact of the scene as is the continuity or flow of action through the scene. Composition affects the viewer's sense of visual balance which in turn can influence his or her feelings toward what is happening in the scene. A certain effect can be created by the particular picture composition.

Some basic rules of composition are as follows:

- Allow sufficient head room and border around the subject. TV sets are often adjusted to different sizes so be sure to allow extra head room for your subjects.

- Use a variety of camera angles. Try to minimize use of the standard tripod shot. Interesting angles will make a production more effective.

Picture Impact

A close-up shot has the greatest viewer impact, especially in video because of the small size of the TV set. Long shots or complex scenes will convey little or no information to the viewer. Keep in mind, though, that too much of one thing, even a close-up, may detract from the overall effect of the production.

Continuity

A production should have continuity — it should have a logical flow from scene to scene and from beginning to end. The camera technique should be consistent, and each scene should lead smoothly from one event to another. Good continuity comes with practice, experience and a well-planned production. It will be well worth the effort to read any of the fine books on film and video camera technique and esthetics. Check your local media bookstore.

The Camera As A Mood Creator

One need only watch any good film or TV drama to see how the camera position and movement set the mood. Slow movement creates a feeling of serenity or perhaps tragedy whereas rapid movement implies fear, suspense and excitement.

It is important to use a tripod to avoid shaky camera work as this always looks amateurish. A hand-held camera or the use of a shoulder brace can be quite effective if used imaginatively to follow a man walking or running down the street. Again, camera movement should enhance the action of the scene, not distract from it. A low camera angle (camera located below the subject) will distort the image, creating a feeling of inferiority or subservience, whereas a high camera angle (camera located above the subject) will create a feeling of dominance or superiority.

Think of the camera as an electronic paintbrush. As it zooms in, moves right or left or up and down, it selects certain images and excludes others, and by its movement an impression or interpretation of the scene is gradually created. The result should be a tapestry of images and feelings.

Straight On

Side Angle

High Angle

Low Angle

45 Degree Angle

Wide Angle

The viewer should feel a part of the action. The camera should not call attention to itself — rather, the scene and action should draw the viewer into it as if he or she were really there. The camera and operator merely exist as an unseen, unnoticed vehicle between viewer and event. A skilled camera operator can bring real life, excitement and interest to an otherwise dull production.

Zoom Lens Operation

Open the lens IRIS(A) for the best light. Turn the ZOOM RING (B) to maximum magnification (full close-up or telephoto). Next, turn the FOCUS RING (C) until the focus is sharpest. Now it should be possible to zoom back (wide angle) with the zoom control and the picture should stay in focus while zooming, provided the camera to subject distance does not change.

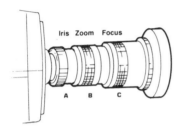

Zoom In

Focus

Zoom Back

Camera Vulnerability

The camera, in particular must *NEVER* be pointed at the sun or any unusually bright light source. Otherwise, the camera tube will immediately be BURNED. A Burn means that excessive amounts of light have destroyed the photosensitive surface of the tube and eliminated its ability to respond to changes in light. A black spot or streak will appear in the picture which, in the case of a severe burn, will remain there permanently. Less severe burns may eventually fade away after a few days or weeks. A permanent burn can only be fixed by having the camera tube replaced. This costs about $100 to $300, including parts and labor. Auto-iris lenses greatly reduce the chances of burning a tube.

Normal

Burned Tube

How To Avoid Burns

The bright sun is a potential burn lurking behind trees and buildings just waiting for a video camera to pan up into its view. Chrome car bumpers reflecting sunlight and sparkling ocean waves reflecting the sun in late afternoon are notorious camera tube killers. The tubes used in expensive TV studio cameras are burn resistant but cost several thousand dollars!

The tubes used in home video cameras are very inexpensive by comparison but can be burned easily by a careless camera operator.

The video camera is most vulnerable when used outside, so it's best *always* to keep the lens capped when the camera is not in use. If the primary use is inside the home, there is very little danger of burning the tube. If shooting outside, try to be aware of the position of the sun and try to avoid shooting it with the camera. Generally speaking, if you use care and caution, a camera tube should last several years without needing replacement.

149

A camera tube may need replacement when the following symptoms occur:

- A permanent burn persists on the tube.
- The camera can no longer be focused.
- The camera's picture is dark and without contrast.

CAUTION: The camera tube should be replaced only by a competent video technician as damage could otherwise be done to the camera.

How to take care of your camera

DO NOT point the camera at the sun — instant burn! Buy or make a case for the camera if it is to be transported frequently.

DO NOT store the camera in a *face-down* position. Always store the camera in a case, if possible, and in a *horizontal* position. Otherwise, small flakes from the camera tube will eventually settle on the tube face creating annoying spots in the picture.

ALWAYS keep the lens cap *ON* when the camera is not in use. Some lenses feature a CLOSED or *C* position which completely closes the camera iris, protecting the camera tube from the light when not in use.

Editing In The Camera

Most TV and film productions rely on the process of editing the tape after shooting to create the desired sequence of long shots, medium shots and close ups. However, the home video producer does not usually have that option. At least 2 special sophisticated VCRs called ELECTRONIC EDITING VCRs are needed in order to precisely edit videotapes. *(See Chapter 9 — Editing.)* If electronic editing is not possible, all the editing must be done as you shoot. This technique is called IN CAMERA EDITING, although the editing is not done physically in the camera. This is film terminology, because the film in a film camera can actually be started and stopped in the camera, resulting is a kind of edited film. In video, the tape is started and stopped by the ON/OFF switch on the camera or VCR, and this is called In-Camera Editing (at least until someone coins a new phrase for video).

The following are two methods which you can consider using to simulate an edited tape:

Method #1 Fading In and Fading Out

Step 1 Close the camera lens aperture to the position marked *C* or turn the lens f-stop to its smallest position — F16 or F22. Or place your hand or a card in front of the lens.

Step 2 Start the VCR and allow it to run for 5 or 10 seconds.

Step 3 Slowly open the lens aperture or remove your hand from in front of the lens. As the picture fades in, cue the action to begin.

Step 4 At the end of the scene, close the lens aperture or block the lens and the scene will fade out.

Step 5 Let the tape run for 5 or 10 seconds more and then stop the VCR.

Method #2 Fading In With Sequential Scenes

Step 1 Close the camera lens.

Step 2 Start the VCR.

Step 3 Open the camera lens and cue the action to begin.

Step 4 At the end of each scene, place your VCR in the PAUSE mode or stop the VCR.

Step 5 Set up the next scene.

Step 6 Restart the VCR and cue the action to begin again.

Step 7 Repeat this process to the end of the tape.

Step 8 Close the lens aperture at the end of the last scene and allow the VCR to run for 20 or 30 seconds.

NOTE: It is usual to have a few seconds of distortion in the picture when you stop and start the VCR. This distortion is called a GLITCH by video people. Most portable VCRs produce very clean transitions between scenes when the VCR starts and stops. This makes it possible to create a cleanly edited in-camera tape.

SOUND ADVICE

One of the most significant advantages of video is its sound recording capabilities. Because the sound and picture are recorded on the same piece of magnetic tape at the same time, the sound will always be in perfect SYNCHRONIZATION (SYNC) with the picture at all times.

Since most videotapes consist of great amounts of dialog, the importance of recording good sound is obvious. The effectiveness of your tape can be severely compromised if the sound quality is poor. Recording good sound, though, is often much more difficult than recording a good picture because a video camera can take a good picture even if it's 30 feet away from the subject, but the microphone that records the sound must be within several feet of the subject. The subject's dialog at 30 feet may be virtually unintelligible, but there are ways of dealing with these problems.

How Sound Works

Sound starts as variations in air pressure. These variations are sensed by a very sensitive diaphram (A) located inside the microphone and converted into electrical information (B). This information is then relayed to the audio amplifier inside the VCR (C) and transferred to the videotape through the audio recording head (D).

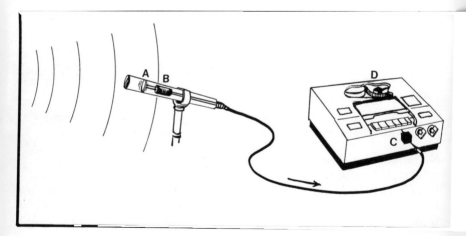

The sound is then stored by the videotape on the audiotrack and later played back by reversing the process.

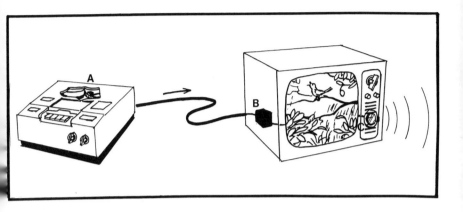

The tape moves past the audio playback head (A) which picks up the audio information and transfers it to the TV set audio amplifier (B) where it is amplified and changed back into air pressure variations by the speaker (C) which is really a microphone in reverse.

Creative Sound

The creative use of sound is another whole art and science which is often totally neglected by most TV and video people, but used with great genius by certain filmmakers. One need only experience *Star Wars* in a good theatre with 6-track dolby sound to hear what a master of creative sound, such as George Lucas, can do with the medium. TV people argue that since the TV speaker is so small, why bother with creative quality sound because you can't hear it anyway. However, VCRs can be plugged directly into stereo systems for high quality sound reproduction. The smaller the playback speaker, the more important it is to have decent sound in order to overcome some of the speaker's shortcomings. The point is not to ignore the rich presence of environmental sounds and creative music and to make an effort to use a good microphone so you can get good quality dialog. The imaginative use of sounds other than just dialog can add a professional touch to your tape.

Naturally, the recording of professional quality sound requires a knowledge of microphones and recording techniques and on-the-job experience. In other words, these things are not gained overnight and without some expense. There are many good books written on sound that will be of value to the recording enthusiast. Also, most home sound recording gear can be interfaced easily with home video equipment. By using a minimal amount of equipment and following some simple rules and guidelines, the beginner can improve his sound recording skills considerably.

Types of Microphones

Let's start with the microphone. There are several types which are intended for different kinds of applications. It is important to use the correct microphone for the correct application in order to insure the best quality sound.

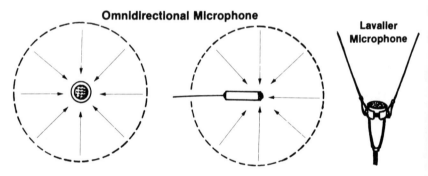

Omnidirectional Microphone

Lavalier Microphone

OMNIDIRECTIONAL MICROPHONE   The omnidirectional microphone picks up sounds from nearly all directions at all times. This is the most common type of cheaper microphone which comes built-into most audio cassette recorders and portable video cameras. Because it has such a wide PICKUP PATTERN and must pick up all sounds, it cannot be selective. Consequently, undesirable environmental sounds such as traffic noises, airplanes, lawnmowers and motorbikes often severely affect the quality of the sound.

A popular omnidirectional microphone is the LAVALIER which is hung around a person's neck during a group discussion. The lavalier also affords greater mobility to the speaker.

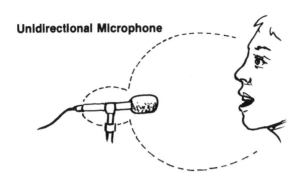

Unidirectional Microphone

UNIDIRECTIONAL MICROPHONE — The other type of popular microphone is the unidirectional microphone which has a narrow range of pickup and is very selective about what it hears. Most high quality hand-held, stand, PA (Public Address) or shotgun microphones are unidirectional. The sound recording quality of this type is the best, but some mics must be placed very close to the sound source (about 6 inches) and must be aimed directly at it, otherwise the sound quality will deteriorate rapidly. Unidirectional microphones are able to eliminate most of the unwanted extraneous sounds that are present in a recording environment.

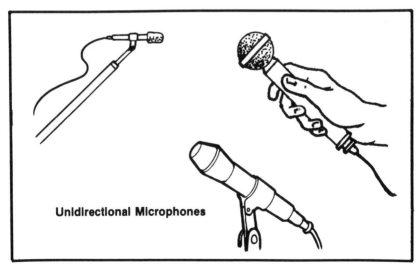

Unidirectional Microphones

155

Shotgun Mics

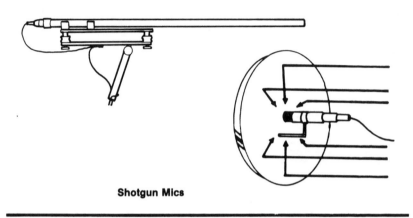

Shotgun Mics

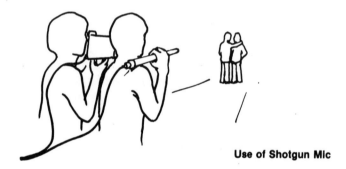

Use of Shotgun Mic

There is one kind of mic that is able to pick up good sound without being close to the sound source. This is the SHOTGUN MIC, and it has an extremely narrow range of pickup and can achieve the effect of sounding like it is placed close to the speaker even though it may be 30 to 50 feet away. Good shotgun microphones are very expensive ($400-$900), but Comprehensive Video has a $69 shotgun mic they say will pick up sound as well as other units costing many times more.

Use of an External Microphone

Even though most portable cameras have a built-in microphone to record the sound, the resulting quality is often fairly poor because the mic ends up being too far away from the sound source. You will get much better sound if you use an

EXTERNAL MICROPHONE, which is a second mic plugged into the MIC IN or MICROPHONE plug on the VCR and placed up close to the sound source. When the MIC IN jack is activated, it cancels out the built-in mic in the camera. Also, you will probably need a long microphone extension cable. Connect an earphone or headset to the VCR EARPHONE jack to monitor the sound.

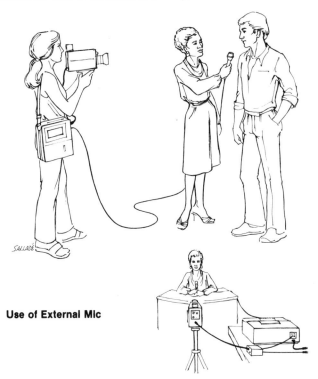

Use of External Mic

Microphone Design

There are 2 basic types of microphone design: the DYNAMIC MICROPHONE is merely a precision diaphram that vibrates when air pressure waves strike it, and the newer CONDENSER MICROPHONE actually amplifies the sound electrically within the microphone. The condenser mic is usually much smaller and considerably more sensitive than the dynamic mic but it requires a battery. So if you select a condenser mic, make sure the battery is good and is correctly installed.

ALWAYS BE SURE TO CARRY SPARE BATTERIES!

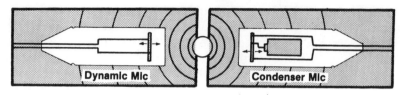

Audio Adapters

Most home video recorders use one of two types of audio connectors as an input plug for the microphone. The Beta format VCRs use the small MINI PLUG whereas the VHS recorders use the larger PHONE PLUG. Microphone and other audio adapters are available from most electronic stores like Radio Shack and Lafayette. Audio adapters and accessories designed specifically for video are also available from your local video dealer or from Comprehensive Video.

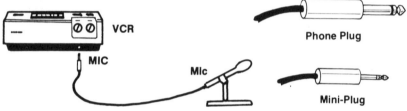

Other Audio Connectors and Connections

Both Beta and VHS systems use an in-between size plug called a PHONO or RCA PLUG which is located on the back panel of the VCR. It is used for connecting the sound from the VCR to a stereo system or another VCR for dubbing or editing purposes. These audio connections are labeled AUDIO IN and AUDIO OUT, and the plugs are different from the microphone plugs so you can't confuse them. The idea of different plugs is not necessarily to confuse you or make you buy lots of audio adapters but to prevent accidental wrong connections.

Microphone Impedance

Impedance is the measure of the microphone's resistance to the flow of electricity. Every input connection has a certain amount of impedance. Therefore, the impedance rating of the microphone should match fairly closely the impedance of the particular microphone input.

All home VCR mic inputs are rated at 600 OHMS which is termed LOW IMPEDANCE as opposed to 2,000 to 10,000 OHMS which is termed HIGH IMPEDANCE. All good quality microphones are low impedance. The best thing to do is just to try whatever microphone you have and make a sound test. If the sound is full, rich and has good strong volume, then use that microphone. If the sound is weak, garbled, and has little or no volume, then it probably is broken or has the wrong impedance. You can't really hurt the VCR or microphone by trying them together even though some microphones will have the larger Phone plugs, and others will have the smaller Mini plugs. Any mic can usually be plugged into the microphone input plug if the proper adapter is used. Some mics will work better than others.

Probably, you will need extension cables for your microphone so you can get the microphone close enough to the sound source. Also, a wind screen is a must if you are recording outdoors, especially on a windy day. A piece of foam rubber or a heavy sock is probably a necessity, and a boom is a great help for recording in situations where it is either too difficult or too unsightly to have a mic stand or pass around the microphone. You can make your own boom mic with a few accessories from Radio Shack and a broom stick.

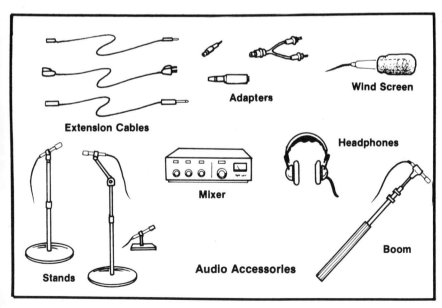

Extension Cables

Adapters

Wind Screen

Headphones

Mixer

Stands

Audio Accessories

Boom

Occasionally, you may come across a situation where there are several sources of sound such as a panel discussion or a play. Often the only way to record something like this with good sound is to use several mics and blend them together into one sound with an AUDIO MIXER. However, this approach requires several matched mics, a whole assortment of mic cables and a mixer. The mixer alone can cost from $40 to $300.

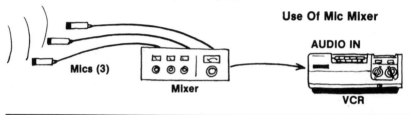

Use Of Mic Mixer

AUDIO IN

Mics (3)

Mixer

VCR

Typical Sound Setups

Now, let's take a look at several typical sound recording setups and evaluate the probable quality of the results.

Option #1

- Microphone is in the camera.

- Sound quality will probably be poor, but this arrangement affords good camera mobility and audio simplicity.

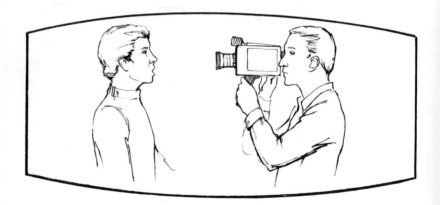

Option #2

- An external uni-directional microphone is used.

- Sound quality will be excellent, but you may need an extra person to hold the mic, and an extension cable is required.

Option #3

- A boom mic or shotgun mic is used.

- The sound quality will be good to excellent.

- The camera has good mobility.

- An extra person is needed to hold the microphone and possibly extra cables will be required.

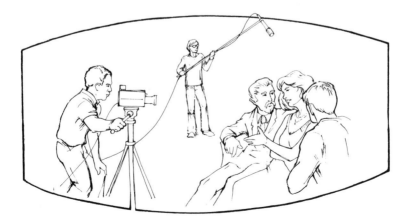

Option #4

Use of Multiple Microphones and Mixer System

- Excellent quality sound is achieved, but an extra person will be required to run the mixer. Also, extra cables, mics, and a mixer will have to be set up.

- This is a complex system that can break down.

Audio Production/Sound Mixing and Voice Overs

You have quite a lot of audio recording flexibility even with a simple home VCR. The most basic way to record sound is to use the camera's built-in microphone or an external mic to capture whatever sound accompanies what the camera is shooting. You can also add sound later to what you have already recorded by using the AUDIO DUB feature on the VCR. This feature allows you to add new sound to your tape without erasing the picture. However, the old sound will be erased where the new sound is added.

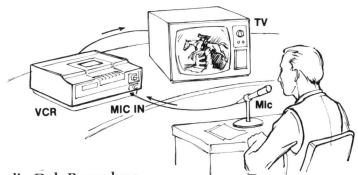

Audio Dub Procedure

NOTE: *Some Beta format VCRs do not have the audio dub feature.*

Step 1   Connect the microphone to the VCR through the MICROPHONE input. If the mic is built into the camera, just connect the camera to the VCR.

Step 2   Playback your pre-recorded tape and pause the tape at the point where you want to record the new sound.

Step 3   Prepare your new sound and turn down the volume control on the TV set.

Step 4   Place the VCR in the AUDIO DUB mode by pushing down the AUDIO DUB button. Release the PAUSE control. Start talking into the microphone or playing your music as the new sound is being recorded by the VCR.

Step 5   When you have recorded the new sound, *immediately STOP* the VCR.

Step 6   Rewind the tape and check to see if the recording was successful. If the new sound is not correct, repeat the process.

NOTE: This process can be repeated any number of times; however, be careful not to push the RECORD button accidentally as this will erase *both* the picture and the sound.

An audio dub can be a narration added to visuals taped earlier or it can be live or taped music fed into the VCR from an audiotape recorder. An audiocassette recorder cannot be plugged into the MIC INput because the output impedance of the audio recorder will not match the input impedance of the VCR. Rather, plug the output from the audio recorder or player into the AUDIO INPUT or LINE INPUT plug on the back of the VCR. Also, note that you *cannot* use the MIC INput and AUDIO INPUT or LINE INPUT plugs simultaneously. The MIC IN or MICROPHONE plug always takes preference over the AUDIO INPUT or LINE INPUT plug and will shut off if both inputs are used at once.

Music Recording With a VCR

Music can add a whole other dimension to your tapes. The right music can give your tapes a professional feeling and impact. There are 2 basic ways to dub prerecorded music onto a VCR.

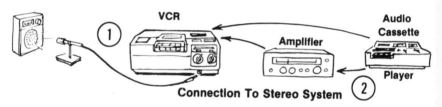

Connection To Stereo System

Method #1 simply involves placing a microphone in front of a speaker and recording the sound. A better but more complicated way is the direct recording method (#2), where an audiocassette recorder or audio amplifier is plugged into the AUDIO INPUT of the VCR. This requires special audio dubbing cables.

Anyone who gets really involved in adding sound to a tape will soon want to have the music mixed with the dialog or narration. This is called mixing sound or having sound-on-sound. With ½-inch VCRs you can only record the new sound and erase the old sound or just keep the old sound; therefore, a combination of sounds will have to be mixed on a separate audio recorder first or several sounds recorded simultaneously by the microphone or mixer live.

A typical sound tape with audio dubbing might look like this schematically.

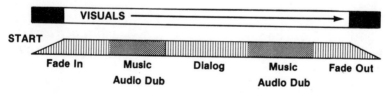

164

Like shooting, effective and successful sound requires that you *plan ahead*. If you want music mixed with your live dialog, make a music tape beforehand and have it playing in the background while you are recording your tape. Be sure to have the correct microphones and extra batteries for the microphones. And don't forget extension cables, booms, wind filters and a mixer if necessary. Often a good headset or an earplug is required for monitoring the sound. If problems arise, *see Chapter 10 — Maintenance and Troubleshooting*.

BRIGHT IDEAS — Lighting

Lighting is another very important factor in the creation of a good videotape. No matter how good your video camera, poor lighting will produce a poor quality picture. This in turn will have an effect on the viewer.

Because the TV set shows only 2 dimensions, the third dimension — depth — must be created by your lighting. Like camera operation and audio recording, some people devote whole professional careers to the development and perfection of creative lighting skills. Lighting, perhaps more than anything else, determines mood and feeling; therefore, the proper lighting is a crucial component of any serious TV program or feature film.

The average home producer does not have the time, equipment or need to take lighting quite so seriously. The main objective is to get a picture that is pleasing to the eye and has good detail. B&W cameras are quite sensitive to light and are able to take good pictures even in the low lighting conditions found inside the home. Color cameras, however, are more critical and require special settings and filters for different lighting conditions.

Lighting Conditions

Probably the best lighting condition is a bright, cloudy day. Shadows are few and the lighting is fairly even. Bright sunlight tends to create tremendous contrast — shadows are too dark and areas that face the sun are too bright. Color cameras, though, love sunlight as the colors are rich and vivid. And the picture will be very sharp.

In nature, the sun is the primary light source. The sun's light is reflected and diffused many ways, providing secondary illumination. In trying to illuminate a subject artificially when indoors, the picture will look natural if the principles of natural lighting are used.

How to Light

The basic method of lighting is called the 3-POINT method. A single, main source of light is generally located in front and above and to the right or left of the subject. This light is intended to roughly simulate the sun and is called a KEY LIGHT. Other smaller lights are then used to simulate secondary illumination or reflected light and are known as FILL LIGHTS. A third, even smaller light, called a BACK LIGHT may be used to separate the subject from the background and really provide a 3-dimensional effect.

Good Lighting

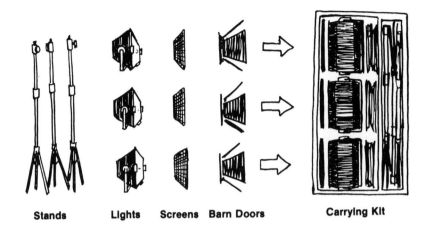

Stands   **Lights**   **Screens**   **Barn Doors**   **Carrying Kit**

Professionals use special QUARTZ LIGHTS which provide a great amount of light from a small lamp. Quartz lights come in all sizes and there are nice 3 and 4 light kits that can be purchased for $300 to $800. These kits include DIFFUSION SCREENS which allow you to control the amount of light given off by the lamp, stands to mount the lights on and BARN DOORS which make it possible to direct the light toward the subject.

Certainly a full 3 or 4 light set-up will enhance any production and really make it look professional if used properly. However, 3 quartz lights will draw at least 1500 watts of power and may blow out your fuses unless you plug the lights into different circuits. You can do this by buying heavy duty AC extension cables and plugging some of the lights into wall plugs in separate rooms.

B&W cameras do not really require such an elaborate lighting set-up, but most color cameras do need something more than the average household level of light if you want to have a crisp and colorful picture.

The least expensive set-up includes 2 or 3 photographic lamps (250 or 500 watts) which cost about $20 apiece and a few heavy duty extension cords which can be purchased at most discount stores. Use these lights to illuminate your subject in addition to room lighting.

Also, you can minimize the need for artificial light by shooting in a bright sunny living room during the day and using the natural sunlight. You may have a problem mixing sunlight and artificial light if you have a color camera because of the mixed color temperature of daylight and indoor light. As we mentioned earlier, color cameras must be properly set for the dominant lighting conditions, and a mixture can confuse the camera. However, the Color Temperature Selector dial on the camera might be adequate. If not, use your White Balance control for precise color adjustment.

Color Temperature Control

The relationship of the brightest area to the darkest area is known as the CONTRAST RATIO. The idea of lighting *any* scene is to minimize this ratio. Thus, an evenly lighted scene will provide good blacks, grays and whites which will result in good detail in black and white and a good gradation of color.

If, on the other hand, you want to create dramatic and powerful scenes, then use contrasty lighting. A single bright light, for example, placed either high above or below the subject in a dark room will create a certain mood. A low-angle placement of a light can create a feeling of mystery whereas a bright, even illumination can suggest gaiety. Simply stated, light can make the subject credible or incredible, effective or ineffective.

The really nice thing about video is that you can experiment and see right on your TV set what your lighting looks like. Just keep moving the lights until you get the effect you want. What you see is what you will get.

Lighting Examples

One easy trick to use when shooting in relatively dark rooms such as a girlfriend's or boyfriend's bedroom is to replace the standard bulbs in the room lamps with bright photographic bulbs available at any photo store. This will preserve the natural lighting effect but will increase the overall level of light in the room. For best effect though, you might want to add one photographic keylight also.

The Problem of Killer Backlighting

The two greatest lighting problems are insufficient light and severe backlighting. The former creates a poor gray overall picture. Severe backlighting causes the camera's automatic light adjusting system to black out the detail in the subject if the subject is in front of a brightly illuminated area.

Situation

Situation Result

Poor Subject Placement

No Detail In Picture
Killer Backlighting

Correct Subject Placement

Good Detail In Picture

All video cameras contain built-in light sensing circuits that automatically cause the camera to adjust to the amount of light. However, the automatic circuit works best when the lighting is relatively uniform and constant. It usually has problems dealing with severe backlighting because it will only adjust to the brightest area of light in the scene. New auto-iris lenses, though, cope remarkably well with contrasty scenes. If you have an electronic viewfinder and can adjust the auto-iris lens manually or have a Back Light Control switch, perfect light exposure is possible even under difficult lighting circumstances.

Movement and Lighting

This is a real problem in motion photography. If only one area is well-lighted and the subject moves away slightly, he may find himself in darkness. Consequently, movement must be planned in advance, and lighting may have to be set up for several places along the subject's line of movement. Possibly several key lights and fill lights will be needed. The camera's compensating circuitry will be able to adjust somewhat to the differences in light, but it has its limits. You can, of course, open or close the lens aperture to adjust the amount of light, also. If shooting outdoors, you will have to avoid shooting into dark shadows or heavily backlighted areas such as a bright sky background which may cause a loss of detail in the picture or have a different color temperature shifting the color of your scene.

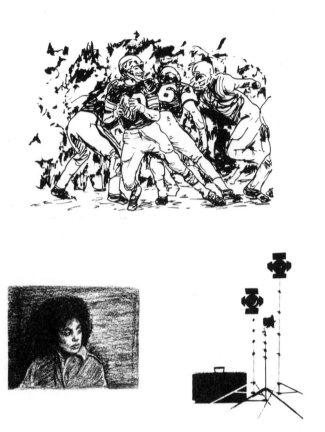

Again, depending on your camera and your circumstances, you may not have to be overly concerned about the lighting. Often a single household floodlight or photographic light aimed at the subject or on the ceiling above the subject will raise the room illumination sufficiently to provide reasonably good pictures. Lights, though, do create cables for people to trip over and hot lights can be very hazardous. So be careful. If you are fortunate to have professional quartz lights, remember never to touch the bulb when first installing it or "re-lamping". Invisible grease on your hands will cause the bulb to remain marked. Always place a piece of paper between your fingers and the bulb.

SIMPLE GRAPHICS FOR THAT EXTRA TOUCH

Graphics can add a nice professional quality to your program and can be done simply and quickly.

The Essential Area

The television screen is a fixed size. This means that when videotaping a piece of art work, it must be a certain height and a certain width to fit on the screen. The relationship of height to width is called the ASPECT RATIO and in TV it is 3:4. The ESSENTIAL AREA is that area within the 3:4 ASPECT RATIO.

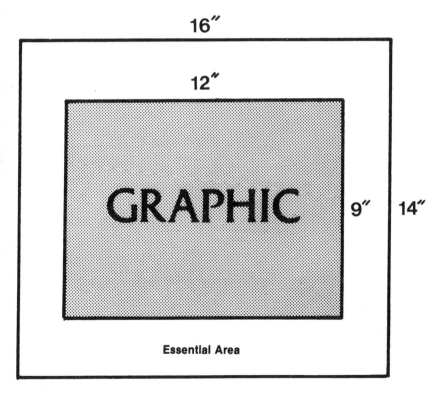

Essential Area

When constructing a graphic for a video program, use a piece of poster board 14 inches by 16 inches. It is best to use an off-white or blue colored poster board because it is easier to light for shooting. Next, draw a light outline 9 inches by 12 inches. This is the ESSENTIAL AREA where the graphic is to be placed.

Graphic Method #1 — Magic Marker and Hand Artwork

There are any number of ways to create graphics. The simplest is just to use a magic marker or wide, felt-tipped pen and a piece of paper and shoot that with the camera. Remember that the writing must be large and it must fit *inside* the essential area.This means that you will need several graphics to give credit to Peter, Mary, Howard, Mrs. Osborne, Maury the cat, Zeke the dog and all the others who took part in the big production. One way to do this is to make several cards and hold them in a pile and shoot them one-by-one, or make a large list and slowly pan the camera down the list. But, the list must be curved so the print doesn't go out of focus. Another way is to attach the list to two rollers and crank it along.

Shooting A Credit List

Graphic Method #2 — Press-On Letter Graphics

A very wide range of press-on letters and artwork is available at most graphic art or artist supply stores. Popular manufacturers include *Zipatone*, *Paratype* and *Format*. Hundreds of different styles and sizes of letters can be purchased in sheets. Generally, you will want 36 point letters or larger. The letters come in an extremely wide variety of type faces so you should be able to find just the right kind of type to express the character of your program.

174

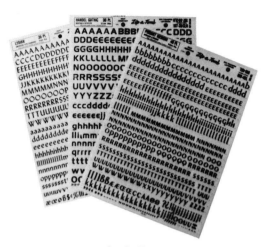

Press-On Letters

The technique of using press-on letters is simple. Place the letter sheet on your graphic card and rub the back of the appropriate letter which is set in the correct position. The wax coating on the back of the type sheet causes the type to adhere to your paper or poster board. Use a dull pencil, and rub the letter in a firm rotating manner until the letter sticks to the paper. If the letter is pressed too hard, it may crack. If such a problem occurs, use a piece of scotch tape or masking tape to lift the damaged letter from the paper. Be careful though, a slip of the tape can bring up a portion of a neighboring letter.

When choosing letter types, avoid styles that are unnecessarily elaborate as they will only confuse the viewer and clutter the screen. Keep the letters close and try to line them up parallel in the horizontal and vertical planes. A good rule is to space each letter the width of the letter "i" and space each word the width of the letter "e." For durability and ease of shooting, use poster board or heavy cardboard to mount your graphics. White letters on black often look much better than black letters on white.

For even more variety, do not hesitate to mix "stills" (photos you may have enlarged from snapshots taken with your instamatic or SLR) with live video action.

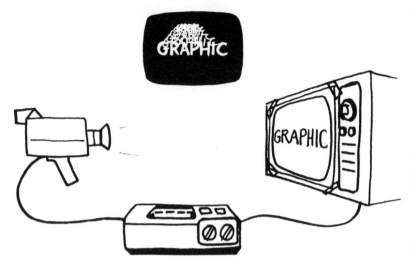

Video Feedback Graphics

Method #3 — Video Feedback Graphics

Secure some clear acetate and draw your graphics on it or use the press-on letters. Next, place the acetate on the face of your TV set. Turn your equipment on and shoot the TV set with the camera while tilting and moving the camera from side to side and front to back, experimenting with angles to get the best effect. This effect is usually a real crowd pleaser.

Bringing it All Together

Creative camera technique, good sound and adequate lighting will really help a tape to look professional. Bringing it all together, of course, will require some time and experimentation. Tape is cheap so you have that option. You do not need lots of fancy expensive video equipment although it sure helps sometimes. A very effective tape can be made with a $300 camera, a good $30 unidirectional microphone and $40 worth of photographic lights properly placed. A successful tape is really determined by what the people in front and behind the camera do rather than what the equipment does. So, don't be discouraged because you can't afford sophisticated color cameras and fancy editing systems. A little personal ingenuity and imagination can go a long way toward making a powerful videotape.

9

Editing and Dubbing

The Need For Editing

You may find after 6 months or so, that you would like to recycle and reuse some of your tape in order to keep tape costs down. You may also be looking forward to finally erasing old Aunt Harriet's interminable 45-minute luncheon address to the Gopher Springs Jr. Women's Auxiliary Club, which will make the tape available for something a little more stimulating such as the Olivia Newton-John special coming up next Tuesday night.

Unfortunately, you remember that Aunt Harriet's tape also has that classic sequence of your next door neighbor's son Wilbur Wilson driving his father's new Ford Station Wagon into the swimming pool because he didn't know how to handle a standard shift. You just happened to have your video recorder and camera set up around the pool for taping Suzy Wilson's diving lessons when Wilbur and the car crashed through the hedge and landed in the pool. You got the whole event on tape. It was really great, and you certainly can't recycle that footage. It's real academy-award winning stuff.

So, how can you send Aunt Harriet's dismal dialog off into the ethereal cosmos forever but preserve Wilbur Wilson and his underwater car for posterity?

Video Editing

The method commonly used in film and video to keep or eliminate sections of program material is, of course, called editing. Although the result is the same, editing videotape is a radically different process than editing film.

Essentially, the process of editing videotape involves simply *copying* onto a second tape those segments of the original tape which you want to keep. These desired segments of picture and sound can be assembled in chronological order, or in any other order, onto the second tape — the last scene first, then the third scene, the first scene, and so on.

After the scenes are copied on the second tape, the original tape can then be used again for shooting new scenes. The recorder always automatically erases the tape as it records on it. Sounds simple doesn't it? You are about to ask, "but doesn't it require a second VCR to make a second tape?" Yes, that is the case. You always need two VCRs to edit or copy a videotape because it is not advisable to cut and splice videotape. Once the videotape is physically cut, it is ruined permanently at that point, even if spliced together. The tape might possibly damage the VCR when the spliced part of the tape passed through the VCR's internal mechanisms. The tape must be continuous and smooth as the VCR greatly prefers only perfect tape running through its innards.

In order to copy a tape yourself, your options are to buy, borrow or appropriate a second VCR. You may want to find out who else on your block has another similar format VCR. Who knows what romantic possibilities may be uncovered as you search for a second VCR. In the old days, borrowing sugar afforded a convenient excuse to meet that lovely lady or handsome man next door. Now, modern technology has provided us with a much sweeter line, "Do you mind if I bring over my Betamax and make a dub tonight? The sugar excuse was only good for 5 minutes, but the possibilities afforded by copying a 2 or 4-hour videotape boggle the mind. It seems television just might bring people together after all.

Dubbing Vs. Editing

As we mentioned, the copying or DUBBING of videotape requires two machines, one for playback and one for recording. Videotape copying is just like the process of copying audiotapes or recording tapes from records. The simplest form of this technique is known as STRAIGHT DUBBING. Technically, dubbing could be described as the copying of a tape in its entirety without really changing the sequences or the time length of the scenes. EDITING is the process of actually altering the sequence of scenes, shortening, lengthening or eliminating scenes altogether. Any two VCRs can be used for straight dubbing, assuming one is a recorder. Simple deletions and the rearrangement of segments can also be accomplished with ordinary home VCRs by starting and stopping the second recording VCR at the appropriate spots and re-recording only those portions of the tape that you want to keep. This is a form of simple editing and will work quite satisfactorily.

Glitches

In both film and video, the individual frames of information are copied one at a time, but the successful reproduction of film frames does not depend on the speed the film is running. Videotape, however, must run at a specific speed of 30 frames per second because the TV system will only work at one specific speed. Film can be run at any speed, and the picture will remain perfectly intact; the speed of the perceivable action will, of course, appear faster or slower, and the sound will change.

In video, though, speed is the crucial element in editing and dubbing. The playback machine and the recording machine must both be moving at full speed for the copying to be successful. If the videotape moves too slowly or too fast, picture and sound distortion will result. Often, a slight variation in the speed of a VCR will cause it to lose its picture.

But, a VCR isn't always running at full speed. When it starts up, there is a split second or so when it is "coming up to speed". Consequently, the recorded tape will often show some distortion at each scene start and stop point. This distortion is known in video jargon as a GLITCH. These glitches become recorded into the tape permanently until the tape is erased and recorded over again.

Normal

Glitch

Most portable VCRs have rapid start/stop systems that minimize or eliminate the distortion or glitch between scene transitions when the camera is plugged in and the VCR is being started or stopped by the camera's remote trigger switch. Thus, by editing in the camera as you shoot, you can end up with a smoothly edited tape even though the VCR was stopped and started many times.

The Process of Editing

Film is cut physically at the point where the edit is to be made. The person who is editing holds the film up to the light or places it on an editing device known as a MOVIEOLA. The exact edit point is then selected by moving the film along frame-by-frame. The cut is then made between the selected frames, and the new segments are then spliced together.

Initially, videotape was also spliced physically in this manner, but since the frames on the tape are invisible to the eye, and the tape has a variety of other information on it, successful splicing was very difficult and once the tape is cut it is effectively ruined. However, there are video splicing kits available. One is the "Editall" which can be purchased from Comprehensive Video Supply Corp. for $39.95.

In video, then, the splicing is done electronically by using a special EDITOR VCR. Editing of segments from several tapes is usually done on an elaborate ELECTRONIC EDITING SYSTEM which involves 2 VCRs and a special AUTOMATIC EDITING CONTROLLER which runs the VCRs. But we will get into this a little later.

How Video Editing Works

Let's say you have a total of 3 hours of Cheryl's first big little league game on 3 different tapes. You would like to edit these 3 hours down to 1 hour of the best action footage — her grand slam home run and her fine pitching.

First, you will need to locate those segments on the 3 tapes and perhaps time them. These segments will then be placed on the PLAYBACK VCR and called your MASTER TAPE FOOTAGE. Next, you will transfer the master tape footage to the editor VCR which contains a separate blank tape called the EDITED MASTER TAPE. Thus, your 3 hours of tape become 1 hour of tape, and you can reuse the original. Later, if you wish, you can create copies of the edit master directly and give these copies to friends or use them for Cheryl's portfolio.

Everytime you copy a tape, it loses some quality. The more you copy it, the faster it degenerates. However, you lose much less quality if you just keep copying the original tape because the copies are only one GENERATION removed from the original tape. The copy is known then as a SECOND GENERATION TAPE. If you make a copy of the original and then reproduce that copy, you will then have a THIRD GENERATION tape and so on.

Here are some ways to minimize the quality losses during copying:

- Try to shoot in good light or add artificial lights, especially if you're shooting in color.

- Make sure the camera is working properly, is correctly focused and the lens aperture is correctly set.

- Use only good videotape.

- Use a good external microphone and have it close to the sound source.

- Make sure all connections are correct and tight.

Tape Copying Methods

A big part of the editing process is the task of locating the segments of the tapes that you want to edit. Finding these segments involves watching the tape and noting where the scenes are by using the tape counter as a rough reference guide.

If you are going to rearrange a lot of scenes, then you may want to prepare a simple editing script. It should include at what digit point each segment is located, the length in minutes and seconds of each scene and how the scenes are to be ordered on the finished tape. This kind of preparation will prevent confusion during editing and save time.

Basic Editing Methods

The basic method of editing is called ASSEMBLE EDITING which is just the simple linear assembly of sequences. For example, segment A is followed by segment B which is followed by segment C and so on. An assemble edited tape might look like this:

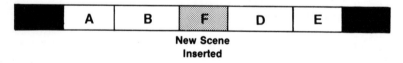

	Time ———————————————→					
START	Scene	Scene	Scene	Scene	Scene	END
	A	B	C	D	E	
30 sec.	5 min	10 min	8 min	3 min	4 min	30 sec.

Assemble Editing

Original segments or scenes do not necessarily have to be assembled in the same order as they were shot. For example, scene C could have been the first segment on the original tape and scene A could have been located in the middle of the original tape.

The other process of editing is called the INSERT EDITING method which allows scenes to be added to an assemble edited tape. Only sophisticated electronic editors can do this, though.

	A	B	F	D	E	

**New Scene
Inserted**

Insert Editing

Both the picture and the sound are usually edited simultaneously, but new sound can be added later to the tape by using the AUDIO DUB feature on most VCRs. Also, good electronic editors allow picture and sound to be edited separately in all kinds of combinations.

Shoot To Edit

If you intend to edit your tapes on an electronic editing system, and if you desire to have really clean edits between the scenes, you must "SHOOT TO EDIT." This is a process whereby the cameraperson or VCR operator starts the VCR and allows it to run at least 5 to 10 seconds prior to the start of the scene and keeps the VCR running at least 5 to 10 seconds after the scene ends. This extra running time allows the VCR to "get up to speed" and function smoothly at the start or finish of each scene. When editing, the editor VCR needs this PRE-ROLL time on the recorded tape in order to lock up to the tape and produce a clean glitch-free edit at the edit point.

If you try to make an edit at the same point on the tape where the VCR was started or stopped, the glitch at that point will make it impossible to make a clean edit. Edits cannot be made over glitches — only before or after them. Also, when glitches are copied, they often tend to be worse on the copy than on the original tape.

How To Make A Simple Dub

Dubbing is the easiest and simplest way to copy a videotape. Two VCRs are required, and they must be connected together in the correct manner with the proper cables and connectors.

Be sure to use only 75 ohm COAXIAL type cable for the video connections. *Do not* use the 50 ohm CB radio type cable which looks similar. You will need audio and video cables with RCA/PHONO connectors on each end. The proper dubbing cables and connectors can be purchased from large video dealers or ordered from Comprehensive Video Supply.

Dubbing Procedure

Step 1   Connect the VCRs together. You will need 2 connector cables with the correct plugs on them. One cable is for audio and one cable is for video. Also, it helps to have each VCR plugged into a TV set so you can see where you are on the tapes. Make sure the OUT on the Playback or Master VCR is connected to the IN on the Recording or Editing VCR. The VIDEO OUT on VCR A should be connected to the VIDEO IN on VCR B and the AUDIO OUT or LINE OUT on VCR A should be connected to the AUDIO IN or LINE IN on VCR B.

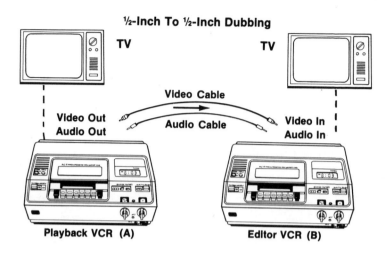

½-Inch To ½-Inch Dubbing

TV | TV

Video Cable

Video Out | Video In
Audio Out | Audio In

Audio Cable

Playback VCR (A) | Editor VCR (B)

Step 2 Place the master tape (tape to be copied or edited) on the Playback VCR (A) and a blank tape on the Recording VCR (B).

Step 3 Rewind your master tape to a point 10 seconds or so before the beginning of the first segment. Make sure the blank tape on the copying VCR is also set at the beginning.

Step 4 Make a test!

Start the recording VCR (B) and place it in the RECORD MODE and also start the playback VCR (A). The dubbing will now begin. Record 1 or 2 minutes of tape and then rewind and play back the results. See if the picture and sound are okay and the tape started at the correct time. If not, start one of your VCRs earlier or later. If the picture and sound are not okay, check your connections. Also keep in mind that some slight picture degradation will take place when a tape is copied. But this should not be extremely significant.

Step 5 If the test was successful, rewind both tapes again and repeat Step 4. Allow the VCRs to continue running for the length of your tape.

Step 6 When the tape is finished, rewind and play back the tape to see if the recording was successful.

How To Edit With Any Recording VCR

Some editing can be done with any recording VCR as a second or editor VCR. Merely by starting and stopping the machine at certain points you can selectively copy a tape and create a kind of edited program, although the scene transitions will probably have glitches in them.

Start-Stop Editing Procedure

Step 1 Connect 2 VCRs together in the same manner as for straight dubbing. Make sure the VIDEO OUT from the playback VCR is connected to the VIDEO IN on the recording (Editor) VCR. Check to see if the AUDIO OUT of the playback VCR is connected to the AUDIO IN on the recording VCR.

Step 2 Load your master (original tape) into the playback VCR and load a blank tape into the editor VCR.

Step 3 Make a quick test recording. Play back any scene on the master VCR and place the recording VCR in the RECORD mode. Record 30 seconds of picture, rewind and play back the tape. Check for satisfactory sound and picture. If it didn't work right, check your connections.

Step 4 Locate the starting point of the first scene that you want to copy. "Cue it up." This means rewind it sufficiently so that when both VCRs are "up to speed," and the tapes are threaded, the scene will be recorded as close to the actual beginning as possible.

NOTE: This will take some experimenting. Use the digit counter as a rough guide. You may have to PRE-ROLL (rewind) your tapes several digits early to have the picture start at the correct point. The number of digits that you pre-roll your tapes may change as the amount of tape on the reels changes.

Step 5 Start both VCRs and place the editor VCR in the RECORD mode. The tape is now being copied.

Step 6 Stop the editor VCR exactly where you want your scene to stop.

Step 7 REWIND or FF (Fast Forward) the playback VCR until you locate the beginning of the next segment to be copied. Cue up the new segment as in Step 4. You may want to rewind the tape a small amount on the editing recorder VCR so that the second scene immediately follows the first. But, be careful. If you accidently erase the last part of the previous scene, you will have to record it all over again. (You may want to experiment a bit with this whole process before you begin your "good" edited tape).

Step 8 Start both VCRs again and place the editor VCR in the RECORD mode. The new scene will be recorded.

Step 9 Continue with this process until you have assembled your entire program.

Helpful Hints

•Experiment first to find the optimum pre-roll time.

•Don't try to edit scenes together too precisely as this can be very frustrating and time consuming.

•You may want to allow 5 to 8 seconds of BLACK between scenes to provide a cleaner transition. Just place the playback VCR in PAUSE mode for 2 to 5 seconds while the recording VCR continues to record. Or connect a camera to the editor VCR, turn on the camera and cover the lens. Record 5 to 8 seconds from the camera or add a graphic if you want.

•Make sure your blank tape is long enough. It's quite disconcerting to get well into your edited tape only to find out that the editor VCR suddenly shuts off in the middle of a segment because you thought you had a longer tape in the machine or you miscalculated the total time of your segments to be edited.

PAUSE Control Editing Procedure

Trying to get both VCRs pre-rolled accurately can result in total frustration, accidently erased scenes and damaged tape. Here's another method that is much easier if your VCR has a still frame type PAUSE control and if the RECORD, PAUSE and PLAY controls can be operated simultaneously. This works quite well with portable VCRs such as the JVC HR-4100AU. It should work fairly well too if your PAUSE control does not actually display a picture.

Step 1 Connect two VCRs properly for editing.

Step 2 Play your master tape until you reach the point just prior to the beginning of the scene you want to copy. Push the PAUSE control on the playback VCR. The VCR will stop.

Step 3 Play the tape on your recording editor VCR until the last scene of the previously edited sequence just ends. Push the PAUSE control on the editor VCR. The machine will stop. Both VCRs are now cued up.

Step 4 Push the RECORD button on the editor VCR.

Step 5 Release both PAUSE controls on both VCRs simultaneously and the new scene will be copied. Stop the VCRs when the scene ends.

Caution: Do not hold either VCR in the PAUSE mode any longer than necessary as the tape might become creased or the videoheads clogged and the tape and head life diminished. Experiment with old tape before trying the big one.

Electronic Editing

Electronic editing is about the only way to precisely edit a videotape. The common electronic editing system includes 2 VCRs, and usually both of them are special electronic editing VCRs. The electronic editing VCR is unique because it contains a CAPSTAN SERVO, which is an extra motor and drive system, and additional electronics. The capstan servo allows the editor VCR to "lock up to" the playback VCR. Thus, the editor VCR can speed up or slow down to match the speed of the playback VCR and then make perfect edits.

But a capstan servo alone is not enough. Most home VCRs have capstan servos but cannot edit. As well as the capstan servo, an editor VCRs needs special editing switches and circuitry. But for really precise editing, the VCRs need the editing controller accessory as well.

Once you have located the exact edit point, you merely push the EDIT button which starts and completes the editing process. Both VCRs are backed up and prepared for the edit. The VCRs then start up and move along at the correct speed. When the edit point is reached the editor VCR makes the edit automatically without glitches. The editor VCR is able to do this by electronically "locking up" to the playback VCR, so when the EDIT button is activated on the controller or the editor VCR, segments of picture and/or sound are instantly and perfectly transferred from the playback VCR to the editor VCR.

Electronic Editing Procedure

Step 1 Connect both VCRs together, connect the editing controller to the VCRs and connect two monitors or TV sets up to the VCRs.

Auto-Edit Programmer Editing

Step 2 Load the playback VCR with the master tape and the editor VCR with a blank tape.

Step 3 Make a test.

Play both VCRs and push the RECORD or EDIT button on the editor. Record 30 to 60 seconds of picture and sound on the editor VCR in order to check the picture and sound quality.

Step 4 If everything is working correctly, REWIND both tapes and locate the first scene to be edited from your master tape. Most editing controllers feature a slow SEARCH mode which allows viewing the tape in slow motion so you can precisely locate an edit point.

Step 5 When the scene has been located, note the location on the VCR digit counters or digital readouts.

Step 6 When the edit points have been located on each tape, press the PAUSE button for both machines.

Step 7 Make a test run of the edit by pressing the PREVIEW or REHEARSE button.

Step 8 If the preview edit was satisfactory, simultaneously press the AUTO EDIT and ASSEM button for an assembly edit and AUTO EDIT and CUT IN for an insert edit. The machines will make the edit at the right time. Stop the machines when the segment is finished.

Step 9 Rewind and replay the scene in order to check the edit. Is it clean? Did it start at the right time? If not, repeat the process.

Step 10 Locate the next segment to be edited on the master VCR and locate the end of the previous edit on the editor VCR.

Step 11 "Cue up" both machines at their proper points — the start of the new segment on the playback VCR and the end of the previously edited segment on the editor VCR.

Step 12 Start up both VCRs and either preview the edit or make the edit.

Step 13 Continue with steps 4 through 12 until you have completed your tape.

Auto-Edit Programmer Editing

Once you have located the segments you want to edit, an automatic editing system such as this allows you to assemble your sequences easily and rapidly. The advantages of such an editing system are many: the machinery does all the manual work of finding the tape segments, preparing the tapes for editing, and actually making the edits. You can even have the machines do a test edit and see if that's what you want. This is called an EDIT PREVIEW or EDIT REHEARSAL feature.

Generally speaking, these systems are way out of the range of the home video user since they cost from $4,000 to $100,000 depending on quality, features and types of equipment. The people who own such equipment are schools, universities, corporations and TV production companies. However, in most major cities, you can rent time on these editing systems by the hour. Then you have the choice of either editing your own tapes or hiring professionals to do your editing for a fee, usually $25 to $50 per hour. If you have looked at your master tapes and have decided beforehand how you want to edit your tape, it may take only 2 or 3 hours to complete a simple edited tape with maybe 10 to 20 edits in it.

The disadvantages of the editing process include the high initial costs of sophisticated equipment and the somewhat difficult job of operating the equipment. Video editing requires a personality that is calm and well organized and a flexible mind that can deal with several things simultaneously. Also, a sense of split second timing is necessary. Much can be done creatively in the editing process so that good results can be very satisfying and even exhilarating.

The automatic editing systems allow you to watch the scenes that will be edited at a slower speed so you can easily locate the exact point where you want to make an edit. This slow speed or SEARCH MODE is a feature found only in the more expensive 3/4-inch U-Matic editor VCRs and is activated by the special AUTOMATIC EDITING CONTROLLER. An editing controller must be used with specific editor VCRs. The controller essentially serves as the "brain" which tells the VCRs what to do — how to locate a scene, back up the tapes, what kind of edit to make, and when to make the edit. Some editing controllers even have a joystick device which allows you to go forward and backward one frame at a time on the VCRs. This allows very accurate editing.

Editing Options—Hardware

½-Inch to ½-Inch Videocassette This method is the simplest and the least expensive. Two ½-inch VCRs are used for editing. One unit serves as a playback machine and the other serves as an editor. Unfortunately, neither Beta nor VHS offers a true home ½-inch editing system, so your edits will be a little rough. There will be noticable picture quality degradation when copying from ½-inch to ½-inch.

Connecting 2 deck-type VCRs together will work well, but editing to a portable such as the JVC HR-4100AU will produce very good results. The Sony SL-3000 does not have nice audio and video inputs like the VHS portables, so you will need a Sony 14-Pin adapter box to provide the necessary inputs into the machine.

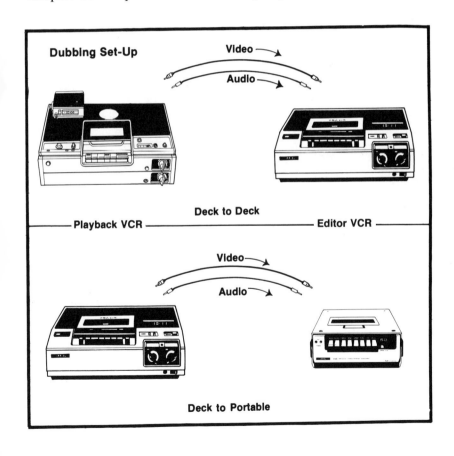

Dubbing Set-Up

Video

Audio

Deck to Deck

Playback VCR —————————— Editor VCR

Video

Audio

Deck to Portable

½-Inch To 3/4-Inch Editing With Auto-Programmer

½-Inch To ¾-Inch. One way of obtaining higher quality and much greater editing flexibility and control is to use a ½-inch VCR as a playback machine and a ¾-inch industrial editor VCR as a recording machine. For example, the Sony SLO-320 Betamax will connect to the RM-430 or RM-400 automatic editing controller which allows the Betamax to be used as a playback or recording machine with the Sony VO-2850 or VO-2860 ¾-inch videocassette editors. The editing is done on the ¾-inch VCR and then dubbed back down to the Betamax format. This way you end up with a third generation tape, but the quality loss is less than editing from ½-inch to ½-inch.

VHS Editing

As mentioned in *Chapter 11, Industrial VCRs,* Panasonic makes the NV-8170 and NV-8200 VCRs for operation with their ¾-inch editing VCRs and automatic editing controller. You could also edit between the NV-8170 ½-inch player and the NV-8200 recorder if you have the controller option and get the advantage of the second soundtrack for mixing music and a voice narrative. However, these ½-inch machines are not true editors and your quality will not be as good as editing up to the ¾-inch VCRs.

But, like the Betamax editing system, you can do very good quality and precise editing with your VHS tapes by editing from the NV-8170 or NV-8200 to the ¾-inch editing VCRs through the auto-editing controller. Then you dub your tape back down to the VHS format again. The advantage of the VHS system vs. the Betamax system is two fold: The VHS industrial editing system is compatible with all 2-hour (SP) mode home video recorders, and the NV-8170/8200 VCRs also have the 2-track stereo sound capability. The Betamax industrial system is only compatible with 1-hour X1 playback Beta VCRs and has only one sound track although you could dub your final copies to the Beta II format.

Basically, any ½-inch VCR can be connected to any ¾-inch VCR but you cannot use the auto-controller edit programming system unless you use the specific editing VCRs.

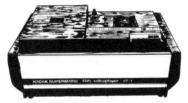

Kodak Videoplayer

Super-8 Film to ½-Inch Videocassette. Kodak made a unit called the KODAK VIDEOPLAYER which allows direct recording of Super-8 film onto any VTR and playback through any standard TV set. The cost is about $1,900 and it performs quite well. By transferring your films in a certain sequence, you can in effect create an edited sequence of Super-8 film on videotape. Unfortunately, this unit has gone out of production, but there are used units floating around. Otherwise, you can transfer your Super-8 to video by taking it to a commercial transferring facility.

Do-It-Yourself Film Transfer

Several manufacturers offer film transfer devices and accessories that work quite well for transferring film, slides and photos to videotape. Prices range from $90 to $150 for a telecine adapter which can be very simple like the JVC or Quasar or more

JVC Telecine

Quasar Telecine

elaborate like the Sony. (*See Chapter 3, How To Operate Your VCR-VCR Accessories.*) However, Fotomat will provide more professional results and can add dissolves and color correction to slides. Sony also offers a high quality film transfer service.

Commercial Editing Facilities

If you want to do some fancy editing, you might want to look into commercial video editing facilities. Excellent high quality and very sophisticated video editing facilities are available in most major cities. Here you can do just about anything with your tape, for a fee of course. Shop around as prices vary considerably.

As you get into the big systems, for example, the 3/4-inch and 1-inch VTRs, you will discover that prices go up fast, but the quality is really excellent. However, the inherent picture quality limitations of ½-inch home videocassette recorders and the resulting tapes probably do not justify buying time on big editing systems for the editing of ½-inch videocassettes. The home ½-inch VCR format was never intended to be used for professional quality master production.

If you are considering an important videotape production requiring editing and many copies, you should explore shooting and editing *entirely* with 3/4-inch VCRs. If this is the case, your best bet will probably be to rent 3/4-inch equipment. But at this point, video gets a lot more complicated and costs can add up fast. Do some research first and talk with professionals in the video production and editing business so you know what you're getting yourself into.

10 Maintenance and Troubleshooting

As we mentioned earlier, machines, like people, will respond better to tender loving care than they will to violence and abuse. VCRs, in particular, are delicate and cannot tolerate excessive moisture, dust or rough handling. The alignment of mechanical mechanisms inside the VCR is critical to proper tape recording and playback, and if these mechanical mechanisms go out of alignment, problems will result. Certain VCRs, like the Panasonic and RCA machines, are built on a solid, die-cast chassis and will tolerate greater stress.

VCRs are built to be strong and dependable, but there are limits. Video equipment must be treated more carefully than film equipment because video recorders have so many electronic and mechanical parts. Also, video cameras have a delicate light sensitive tube.

Cleaning The Camera Lens

Eventually, dust will settle on the lens, especially if the camera lens is not capped and the camera is not stored in a case or covered. Clean the lens while it is on the camera with lens cleaning tissue or compressed air available at any photo supply store. If spots still persist in the picture, you may have to clean the face of the camera tube.

Camera Tube Cleaning Procedure

Step   1   Remove the lens carefully by holding the camera firmly and gently turn the lens counterclockwise.

Step   2   Soak a Q-tip or similar cotton swab in the lens cleaning solution (available at photo stores) and gently wipe off the face of the camera tube surface which should be visible when you remove the lens. Be careful not to get more dirt or pieces of cotton on the face of the tube. You can also try compressed air to remove debris.

Step   3   Tilt the camera body carefully and angle the tube surface in order to see if there are any remaining dust particles on the tube face. If so, continue cleaning.

Step   4   Replace the lens, turn the camera on, activate the VCR and TV set, and check the camera's picture to see if it is clean. If not, repeat the camera cleaning procedure. If spots still persist, they may be burns or objects inside the tube, and the tube may have to be replaced.

Care of The Video Recorder

The VCR is the only component of the video system which contains any moving parts. Occasionally, drive belts, switches and knobs may have to be replaced, and mechanical adjustments may be necessary if the machine is used heavily. A reasonably well cared for VCR should run for many years without any major expense because the Japanese, who make all these machines, are perhaps the world's best experts at making rugged consumer-oriented electronic and mechanical products. The Japanese take great pride in the craftsmanship and detail that go into their products, and the buyer of these products will definitely reap the benefits.

VCRs like the Panasonic VHS Omnivision and RCA systems use the direct-drive motor and a die-cast chassis which increase reliability. The major problems that VCRs have to face are dust, moisture and accidents.

Vital VCR Precautions

- Be sure to find/buy/make a cover for your VCR that will protect it from dust and moisture.

- If you live near the ocean, try to protect your VCR from the salt in the air.

- Operate the VCR in a horizontal position only.

- Protect the VCR (and people) from cigarette smoke as it is damaging to vital parts.
- *DO NOT* place any junk food or liquids such as beer or diet soda on or near the VCR as someone might jar the machine and cause the liquids or foods to fall into it. If the VCR is caused to ingest such toxic substances, it may prove fatal to both the VCR and its owner's pocketbook.

Cleaning The Video Recorder

Video works by recording a series of VIDEO, AUDIO and CONTROL TRACKS on the videotape as the tape moves past the various recording heads. There are VIDEO HEADS, AUDIO HEADS and CONTROL TRACK HEADS inside the machine which can become clogged with use. Eventually, oxides fall or wear off the videotape and collect on the heads causing deposit buildups which in turn impair the efficiency of the recording and playback process. This will show up as a marked deterioration in picture and sound quality. In extreme cases, the picture may disappear altogether.

One Clogged Head   **Two Clogged Heads**

Inside the VCR are 2 rotating video heads mounted 180° apart inside a circular head drum. Poor quality tape or heavily used or damaged tape can completely clog one or both video heads. Half the picture may disappear or perhaps the whole picture may disappear, but sometimes these symptoms will soon clear up as the tape continues to play. If the heads do become clogged or the picture begins to deteriorate noticeably, you may need to take your VCR to your service center.

VCRs will occasionally need servicing every 8 months or so if used heavily. Repair bills are likely to be expensive—$50-$200—even for a routine check up. Video heads will need replacement after about 1000 hours of use depending on the VCR and how it is used. Video head replacement will cost about $200. You might consider extended warranty plans usually offered by speciality video dealers.

The quick and easy way to clean your VCR heads is with a Cleaning Cassette. TDK, Fuji, Scotch and Allsop all make non-abrasive cleaning cassettes which are merely inserted in the VCR and run for about 10-30 seconds.

Cleaning The Video Heads

It's not a good idea to personally disassemble or try to clean your VCR. Instead, take it back to your place of purchase or to a TV or video service facility and have them do it for you. If you do feel like digging into it yourself, you will need a phillips screwdriver, some head cleaning solution or rubbing alchohol and cleaning swabs (non-cotton foam type). You may also void the warranty by personally working on the machine. But if you insist, a company called NORTRONICS *(See Manufacturer's Appendix)* has a nifty VCR head cleaning kit specifically designed for home VCRs. It includes excellent easy-to-follow instructions. The Nortronics Kit can also be ordered from Comprehensive Video Supply.

Head Cleaning Procedure

Step 1 Make absolutely sure the VCR is turned *OFF.*

Step 2 Remove the screws from the top cover of the machine using a narrow-tip phillips screwdriver while being careful not to damage the screw heads. If your machine is a Sony Betamax, you will need to remove the TRACKING knob in the lower left-hand corner. It will pull directly off the shaft.

Step 3 Press the EJECT button to raise the cassette compartment and carefully remove the cover from the machine.

Step 4 Clean each of the two video heads by rotating them into position by turning the motor fan shroud. This will rotate the entire video head assembly into position.

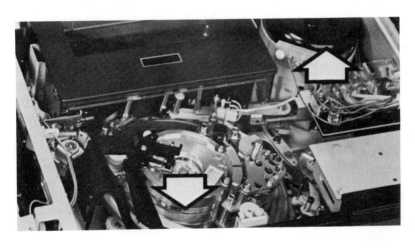

Step 5 Spray a cleaning swab with the head cleaning solution. *Very carefully* clean each head by using a back and forth HORIZONTAL motion *only* in the same plane as the tape travels. *DO NOT rub the video heads vertically as this may easily cause severe head damage.*

Step 6 Clean the video erase, audio and control track heads. These are stationary heads that are more rugged than the brittle video heads. On Betamax VCRs, these heads are located in the large assembly next to the circular head drum. They look like regular audio heads. VHS machines have the stationary heads located on the tape path to the right and left of the head drum cylinder. Spray the swab with the head cleaner and clean the heads and tape guides until all deposits have been removed.

Step 7 Replace the cover and all knobs on the VCR, turn the machine on and play a tape to confirm that everything is working ok. If it isn't repeat steps 5 and 6.

Cassette Tape Repair Procedure

If the tape becomes damaged or you have to cut off a piece which got jammed in the machine, repair the cassette tape in the following way:

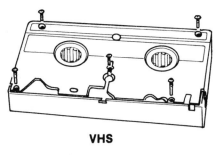

VHS

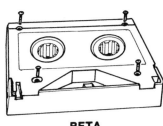

BETA

Step 1 Use a narrow-tip phillips screwdriver to remove the screws that hold the cassette together.

Step 2 Carefully grasp the cassette and turn it over so the label faces you.

Step 3 Depress the front panel release catch on the left side of the cassette and open the tape protector panel.

Step 4 While holding the spring loaded tape protector panel open, carefully lift the top cover of the cassette off the body of the cassette.

Step 5 Splice the remaining good tape together or onto the leader.

    A.   Cut off the bad tape and overlap the ends of the good tape together

    B.   Cut the tape at the right angle.

    C.   Join the ends together.

    D.   Carefully apply the video splicing tape.

NOTE: Use video splicing tape only. *Never* use audio splicing tape!

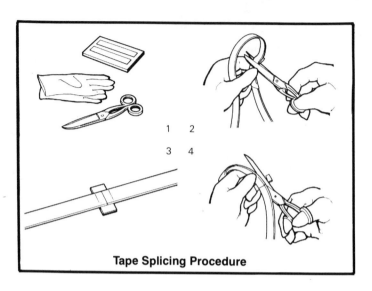

Tape Splicing Procedure

Step 6 Rewind the tape carefully by hand back into the cassette, making sure the tape is threaded through the proper tape guides.

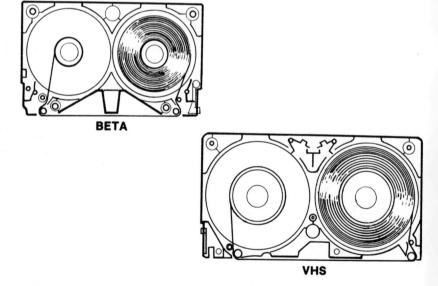

BETA

VHS

Step 7 Reassemble the cassette, replace the top cover and all the screws.

Care of Plugs and Connectors

Although seemingly minor items, your cables and plugs are the lifeline of your system. A broken wire or a weak plug will immediately shut down your system and drive you crazy trying to find out what's wrong.

The following list of do's and don'ts should at least minimize cable and connector problems.

How to keep a good connection:

DO keep connectors and connections free from dirt.

DO color code and mark all cables and perhaps attach a chart of how everything plugs together.

DO keep a few extension cables handy for power, microphone and camera cables.

DO use the best metal connectors and best quality cables you can buy if you are making up your own cables. Use SWITCHCRAFT or AMPHENOL plugs.

DO NOT break a prong on a plug. The equipment will not work.

DO NOT bend the cables excessively. This will weaken the cables and tear the wires from the plug. COIL all wires in 12 to 15-inch loops.

DO NOT try to force connectors together. If they don't fit together easily, you are usually doing something wrong or have the wrong connector.

DO NOT drop your cable plug ends on the floor or step on them.

DO NOT allow your dog to chew your connectors, as this will weaken and eventually break them and may also give your dog indigestion.

DO NOT lose your cables. Replacements are expensive and often impossible to locate on short notice.

Replacement of Parts and Connectors

Usually, a TV-Radio store like Radio Shack or Lafayette Electronics will have some replacement connectors for your VCR, camera and microphone cables and plugs. Another option is to go directly to the manufacturer's warehouse if there happens to be one nearby. You could also send for the plugs and connectors from the manufacturer, but that may take weeks or months.

When you do attempt to replace a connector or a cable, be sure to take the item to be replaced with you or know the identification number of the connector or the name of the plug. Verbal descriptions may be inadequate because there are many kinds of plugs and connectors to choose from. A typical close encounter between a plugless video user and a local electronic shop clerk might go as follows:

"Well, you see, it has a little bulge about this big on the end that fits over a skinny silver sleeve..."

Video and audio accessories and related production items can be ordered from video supply houses like *Comprehensive Video Supply Corp.* As we mentioned, they have a professional catalog which has an incredible assortment of popular and hard-to-find accessories from A (audio and video adapters) to Z (zoom lenses). The catalog contains an extensive film and TV/video book library, and items such as equipment carrying cases and test gear are also included. It's a must for the serious videophile.

Troubleshooting —
What To Do When It Doesn't Work

Psyching Out the Machine

Unlike people, machines can't tell you where it hurts. They just suddenly or intermittently cease to function. When this happens, *PATIENCE NOT PANIC* is the approach to take.

Human Error

Most problems are due to simple human error; probably 80% to 90% of all malfunctions stem from tape misthreading, cables plugged into wrong inputs or outputs, or switches placed on improper modes. *CHECK THESE THINGS OUT FIRST!*

Mechanical and Electronic Malfunctions

The other 8% to 10% of machine problems are due to mechanical failures such as broken plugs or wires, dirty heads, broken switches, etc., which a good mechanically inclined person can fix personally. The remaining 2% or so are due to electronic problems such as component failure, which take a competent VCR service technician and the proper test equipment to fix.

Cosmic Interference and Mental Attitude

Then every once in awhile, strange things happen; usually the "come-and-go" type where your system will suffer severe picture distortion, horrible color quality, or loss of audio minutes before or during the big production. The VCR operator and director often experience waves of nausea and acute mental hallucinations usually accompanied by recurring questions such as "Why me?" or "What did I do to deserve this?"

Assuming everything is properly connected, there is another cause to consider. Even so-called inanimate matter such as electronic circuits and pieces of metal and plastic are all made up of atoms and molecules that must bind together in a certain absolute pattern. A kind of INTERNAL INTELLIGENCE and energy is necessary to maintain this pattern. A VCR has a great variety of moving parts and must maintain a vast multitude of precise electronic levels and critical tolerances that must all function together perfectly 100% of the time. The slightest deviation in one component's performance will often adversely affect all the rest.

The internal intelligence of VCRs and cameras will definitely respond to highly negative or positive emotional fields generated by people. Like organic matter such as plants, animals or people, a video system will respond well to those operators who approach it with care and love. An overly frustrated or negative person will pass those personal frustrations onto the equipment and "strange" failures will inevitably result. This is why equipment "works" for certain people and "doesn't work" for others. *It happens every time.* Thus COSMIC INTERFERENCE may be *your* problem rather than the machine's. If you're convinced the equipment will break down, it definitely will. Be prepared for all contingencies, but approach your production with a positive mental attitude.

VCR Troubleshooting Chart

Symptoms	Check and Remedy
•No Power (Beta VCRs) (pilot lamp does not light)	•VCR may not be plugged in •Timer (on Sony SL-8200 and Zenith VCR) may not be turned on or may be improperly adjusted.
•No Power (JVC VCRs) *(Toshiba VCRs)*	•Turn TIMER/SLEEP switch *off*
•No color on TV set	•PROGRAM SELECTOR, ANTENNA or VCR/TV switch should be set to TV, even if the VCR is turned off. •Are the antenna connections correct? •Is the TV set to the correct VCR output channel — 3 or 4? •Are the correct channels fine tuned on both the VCR and TV set?
•Badly distorted playback picture.	•Adjust the TRACKING CONTROL The video heads may be clogged. (Take unit to service center)
•No recording or playback	•VCR PROGRAM SELECTOR must be in the VCR, VTR or CASSETTE position. •Check for proper connections •Are the plugs broken or weak? •Is the PAUSE switch in the normal position? Release the switch.
•TV Broadcasts cannot be recorded	•Make sure the VHS INPUT SELECTOR is in the VTR/TUNER position and the JVC RECORD SELECTOR is in the TV position. BetaVision and Toshiba VCR CAMERA-TUNER switch must be in the TUNER position. •Check to see if the cassette safety tab has been removed. Unplug camera and microphone from VCR.

VCR Troubleshooting Chart

Symptoms	Check and Remedy
•RECORD button cannot be pressed.	•Check to see if the cassette safety tab has been removed. •Is the DEW indicator lamp on?
•PLAY button cannot be pressed.	•Is the cassette properly loaded? •On Beta VCRs, is the STAND BY lamp off? If not, wait until it goes off. •Is the DEW lamp on?
•AUDIO DUB button cannot be pushed.	•Is the cassette properly loaded? •Check to see if the cassette safety tab has been removed.
•VCR stops in REWIND before end of tape	•Turn the MEMORY or SEARCH switch off.
•REWIND, FWD or Fast Forward mode does not function	•The tape may need rewinding
•No camera or microphone recording	•Are the connections correct? •Is the camera plugged in and switched on? •Is the microphone plugged in? •The VCR INPUT SELECTOR switch must be in the CAMERA position.
•Poor quality camera recording	•Is the lens iris open? •Add more light.
•Cassette will not eject	•Turn the VCR on and push the eject button.
Sound Problems	
•Whistling or screeching sound in the mic recording	•Turn the TV set's volume control down or off. •Move the mic away from the TV set.
•Poor quality sound	•Improper mic or poor quality mic. •Microphone is too far away from the sound source.
•No sound	•Broken mic or cable. •Improper connection.

11 Industrial Half-Inch VCRs

As a home video user, you may at some time want to know what other equipment is available that might complement your home video system. This would be especially true if you contemplate using video in your business. As additional information, this chapter on Industrial ½-inch video systems should be of some assistance.

Although the ½-inch Betamax and VHS video recorders were designed specifically for the home video user, educational/industrial video users immediately recognized the ½-inch home video recorder as a much less expensive means to record and distribute video programming. It was quickly apparent that two ½-inch home VCRs could be purchased for the same price as one ¾-inch video recorder.

This kind of thinking was bad news to the video manufacturers because they had hoped to avoid a situation where their educational/industrial users would begin to use the cheaper home VCRs. The next move by the manufacturers was to try and convince the educational/industrial user that there were better and more appropriate VCRs designed specifically for him. As a result, first Sony and then Panasonic introduced a line of VCRs primarily intended for the educational/industrial user. But, in many cases, there was little difference between the home VCR and the industrial VCR. With some machines, though, there are substantial differences.

The so-called INDUSTRIAL VIDEO SYSTEMS, like their sister home video systems, are divided up into two incompatible formats—BETAMAX and VHS. These industrial video systems are very similar to home video systems and differ mainly in terms of audio and video connectors, specific features and record/play time.

The Azimuth Recording System

All Betamax systems, and VHS systems use the AZIMUTH recording process which permits the video information to be laid down in a much denser configuration of tracks on the tape. This results in more information being recorded. This is possible because of the elimination of the GUARDBANDS during the recording of the tape. GUARDBANDS are separations or spaces between the video tracks that are required in conventional video recording methods to keep the video information from being wrongly played back by a misaligned video head.

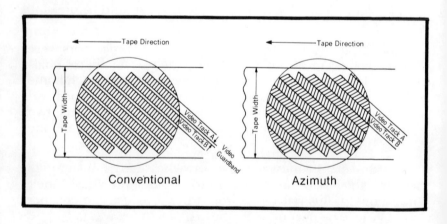

In the Azimuth recording process each diagonal video track is recorded right alongside the other but at a slightly opposite slant of 6°. If one of the two video heads passes over the wrong track due to misalignment, no interference will result. Therefore, the guardbands are no longer needed. (All ½-inch Betamax and VHS systems use this recording process.

210

Loading design

As we mentioned earlier, one big difference between the Beta and VHS systems is the tape loading design. The original videocassette recorders—the ¾-inch U-Matics—use a very long loading path called a U-LOAD design, whereas the Beta VCRs use a shorter version called a B-LOAD design, and the VHS systems use the shortest, M-load design.

The Beta machines thread the tape and keep it threaded through all PLAY, REWIND and FAST FORWARD (FF) functions until the tape is ejected. Then the tape is de-threaded (returned) back into the cassette. The M-Load system, on the other hand, threads the tape only during the PLAY mode, except in special effects VCRs where the tape plays in variable speeds. REWIND, FAST FORWARD, and STOP modes require that the tape be returned to the cassette.

Because the M-Load design has the shortest tape path, it threads very quickly but subjects the tape to 1½ times more tension than the B-load system. The longer B-load design also allows better stability of tape travel around the video head. Less tension and high stability increase tape life and promote more accurate tape tracking and interchangeability—especially important in long playing modes. And because the B-load keeps the tape around the head, Still Frame picture and forward and reverse scanning of the tape are made possible.

On the other hand, VHS tape is subjected to less wear during Rewind and Fast Forward modes because the tape is not traveling around the video head but is instead inside the cassette. This helps head wear and tape life. However, special effect modes on VHS machines do create substantially increased tape and head wear relative to Beta VCRs.

Quality — Usually, true industrial VCRs are of higher quality electronically and mechanically than the home VCRs. Picture resolution and audio quality always should be better in the "faster" 1-hour Betamax or 2-hour VHS modes than in the "slower" or LP modes of the home VCRs. Picture degradation is particularly noticeable in the 6-hour mode VHS VCRs. The difference in picture quality between the home and industrial VCR is due primarily to the fact that more information per square inch can be recorded in the faster modes than in the slower modes. Since better picture and sound quality are deemed more important than long recording times to professional users, the Betamax industrial VCRs are limited to 1-hour only and the VHS industrial VCRs are limited to 2 hours.

Beta Industrial Systems

The only industrial Beta systems currently available are Sony's BETAMAX systems. These VCRs are unique in that all Betamax VCRs can record and playback in a 1-hour X1 mode only. The characteristics of the industrial Betamax recorders and players are as follows:

Recording Time —All Betamax industrial VCRs can only record and playback for 1 hour even though they use the same tape cassette as the 2-hour home Betamax VCR. This is because in the 1-hour mode the tape runs at a constant 4 centimeters per second speed which causes it to use up the tape in the casette in 60 minutes. The 2-hour home video recorder runs at a slower speed of only 2 centimeters per second and thus is able to make the 60-minute tape last twice as long or 2 hours.

Certain home Betamax VCRs have a 2-speed capability such as the older model Sony SL-8200. It is able to play and record in both the 1-hour and 2-hour modes. The newer Sony models, the SL-5400, SL-5600 and SL-5800 VCRs, record in the 2-hour and 3-hour Beta modes but play back in all three modes. The design philosophy here reflects the belief that industrial demands require best picture quality, which the single fast speed produces, and have little need of a recording or playing time of more than 1 hour.

Cost — the Betamax industrial VCRs are usually more expensive than the home VCRs. Industrial recording VCRs start at $1,300 and climb to $1,800 or more for a portable recorder or a recorder with optional accessories. Prices on home recording units can range from $800 to $1,200.

Features — The industrial Betamax line offers a wide range of features not particularly useful to the home recording enthusiast, but of great value to the serious professional user who requires remote control, editing capability, portability, and high quality picture and sound reproduction. Certain Betamax units offer a

212

unique optional MEMORY ACCESS accessory that allows automatic indexing and playing of particular segments of the tape. These Betamax VCRs can also be used with automatic editing devices, and portable VCRs are available. The flexibility of the industrial Betamax line is considerable.

Betamax Industrial Systems

SLP-100/SLO-260

Sony SLO-260

Sony SLP-100

The original industrial Sony ("second generation") Betamax machines included the SLP-100 player and the SLO-260 recorder. Both these units use a mechanical push button control system and have the ability to play back their picture and sound on any conventional TV receiver. The SLO-260 recorder also features built-in TV tuners so off-the-air recordings could be made. These systems are the least expensive units in the industrial Betamax line and are nearly identical to the home VCRs.

The "third generation" of Betamax industrial *1 hour only* VCRs include the SLP-300, SLP-303, SLO-320, SLO-323, SLO-383 and the portable SLO-340. The Betamax 300 series represents a completely redesigned line of industrial ½-inch VCRs and really exemplifies the state-of-the-art in ½-inch video for demanding performance applications. These are not intended to be redesigned home machines. In the 300 series, the TV tuners have been eliminated, a better more rugged tape-threading mechanism has been added, the construction of the unit is better, and many sophisticated features and accessories are available such as stereo sound, multiprogrammable memory access with remote control and true and complete electronic editing. We will look at some of these machines.

SLP-300

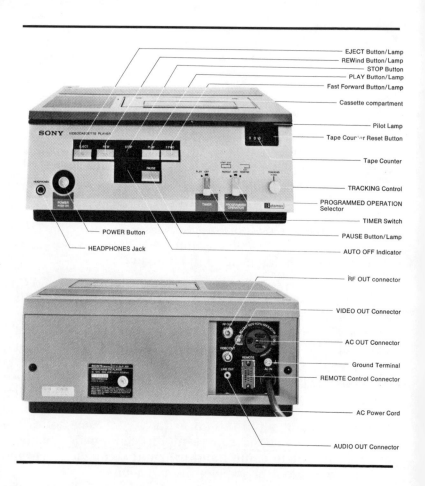

EJECT Button/Lamp
REWind Button/Lamp
STOP Button
PLAY Button/Lamp
Fast Forward Button/Lamp

Cassette compartment

Pilot Lamp
Tape Counter Reset Button

Tape Counter

TRACKING Control

PROGRAMMED OPERATION Selector

TIMER Switch

PAUSE Button/Lamp

AUTO OFF Indicator

POWER Button

HEADPHONES Jack

RF OUT connector

VIDEO OUT Connector

AC OUT Connector

Ground Terminal

REMOTE Control Connector

AC Power Cord

AUDIO OUT Connector

Sony SLO-320

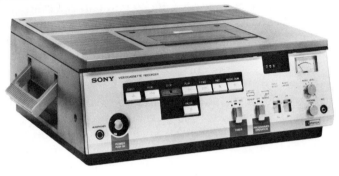

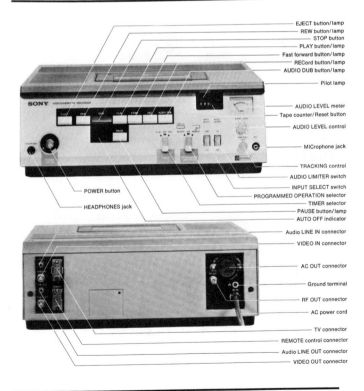

EJECT button/lamp
REW button/lamp
STOP button
PLAY button/lamp
Fast forward button/lamp
RECord button/lamp
AUDIO DUB button/lamp

Pilot lamp

AUDIO LEVEL meter
Tape counter/Reset button
AUDIO LEVEL control

MICrophone jack

TRACKING control
AUDIO LIMITER switch
INPUT SELECT switch
PROGRAMMED OPERATION selector
TIMER selector
PAUSE button/lamp
AUTO OFF indicator

POWER button

HEADPHONES jack

Audio LINE IN connector
VIDEO IN connector

AC OUT connector

Ground terminal

RF OUT connector
AC power cord

TV connector
REMOTE control connector
Audio LINE OUT connector
VIDEO OUT connector

All 300 series non-portable VCRs use electronic solenoid switches with built-in logic circuits so you can push any button and not jam or confuse the machine. The SLO-300, SLO-320, SLP-303 and SLO-323 have automatic rewind and repeat modes for continuous play. The machines use direct drive for capstan servos and head drums for good picture and stability. Also included in all units are RF modulators for playback on any TV set, professional BNC video connectors and 8-Pin monitor connectors (except on SLP-300, SLP-303 and SLO-340). The SLP-303, SLO-323 and SLO-383 have 2 audio tracks for stereo sound, and a BetaScan high speed picture search in forward or reverse with visible picture. The picture may be advanced frame by frame, and a noiseless still picture may be viewed. Manual control of audio is possible on the SLO-320, SLO-323 and SLO-383, and improved assemble editing ability has been added to the SLO-323.

SLP-303

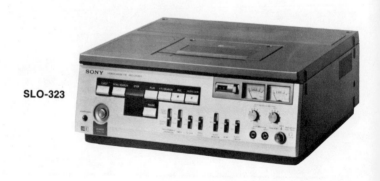

SLO-323

216

The BetaScan high-speed picture search mode operates at between 6 times and 15 times normal speed with visible picture in fast forward and between 5 times and 10 times normal speed with picture in rewind mode. Noise reduction circuitry is also built into the SLP-303 and SLO-323, and both machines include an external sync lock function, a built-in antenna selector, a switchable RF modulator and a soft eject mechanism.

Betamax Memory Access

The 300 series Betamax machines were a big step forward and have always represented the state-of-the-art for some time after their introduction. The SLP-300 player and SLO-320 recorder/player featured the first low-cost AUTOMATIC SEARCH CONTROL. With the original unit, called the RM-300 AUTO SEARCH CONTROL, any segment of the tape could be located rapidly and automatically by means of an electronic indexing system. The VCR does this by counting the control track pulses on the videotape, and the automatic controller serves as the indexing unit. The controller will cue up and play the desired segment automatically and precisely when the index numbers are entered into it.

RM-300
Auto Search Control

Operating the Memory Access System

Step 1 Plug in the RM-300 AUTO SEARCH CONTROL to the REMOTE control connector on the back of the VCR.

Step 2 Insert a prerecorded 30 or 60-minute cassette into the VCR. The VCR will automatically rewind the tape to the beginning and will set the electronic counter at "0."

Step 3 Press FWD and review the tape. Write down a brief description of the scene and note the numbers that appear on the digital counter unit as they correspond to the scene.

Step 4 When you want to locate a specific scene, enter the digital reference number into the RM-300 keyboard. Push the SEARCH button, and the VCR will rewind or go forward until it finds the indicated scene. It will then play the scene back automatically within + or -2 seconds of the actual starting point of the scene. If you want to replay the same scene again, just push the SEARCH button once more, and the VCR will repeat the scene.

The memory access feature is really dynamite. It allows you for the first time to stack many programs on one tape. This drastically reduces tape costs and makes the machine much more usable and flexible. The information for the access numbers is transferred during dubbing so the reference numbers will remain the same for as many copies of the tape as you want to make. Newer model versions incorporate the BetaScan rapid forward and reverse search function.

The search mechanism is quite accurate and works by measuring the electronic CONTROL TRACK PULSES which must be recorded by all VCRs on all videotapes. Control track pulses are electronic signals. They are sometimes likened to sprocket holes on film which keep the film running at a constant speed.

The possibilities and applications afforded by the memory access system are limited only by your imagination. Learning tapes can be keyed to question and answer tests; real estate tapes can be made so a customer can select a particular type of house to view; video dating services can refer to a specific part of researched data. The list of possibilities is endless.

More sophisticated Betamax models, such as the SLP-303 player and the SLO-323 recorder/player, were later introduced with two far more sophisticated PROGRAMMABLE AUTO SEARCH CONTORLS, the RX-303 ($350) and the RX-353 ($400). The RX series will direct the appropriate U-Matic (VO-2611) and Betamax VCRs to remotely stop, advance, rewind, stop again and then play either at pre-selected segment demarcations or at any hour and minute of tape time selected by the operator.

RX-303

RX-353

Both autosearch units have memory capacity of up to 63 segments and may be programmed to recall any 8 segments in any order and programmed for repetition if desired. The RX-353 can be used to record on the tape the audio tones by which segments are demarcated as well as to recall the segments as desired individually or in any programmed sequence. The RX-303 *does not* allow for recording of programmed audio tones on the tape, so programmed operations must be manually reentered in the programmer. Both units provide rapid access to any spot on the tape, may be programmed to search in either direction, will command the VCR to skip and review segments in the programmed sequence, can interrupt the program sequence at any time and are easy to operate once the control functions are understood.

Such remote control flexibilty makes them ideal for training and instructional applications. Because the program information is stored in the form of an audio tone recorded prior to the video on the tape, existing tape libraries can be indexed with the RX-303 and RX-353. Although the RX-353 is required to record the master program sequence, duplication of programmed tapes can be accomplished with any VCR.

Editing With Betamax

All the 300 series VCRs except the SLO-340 can be used in some capacity for editing. However, there is only one machine that is a true full function editor, the SLO-383. The long-awaited SLO-383 editing Betamax recorder includes the BetaScan variable high-speed picture search capability as well as an edit preview mode when used with the RM-430 editing controller. The SLO-383 allows independently selectable insert editing with video, audio channel 1 or channel 2 or simultaneous assemble editing. Direct drive motors for head drum and capstan maintain precise tape movement.

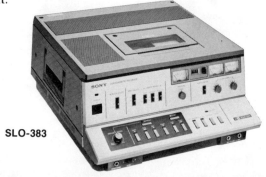

SLO-383

Sophisticated editing with the SLO-383 is possible because it uses a set of special ROTARY ERASE HEADS which insure precise erasure and VERTICAL INTERVAL SWITCHING to eliminate any visual disturbances at the point of the edit. Other professional features are a FRAME SERVO SYSTEM which adjusts the tape so the editing is done with a complete frame of information at the head or tail of an edit, special DUBBING CONNECTORS and circuit which reduce signal deterioration when copying tapes or editing, an ability to reference the VCR to an external sync source, audio limiters for precise sound control and a soft eject mechanism. The SLO-383 will also accept the RM-300, RX-303 and RX-353 Memory Access Automatic Search Controls.

Betamax Editing System

SLO-383   RM-430   SLO-383

RM-430 Automatic Editing Controller

Any 300 series VCR except the SLO-340 can be used as a player VCR in an editing system. The SLO-320, SLO-323 or SLO-383 can be used as the recorder/editor. However, only the SLO-383 is a true editor that will provide really clean edits every time and also perform insert edits. In all cases, the RM-430 Automatic Editing Controller must be used to cue up the various VCRs and perform the edits. The ideal is to edit from a SLO-383 to a VO-2860 3/4-inch editor, using the dubbing connectors to obtain best quality. Next best is editing between 2 SLO-383s. Third best is editing from an SLP-303 or SLO-323 to an SLO-383 editor. The full system of 2 SLO-383s and RM-430 could cost about $8,000, so this is serious business. But, you can do some very nice editing.

SLO-340

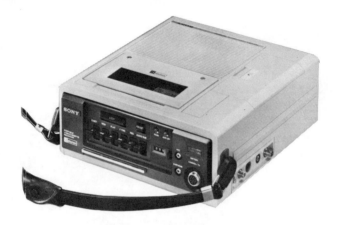

The unique SLO-340 was the first portable Betamax recorder. It is a compact 20 lb. unit that will operate for up to 90 minutes on one fully charged battery. The machine will record in either black and white or color. Of course it holds only one 60 minute tape at a time, so you would have to change tapes after 60 minutes of continuous recording. You can also easily change rechargeable battery packs for greater recording time. The casette tapes are completely interchangeable with any other 1-hour Betamax VCR.

The SLO-340 contains a variety of nice features. Like most portable VTRs, the recorder may be powered by a rechargeable built-in battery pack. For this particular VCR, the battery is the BP-60 battery, which is, strangely, an optional accessory. Or, you may power the VCR with the AC-340 AC power adaptor (included) or with the DCC-3000 car battery adaptor (optional).

Also, the SLO-340 is a one-button operation. An automatic interlock prevents damage to the machine if you try to press the wrong button. Automatic circuitry maintains the proper audio and video levels to assure optimum recording. An audio dub feature is provided so you can add a narration later, and the VCR includes a built-in RF Converter so you can play back the picture and sound through any conventional TV set.

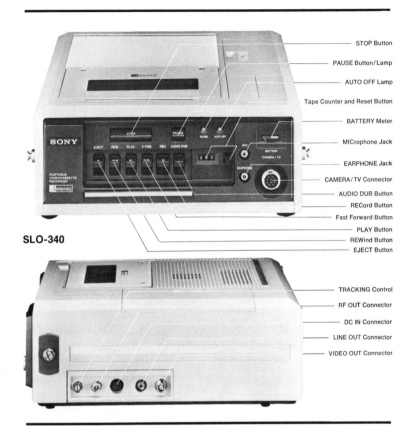

STOP Button

PAUSE Button/Lamp

AUTO OFF Lamp

Tape Counter and Reset Button

BATTERY Meter

MICrophone Jack

EARPHONE Jack

CAMERA/TV Connector

AUDIO DUB Button

RECord Button

Fast Forward Button

PLAY Button

REWind Button

EJECT Button

SLO-340

TRACKING Control

RF OUT Connector

DC IN Connector

LINE OUT Connector

VIDEO OUT Connector

The VCR starts and stops rapidly when you activate the on/off trigger switch on the camera, and a clean "edit" is achievable about 60% of the time. The SLO-340 is **not** an editing machine with a built-in backspacer comparable to true editors like the JVC CR-4400U, Panasonic WV-9400 or Sony BVU-50 ¾-inch or Akai VT-350 ½-inch VCRs.

The SLO-340 will accept either a black & white or color camera. The cameras that interface most easily with it are the AVC-3450 black and white camera and the DXC 1610 color camera. The AVC-3450 weighs less and is more light sensitive than the DXC-1610; that is, it will take pictures in much less light. Also, it is about one-fifth the cost of the DXC-1610.

VHS Industrial Systems

Panasonic VHS System

The Panasonic VHS systems utilize a unique DIE-CAST CHASSIS which means that the critical components are mounted onto a one-piece annealed aluminum chassis, thereby creating a VCR which is strong and rigid, yet lightweight. The Panasonic VHS design also features a DIRECT DRIVE HEAD CYLINDER MOTOR (DDC) which provides greater picture stability and less jitter than belt-driven cylinders. All motors in the VCR run on DC current which allows the machine to be used on either 50 or 60 cycle power systems without modification.

NV-8150/NV-8300, NV-8160/NV-8310

Panasonic's first industrial VCRs were the 2-hour only OMNIVISION II NV-8150 player and the NV-8300 recorder/player. Both these models were later replaced by the NV-8160 player and the NV-8310 recorder. All industrial Panasonic VCRs use standard industrial video and audio connectors: BNC plugs for video, RCA plugs for audio, and 8-Pin connectors for monitors.

The NV-8150 is compatible with any 2-hour VHS system. It features a noise compensator, die-cast chassis, direct drive head cylinder, capstan servo system, and DC motors which permit operation on either 50 or 60-cycle electrical systems without modification. The RF Converter, necessary for VCR playback on a conventional TV set, is optional. An 8-Pin plug and BNC connectors are provided for connection to TV monitors and other VCRs. An auto-search mode stops the tape when the tape counter reaches "00."

The NV-8300, the recording version, employs all the features of the NV-8150, the capstan servo, direct drive system, die-cast chassis, noise compensation circuits, DC motors and easily removable side panels. In addition it has built-in TV timers and a Tuner/Timer so the recorder can automatically record off-the-air programs while left unattended. An Audio Dub mode is included, while the RF Converter is optional. Professional BNC and 8-Pin connectors and RCA/Phono connectors are provided for connection to TV monitors, cameras and microphones.

NV-8300 **Omnivision®️ II**
RECORDER WITH VHF/UHF TUNERS

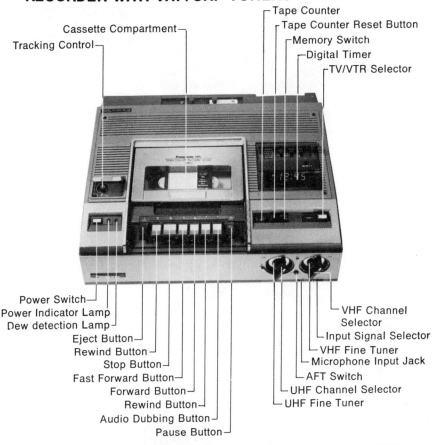

An optional remote Pause control (NV-A181) can be used to temporarily stop the recording or playback of the tape. This can be used with the NV-8300 to delete commercials while recording. Blank tapes are available in 30-minute, 60-minute or 120-minute sizes and cost from $18 to $28.

NV-8300/8310

Panasonic NV-8310

The Panasonic VCRs, unlike their Betamax counterparts, are compatible with the home VHS models in the 2-hour SP mode. Features of these models include Capstan-Servo Direct Drive systems, noise compensation circuits, die-cast chasses and built-in Tuner/Timers on most recorders. Unique features of the NV-8160 and NV-8310 include an adjustable speed control, which varies the playback speed in the Pause mode from 1 to 1.5 times regular speed. A special X2 speed knob provides even faster search of both video and audio. A Still Frame Compensator feature minimizes snowy noise in the Still Frame mode and a Still Frame Advance button is provided.

NV-1000A

Panasonic NV-1000A

The NV-1000A is the only dual-speed 2 and 4-hour industrial VHS VCR. It has a Tuner/Timer but does not have the variable speed functions of the NV-8160 and NV-8310.

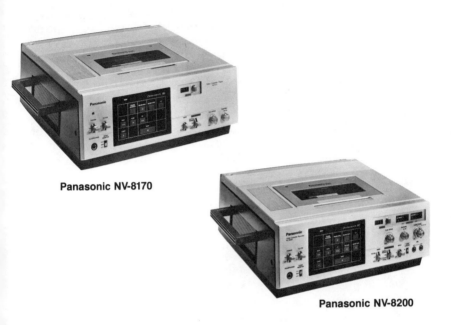

Panasonic NV-8170

Panasonic NV-8200

In response to Sony's highly respected and successful SLP-300 and SLO-320 Betamax VCRs, Panasonic created a similar VHS format VCR. The NV-8170/NV-8200 VCRs are 2-hour SP single-speed machines which are solenoid operated with full logic in the controls; they have a MEMORY REWIND for automatic rewind to a specific spot, an AUTOMATIC REPEAT and an AUTOMATIC REWIND from the end of the tape. The VCRs have a very high quality picture and the quartz-locked direct drive video head cylinder, capstan-drive and three-motor transport system insures good tape stability and interchangeability.

Other features include a Still Frame mode with AUTOMATIC STILL FRAME COMPENSATOR (ASC) for a clean noise-free picture, plus Still Frame Advance and a Variable Speed playback from 0.2 to 1.5 times normal speed. Double-speed playback is also obtained with an X2 button.

The really unique feature of this system, though, is its dual audio track stereo sound capability. This, along with the variable playback speed control, is one feature the Betamax SLO-320 does not have. Dual audio level meters are provided as well as an audio limiter and level control which can be used in a manual recording mode (NV-8200 recorder only).

As is the case with the Betamax SLP-300/SLO-320 models, the Panasonic NV-8170/NV-8200 VCRs also have the RANDOM ACCESS AUTO SEARCH CONTROLLER interface function. Editing is possible when these VCRs are used with the ¾-inch U-Matic editing systems. Both VCRs are lightweight (34 lbs.) and offer great flexibility for the professional video user.

NV-800 Auto Search Controller

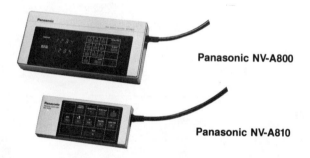

Panasonic NV-A800

Panasonic NV-A810

The NV-A800 AUTO SEARCH CONTROLLER with LED digital display will locate any desired portion of the tape and play back that portion automatically once the correct reference numbers are entered into the controller. Feather-touch solenoid controls operate the controller. A simpler NV-810 REMOTE CONTROL is also available.

½-Inch Editing System

Like the Sony SLP-300 and SLO-320, these Panasonic VCRs can be used to interface with ¾-inch editing VCRs. The NV-820 EDITING INTERFACE ADAPTER is needed with either the NV-8170 or NV-8200 VCRs when used in the editing configuration. Either unit can be used with the ¾-inch NV-9200A or NV-9500A editing VCRs.

Panasonic NV-8410

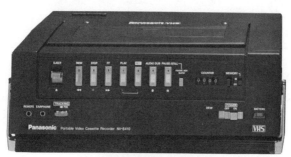

Panasonic NV-8410

The NV-8410 is Panasonic's newest industrial portable ½-inch VHS VCR. It replaces the larger NV-8400. The NV-8410 is very compact and lightweight (13 lbs. including battery), is a 2-hour single-speed machine for optimum picture quality and includes a number of good features.

Like most newer VCRs, the NV-8410 has a full array of solenoid controls with logic so the machine will not jam if you push the wrong button. A special editing circuit (Automatic Assembly Recording) creates good edits without picture roll by backing up the tape slightly before each new edit. Unfortunately, a slight rainbow pattern is frequently seen at the edit point because erasure cannot be perfect without the Flying Erase Heads which are only found on true editing VCRs. Other than the rainbow effect, the edits are perfect.

The VCR has a good still frame mode and an Automatic Still Frame Compensation (ASC) circuit which enables the capstan to reposition the tape automatically so the still frame noise band is removed. The deck has a frame by frame advance feature, activated by holding down the Pause button. This permits viewing the tape at one-tenth the normal speed for slow motion or searching. Pause mode and frame by frame advance can be operated with a remote control.

The NV-8410 VCR can be powered by AC or battery power, and the AC Adapter/Battery Charger NV-B55 (supplied) will operate on 100V/120V/220V/240V AC at 60 or 50 Hz. Such power flexibility makes the VCR ideal for traveling.

Internal features include a quartz-locked direct-drive video head cylinder, a capstan servo, and special hot pressed ferrite heads for durability. The NV-8410 is designed around a single-piece aluminum die-cast chassis which increases durability. Other features are a four-digit tape counter, battery meter, a deluxe carying case with shoulder strap and extra battery case. The VCR includes a built-in handle (very convenient) and an RF converter for playback on any TV set. Professional BNC video connectors are also provided. Somewhat annoying, though, is the lack of an AUDIO IN connector. An audio input attenuator (provided accessory) must be used to feed prerecorded sound into the deck through the MIC IN plug.

An optional matching NV-V240 Tuner/Timer is available which provides a 24-hour digital clock/timer and the ability to automatically tape TV programs off the air.

Panasonic has a large assortment of portable color cameras in various price ranges. The WV-3210 is a TTL 4:1 zoom lens model, the WV-3200 uses an electronic viewfinder and 6:1 lens, the WV-3320 features a 1-inch Vidicon, 6:1 lens and electronic viewfinder, and the WV-3600 is similar but is larger and more sophisticated.

WV-3210　　　　WV-3320

WV-3200

WV-3600

Industrial/Home VCR System Compatibility

The VHS format industrial VCRs are completely compatible with all VHS home VCRs in the 2-hour SP mode. Thus, you can make a tape at work and bring it home to watch on your home VCR. With Sony Betamax machines, though, this is unfortunately not the case at all. Betamax industrial units are all 1-hour X1 mode only VCRs. Since the 1-hour Betamax format was essentially isolated by most Beta II and most Beta III machines, the Betamax industrial VCRs have in essence become a different non-compatible format. To cope with this problem, you could buy two VCRs, one of each format, or transfer your Betamax 1-hour tape to the Beta II 2-hour format. One option is to buy the older model Sony Beta SL-8200 or Zenith JR-9000W dual speed VCRs, both of which playback in the X1 and X2 speeds. The Beta SL-3000 portable VCR also plays back in both speeds but only records in the X1 mode. Fortunately, the newer Sony SL-5400, SL-5600 and SL-5800 home VCRs will play back X1 format tapes.

The VHS format offers complete interchangeability between industrial and home VCRs, but the Beta format does not. Both formats offer comparable models with a wide range of features including editing capability. Sony, though, traditionally has been a year ahead of all others in engineering and design of ½-inch industrial systems. It's not an easy choice, but whatever your decision, you can be assured of good picture quality and system flexibility.

The Big Choice

So, even for video veterans the choice is very difficult. A decision will depend on what equipment, technical services and price factors provide the optimum package that best suits your real needs and future plans.

12 What to Do with Your VCR

Some people consider the applications their $1,000 to $2,500 home VCR system might have before purchasing one, whereas others may buy first and explore possibilities later. Obvious first uses for your VCR are: recording off-the-air broadcasts of cable TV or pay TV programs and the renting, purchasing or trading of pre-recorded tapes from any number of various sources. A camera greatly expands the range of possibilities as it allows the user to make his own programs. Natural recording events include family gatherings, birthday parties, graduations, school plays, little league games, local fairs, bake sales, races, concerts and any other local event that might lend itself easily to video recording. If you are taping events outside the home, a portable battery-powered recorder is almost essential as it is a lot of trouble moving around a 35-pound deck-type model.

Trips and vacations are ideal subject matter for your portable VCR, but you will need extra batteries, a car battery cord, and must charge up your batteries every few days. When on the road you can conveniently play back your tapes on the motel room TV sets to make sure everything is working properly. Be sure to allow for the fact that some motel room TV sets are old and of poor quality so your tapes probably won't look so good as they do on your deluxe RCA, Zenith or Sony Trinitron back home.

Caution: If you do disconnect the motel room TV set from the cable for VCR use, be prepared for a possible visit from the management as motel alarm systems are often built into the TV sets.

How To Make Money With Your VCR

Other than a house, a car or a boat, a home VCR system, particularly a portable one with a color camera, could represent one of your largest expenditures. It would be nice if it could serve as an investment that might provide some return of capital, perhaps even eventually becoming a basis for a livelihood. Most home VCRs are not bought with profit in mind, but they are nevertheless quite capable of producing an income if used creatively for this purpose. Let's look at some possibilities.

Immediate options include videotaping weddings, bar mitzvahs, graduations and other social events for hire. You could advertise your services and set up a small business. You might charge $100 to $300 for the taping (no editing) and also provide one or two free playbacks of the tape. The cost of the cassette or cassettes might be treated as an extra charge. Of course the clients would have to buy a VCR or rent yours for playback.

Other similar tapings might include doing video Christmas and birthday cards (tapes) and sports analysis taping, i.e., golf, tennis, skiing, baseball. You might rent yourself out with camera and VCR on a per/hour fee basis. Another possibility is setting up a video dating service. To do this find an office, set up your camera and VCR in the office, advertise in a local paper or radio station, and as people come in, interview them on videotape. Catalog the interviews for people to come in and look through and hopefully choose someone that they would like to date. This is being done in a number of major cities.

Other areas of community demand could be school plays, school socials, and doing video yearbooks and selling copies of the tapes to student's parents. This may require some editing, which would increase the cost. Another popular area is video security, where you videotape a person's household possessions for insurance purposes.

Trips and tours are a hot item. One resourceful fellow I met books himself and his wife on a cruise boat tour and films everything in super 8. He makes sures to do a professional job of it, getting extra items like colorful signs showing locations, and then he adds graphics and edits the film. He films everyone on the boat as they enjoy themselves on the trip and tells them what he is doing. He then hands out his business cards and takes orders. After editing the super 8 film he dubs it over to Beta or VHS cassettes using Fotomat's super 8 to video dubbing service (which is quite inexpensive). He then sells the copies of the tapes of the cruise to the cruise participants and also to the cruise company which uses the tape to advertise that particular cruise on other cruises. The expenses of taking the trip for the filmmaker and his wife are completely deductible, and he also makes money on the sale of the tapes.

This concept could be done in video almost as easily except for the editing which would be more expensive and troublesome. However, ½-inch videocassette editing should become more feasible in the next few years as better editor VCRs become available.

Another clever idea is recording a local sports event, for example, a softball league game and then playing it back immediately after the game or at a later date on a wide-screen video projector at a popular local bar. Charge an admission fee or ask a fee from the bar owner. The folks that missed the game and the game players and friends can all get together and watch the fun on the big screen or TV set.

Then there is "vanity video" which is the idea of taping people's boats, special cars, motorcycles, houses or horses, and then offering to sell the tape to the owners. There are people who make a good living videotaping horses in particular, by going to the shows that horse enthusiasts attend. Another possibility is setting yourself up as a free-lance business promotional/educational tape-maker where you might go to a local bank, insurance company or real estate firm and persuade them that they ought to do some video training, using you and your recorder. Perhaps you could do small videotapes promoting their services which you could, in turn, get played on cable. The bank or the insurance company would foot the bill for the creation of the tape and your time involved. There are many possibilities along these lines.

Equipment Limitations

The serious video user will very shortly want to make a professional tape to show to groups of people or sell nationally. As a result, the problem of editing will immediately surface. This is an area in which ½-inch VCRs are very limited. It was not really intended that the ½-inch format would be used as a "master production" medium, and thus the lack of image and sound quality and lack of editing equipment poses a shortcoming although "metal" videotape could change this. ¾-inch equipment, on the other hand, is ideally suited to master production and editing, but costs skyrocket relative to ½-inch VCR. The best the ½-inch user can do is to try to carefully plan your shooting, edit in the camera as you go, buy a good camera and microphone, have good lighting and sound and possibly consider transferring your tape to ¾-inch for editing. *Do a test first* to see how your eventual copied tape will look.

Video Business Applications

Video is a natural tool for dentists, doctors and other professionals who have a need for patient educational information and also have people waiting in offices. Why not teach them something useful while they are sitting there? How about preventive health care techniques and vitamin, exercise, and stress information? Waiting time which is normally wasted time could become a constructive educational period.

A manufacturer or traveling salesman might use a portable video player such as the JVC HR-4000 to show a new product or product line or how the product can be used, particularly if it is physically too big to take along. Lawyers use videotape to do depositions for people who can't attend a scheduled court session, or bring "the scene of the crime" into the courtroom by going out and videotaping where the event took place. Video is used frequently by real estate agencies to train their people and show houses to customers in the office.

There are many ingenious utilizations of video being employed by a wide variety of professionals and non-professionals. The possibilities are limited only by personal resourcefulness and budget, and resourcefulness can often compensate for a small budget.

Community Service Tapes

Videotape can be of great assistance to the community. Health care, for one, is an area ripe for expression on video. Tapes can be made with local health clinic staff members, and the programs played back at the clinic, over your local cable TV station, or at hospitals, doctors offices, classrooms or community gatherings. Tapes can be made of local people running for office—their views and platforms—and played at community gatherings. Politically oriented tapes on issues of interest can be used very effectively as part of local fund raising programs.

How about tapes for bedridden senior citizens—taking them to a fair or big event by videotape? Maybe you could get a local grant for this purpose. Again, the list could go on and on. Do some brainstorming and I'm sure some new ingenious ideas will surface.

Education

Perhaps the greatest potential of home VCR is in educational applications—either to learn personally from educational pre-recorded tapes or to produce your own tapes explaining something you know, have done, or can do. The educational applications of industrial VCRs are considerable, and most large corporations have invested substantial sums of money in their own videotape networks. Chrysler has purchased 700 industrial Betamax units for in-house teaching and information dissemination, and General Motors has purchased 10,000 industrial Pioneer "DiscoVision" disc players for training mechanics, sending sales memos, and entertaining customers waiting in showrooms.

Advantages of Video Education

- The world's best expert can be secured to talk about the subject.

- The expert's presentation can be rehearsed until perfect and then taped, eliminating human error.

- The expert is always available on the tape—permanently, 24 hours a day. The program is infinitely reusable and the tape never gets tired or makes mistakes.

- Many copies of the program can be made.

- The program can be shot on location, anywhere in the world if the budget permits. The world becomes the classroom.

- Films, slides, graphics, and other videotape material can be integrated into the program providing a flexibility not possible in a live classroom situation.

- The program can be edited, and time, space, and distance manipulated to create the best effect.

- The program can and should be artistic as well as informative.

- Videocassettes can be played for large groups through a video projector or played privately by one person on a small portable TV set.

- The program can be repeated many times, stopped or advanced forward, for the individual's learning needs.

237

How-To Tapes

Perhaps the most appropriate and most talked about educational application is the how-to use of home video. Subjects abound: car tuneups, minor and major home repair, plumbing, electrical work, interior decorating, gardening techniques, etc. An unending series of cooking tapes will no doubt appear along with an infinite series of arts and crafts tapes—pottery, painting, weaving, macrame, etc. Sports will be big and tapes such as how to improve your golf swing, tennis serve or skiing technique will proliferate.

As we've said, health care is a real natural for video how-to, and with the traditional medical profession pricing itself out of the market, a need exists for a vast quantity of para-medical and alternative health care tapes. Many tapes are already being produced on an amateur basis by health-oriented individuals and groups for local circulation. Hopefully, professionally made health tapes dealing with a wide range of material will soon be available nationally.

It should be pointed out that the local medical clinic, health group or individual practitioner can very effectively produce a basic how-to tape based on his/her own technique and directed toward his/her particular applications. One camera, some good lighting and sound and a logical and cohesive narration, either spoken live on camera or dubbed over pictures, graphics or action can transmit the required information. This is a true do-it yourself area, and the professional can, of course, deduct the cost of equipment and materials.

The really exciting aspect of such do-it yourself video programs is that now tapes can be made on subjects not readily accessible to the vast majority of people. Your own videotapes can represent a means to introduce others to new and unusual subject matter.

Educational/Political Consciousness-Raising Tapes

Consciousness-raising in this sense is defined as the creation of an increased awareness of interrelating factors in one's local and/or global environment. The goal of consciousness-raising is to create a more expanded and evolved mode of thought, feeling, reference and experience.

Ideally, true education should always produce some quantity of consciousness-raising. Successful education might even form the basis for active participation by an individual in a new direction if he/she is so motivated. The function behind any medium's most powerful potential is to influence the viewer to become active in some way relative to the issue the medium presents. Make no mistake about it, video packs an awesome potential. A seemingly innocuous, tiny ½-inch cassette sitting calmly inside the VCR waiting for the Play button to be pressed can be pure dynamite just waiting for detonation. Certain videotapes can permanently alter people's mental constructs, shatter their views of the world as it had previously appeared to them and 45 minutes later, turn them back out into the world with a brand new set of perceptions. Such is the incredible power of a tape creatively crafted for such a purpose.

Video is a powerful tool of information dissemination. It can educate and influence people. There is, however, a very fine line between mere education and political influencing. Fortunately in the U.S.A., we have nearly total freedom of personal expression through media. If a controversial tape steps on a few toes, you may experience some personal repercussions, but assuming you're not libelous, you will not be thrown in jail just for making a tape that challenges the traditional power structure.

Nevertheless, you do have a responsibility for accuracy and the fair representation of people whatever their point of view. Video, like any other journalistic medium, can destroy and defame as well as heal and enthrone. The investigative user must be sensitive to the effect his tape might have on his audience or those persons mentioned in the tape. Certain kinds of educational information often have political ramifications, and it is important for the video maker to realize this. Of course, like it or not, politics is inseparable from life as we are all constantly affected by the decisions that others make for us, despite the fact that we may often have little or no input into the decision-making process. The video maker can steer clear of subject matter that may be volatile, or he may choose to tear into it with great enthusiasm and personal commitment. If you do choose to tackle the controversial or political tape, it might be wise to quickly explore some guidelines that will lend credibility and effectiveness to your program.

Sample Controversial Tape

A good subject to use as our sample is a tape dealing with the effects of a nuclear power plant, waste depository or reprocessing facility on a local community. This is a topic by which everyone is affected, since over half of the American population lives within 50 miles of such a facility, and the rest of the population is upwind or downstream from an associated aspect or byproduct of nuclear technology. Guidelines for such a tape would be as follows:

A. Research what's going on at the facility. What do they do there? Get the facts right!

B. Is it dangerous to humans, plants or animals? (You will gets lots of different, seemingly opposite answers to this question depending on who you talk to.)

C. Just how dangerous is it—is it a critical or insignificant hazard? Will insurance companies insure nuclear power plants? If not, why not? Who pays for the consequences to a local community if an accident takes place? How bad could an accident be? How dangerous is radiation? Is the utility taking all necessary steps to protect the public from known and as yet unknown hazards that may not actually occur for many years? What about the disposal of radioactive waste products? Where do they go and are they being adequately stored for their hazardous lifetime of up to 250,000 years?

How economically practical are nuclear power plants when all the associated capital, energy, health and environmental costs of uranium mining and enrichment, fuel reprocessing, transportation, relocation of native populations, waste disposal, power plant decommissioning and future security are considered? Are all these costs offset by the 30-year life span of a nuclear power plant?

Double check the utility or industry public relations information with research materials from government, other utilities, non-government and other critical sources. Also contact environmental groups, public libraries and book stores for information.

D. If, in your estimation, a hazard does exist in your community, provide supporting data in the form of interviews and/or statistics from credible sources.

E. If your program does show a problem that needs attention, don't just criticize, try to offer imaginative and practical short and long range solutions. This is a big job. Limitations in time, budget and equipment may not allow any great detail for your solutions, but at least they can be suggested briefly. Perhaps a second program can explore the various alternatives, or if there are no easy forthcoming solutions, the tape could invite suggestions from the audience or the community as a method of community involvement. You could also videotape interviews with people who have comments and then play those responses back to a later audience.

F. Get the word out. Don't let your well-researched video labor of love become just another of the many "closet tapes" that many an aspiring videophile, independent producer, and struggling video production company have stashed away gathering dust waiting for some occasion, some day, that might serve as an appropriate forum for such tapes.

Your videotapes can be played back easily to groups using one 19-inch or larger TV set or monitor per 30 to 40 people. Seat them all as close to the TV set as possible. Use a second 19-inch TV set for another 30 to 40 people. For larger groups, a good video projector such as the Sony KP-5000 or KP-7200, Panasonic/Quasar projectors, the Advent 760 or Kloss Video-beam projectors will easily handle 200 to 500 people with the proper seating arrangements and a slightly darkened room. Good projectors can produce a very effective presentation equal or possibly superior to a 16mm film presentation if your tape and sound are good quality. When showing tapes to large audiences try to use an auxiliary sound amplification system with good speakers.

Good places to show your tapes are classrooms, auditoriums, public recreational center, libraries, bank conference rooms, women's and men's clubs, or other community meeting places. Maybe you could play it on your local cable TV. Make up some simple flyers for advertising, try to get free mention from local newspapers and radio stations, and perhaps, if you have the budget, take out display ads. Try to have a discussion group following the presentation and a good speaker or moderator accompany the tape.

Use your tape as the centerpiece for a kind of video town meeting to focus public attention on the issue that you are exploring. You will find you can use this occasion to raise money to help pay for the production of the tape and also raise money for the sponsoring group if there is one. If your tape is good, you will soon get support so you can do another one. Ask for donations and if people think your tape is performing a public service, it's my experience that you can easily raise from $30 to $300 from a group of 20 to 100 people each time you play the tape. You can pay for tapes and equipment quite rapidly this way. You might consider forming a non-profit group to handle donations, purchase more video equipment and make more tapes on public issues. Become a video missionary and present important issues to the public. Show them that television can do something other than just dull everyone's brains and senses.

Responsibility Of The Media

There has been much said, but very little heed paid to the responsibility of the media and its practitioners to provide society with creative inspiration and leadership. Obviously, the traditional television media has spared no expense in entertaining people, certainly not just out of a desire to help the populace feel good but to capture their attention long enough to sell gullible consumers a variety of mostly useless and usually hazardous products. Little or no attention is paid to truly educational subject matter, and anything the least bit political or "consciousness-raising" is avoided like the plague. I was rather astounded to discover that the word "God" is banned on TV except for use by religious broadcasters. Incredible!

It may well be that the job of utilizing the video medium for socially constructive and insightful purposes will fall primarily on the decentralized independent video-maker, who has a personal interest in a clean, safe environment and a healthy and happy future. It may well be that those of you now with portable video cameras and VCRs will take up the challenge to provide society with the kind of quality evolutionary analysis and visionary ideas concerning energy, health, environment, government, inflation, crime, human relationships, spirituality, caring, and love, that the traditional media either doesn't understand, isn't aware of, or manages to avoid most of the time. Sensitive and creative visionaries can point out the things that need to be changed and where society can go from here. A great power lies in the hands of those who hold the camera and microphone. Try to be cognizant of this power and use it wisely for the greater benefit of the whole. To accomplish this would truly represent a great service performed for society and future generations.

13

TV Projection Systems

Just prior to the introduction of home ½-inch VCRs in 1975, several "reasonably" priced, large-screen projection systems began appearing in video dealers' showrooms and in national magazines. TV had finally been liberated from the tiny box that had so long confined it. Now it was possible to have a personal movie theatre in the home and to enjoy the realism of life-size events.

No doubt about it, large-screen TV is exciting. After you watch something like *Godzilla Meets The Turkey Monsters* on a 7-foot screen, it's hard to be turned on by a few 10-inch high figures inside a 15-inch TV set.

Then there's the communal/video groupie aspect of large-screen TV. Although, I'm sure those 10,000 hour riveted-to-the-tube every weekend during football season sports fans don't see themselves as communal video groupies, there is nevertheless a kind of informal massing of bodies that takes place for the weekend ritual of beer, sports and TV viewing.

Now the big-screen phenomenon turns the home into a 50-yard line with all the comforts and advantages of the living room without the disadvantages of the live performance with its distant seats, unpredictable weather, obnoxious traffic jams and packed parking lots. Assuming the neighbor with the video projector is more centrally located than the football or baseball stadium, one might even be able to argue that air pollution would be curbed and gas consumption might be lowered since cars would be driven fewer miles. One might also be tempted to suggest that video projectors could be termed "ecologically advantageous."

Although this might be stretching the point just a bit, the concept of the home entertainment center does invite some interesting sociological and psychological speculation. The idea of bringing people together for a non-stressful and enjoyable sharing experience seems to be advantageous and a step in the right direction in our increasingly mobile society which has suffered such tremendous alienation and fragmentation of home, family and community — primarily due to the impact of television and the car. Of course, you shouldn't need an expensive $3,000 video projector to accomplish this; a simple pot luck dinner could be even more effective. But, if technology can bring people together who otherwise would not make the effort, then let's use the technology rather than do nothing.

As with any standard TV set, the large-screen TV projector can easily be coupled with any home VCR simply by connecting the VCR up to the projector's VHF terminals or the special video inputs on certain better projectors. Even without the video recorder, you can tune in any broadcast program on your projector, but you are limited to the daily diet of garbage commercials and inane TV shows that make up much of the programming. Of course, with a VCR, you can use your automatic timer to record "cream of the crop" TV specials and shows at whatever obscure hours they might be broadcast. This gives you a much greater choice over your programming. And you can wonderfully skip over the commercials by fast-forwarding the VCR.

The really exciting potential of your home entertainment center becomes apparent when you connect the stereo system to your projector and also realize that libraries of videotapes will soon be available. They will feature vast catalogs of movies, sports, how-to subjects, video art, travel, musical entertainment, etc. Special computer cable TV hookups are already installed in test markets which can deliver educational/reference/voting and other special events and computer programming data to your home screen. Of course, "more is not necessarily better" so there needs to be a lot of thought about the usefulness and human impact of such technology.

At present, you can play the sound from your home VCR or video projector through your stereo system quite easily by connecting the AUDIO OUT or LINE OUT from the VCR or projector to one of the AUX IN plugs on your stereo. The result is much greater realism and fidelity of sound than the TV set is capable of reproducing.

Rumor has it and logic dictates that stereo versions of the home VCR will be made available in the near future. It seems that home VCR machines have already been designed for stereo sound, but in keeping with the grand American custom of planned obsolescence, stereo capability for ½-inch VCRs is being kept very quiet at present. Hopefully, current model VCRs can be modified to record and play stereo videotapes when such programs become available.

How Video Projectors Work

Big screen video projectors all work on the same basic principle. They project the picture from a built-in TV set or the video signal from a TV tuner through series of lenses onto a large highly reflective screen.

Thee arc two basic types of projectors, the magnified TV set type and the 2 or 3-tube component color projection type. The magnified TV set type is just an ordinary TV set mounted in a box with a lens that enlarges and projects the TV picture onto a large highly reflective screen. This approach is very inexpensive ($500-$1,500) but never works very well. The image is dark and fuzzy and the colors are very poor. The 2 or 3-tube projection systems, on the other hand, especially the newer ones, produce very bright, sharp and excellent quality images on a large screen. They are also more expensive $2,000-$4,500.

The 2 or 3-tube projection system works by separating the TV picture into its 3 component colors—red, blue and green, amplifying and projecting each color separately through a specially designed tube onto a highly reflective screen, usually 5, 6, or 7 feet wide (measured diagonally). The colors converge on the screen to produce a normal color picture. Because most of the light is projected directly onto the screen instead of being blocked by the shadow mask inside the conventional TV set, the component tube projector systems work much better than the magnified TV set type systems.

Projector Designs

There are two basic designs of projectors—the one-piece kind which combines the projection mechanism and screen into a single unit and a mirror is used to reflect the image onto the screen and the two-piece kind where the projector is located 8 or 9 feet in front of the screen and projects the image onto the screen like a movie projector. Both systems have their advantages and disadvantages. Single unit systems look big and conspicuous and are very difficult to move or transport but eliminate focusing and alignment problems. Two-piece systems are more easily moved but require extra floor space, generally in the middle of the room, and must be properly aligned with the screen. Advent is the major manufacturer of two-piece projection systems with Sony and Panasonic concentrating on one-piece systems.

Brightness and Viewing Angle

Perhaps the most important considerations regarding a projection TV system are the image brightness and viewing requirements of any particular system. All early TV projection systems require a very dark room to produce a good picture, and if you weren't right in front of the center axis of the screen, the picture dropped off rapidly. The newer projectors use improved circuitry and faster and better lenses so viewers can be further to the right or to the left of the center axis of the screen and still see a good picture image. Projectors are always helped by a darkened room and a long narrow viewing environment.

Advent Projectors

Advent Corporation has been the major pioneer in the development of relatively low cost (from $2,500-$4,500), high quality projection systems. The unveiling of the Model 1000A Videobeam in 1975 marked a true milestone in the progress of video technology. Designed for large groups of 20 to 100 people, the 1000A receiver-projector produces a very bright and reasonably sharp picture on a 7-foot, diagonally measured screen.

Priced at around $4,000, the 1000A is too expensive for many home users, and the unit is too big and too complex technically to be practical for most home applications. Realizing this, Advent soon made available two smaller, simpler and less expensive projection systems, the Model 750, with a 6-ft. screen, and the lowest priced Model 710, available with either a 5- or a 6-ft. screen.

In 1978, Advent introduced the Model 760, a significantly improved 3-tube projection system that replaced the Model 750, priced in the $3500 range. The Model 760 is also a 2-piece system consisting of a practical low-profile projector console and a 6-ft. screen. The 760's picture is twice the size and five times the brightness of most single-tube TV set projection systems and twice as bright as the recommended industry standard for movie theatre images.

Advent Model 760

Advent 760

The 760's completely solid state chassis incorporates computer-controlled electronic tuning with keyboard touch and LED channel display. The 5-function wireless remote control unit allows continuous adjustment of the volume and random-access or sequential tuning of 82 broadcast channels. Direct video and audio input and output connectors are provided along with a special audio output for connection to a home stereo system.

In 1979, the Advent Model 760 was followed by the Model 761, a brighter and slightly improved model. Like the Model 760, it also has a variety of inputs for video and stereo equipment interface.

Advent VB125

Also in 1979, Advent introduced their first one-piece projection system, the Model VB125. A low profile 3-tube system, the VB125 is the first projector to mount the major tuning controls on the top front edge of the pull-out drawer. This allows more convenient adjustments of the system. The VB125 also features a computerized digital wireless remote control unit which provides electronic channel tuning, volume and power ON/OFF functions.

The VB125 uses a 5-foot diagonal screen, has very good uniform brightness, a broad horizontal viewing angle and the ability to reject off-axis ambient light. Other very desirable features are a built-in RF selector which allows for easy access to 3 optional video input sources and a high fidelity acoustic suspension loudspeaker for good audio quality. A volume controlled audio output for stereo connection is also included. Price is around $4,000.

One-Piece Systems

The one-piece system began with the Sony and Muntz projectors. The latest refinements of this design are the Panasonic CT-6000V/Quasar PR-6800 and the Sony KP-5000 and KP-7200. The Panasonic/Quasar and Sony KP-5000 projectors have 5-foot screens, and the Sony KP-7200 has a 6-foot screen. All of these systems are very bright, work well even in non-darkened rooms, have a wide viewing angle and produce sharp pictures with good color. All systems also offer multi-function wireless remote control with direct access to any of 82 channels. The units can also be operated by the controls mounted on the front of the cabinet.

The Sony system is unique in that it uses only 2 projection tubes instead of 3, thus simplifying the system somewhat. Direct video inputs are provided, and the screen can be easily removed for transport.

The Quasar projector offers 4 speakers for extended range sound and an attractive solid wood screen enclosure which permits the non-operating set to blend in with the surrounding furniture. All these systems use washable Ektalite screens for good durability and prices are $3,500 to $4,500.

Sony KP-5000

Sony KP-7200

Quasar PR6800QW

Panasonic CT-6000

Widescreen Rear Projection Systems

Quasar "CinemaVision"

Several models of rear screen projection TVs are also available. Panasonic and Quasar are offering several versions of the Model CT-4500 which is a 45-inch diagonal projection design called

"CinemaVision." The system uses 3 tubes, has a wireless remote control, digital channel display, electronic tuning and a stereo-capable two-way four-speaker audio system with separate bass and treble controls. The unit is 27 inches deep and is priced at about $3,500.

Kloss Novabeam

The Kloss NOVABEAM™ is an exciting new projector with picture quality and features comparable to the other top projectors for a considerably lower price ($2,500). The Kloss Novabeam Model One is a two-piece 3-tube system consisting of a compact TV receiver/projector coffee table-like console which houses three newly developed NOVATRON™ projector tubes and all solid state electronics and a free-standing large 6½-foot washable screen.

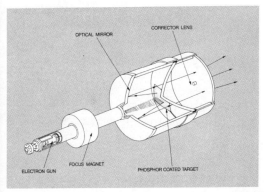

Novatron Tube

Kloss Video Projector

The picture quality of the Novabeam projector is excellent with brightness and image quality that is equal to or better than any other similar projector. The Novabeam uses more efficiently designed projector tubes which improve picture brightness and reduce manufacturing costs. A wireless remote control is also provided. The Novabeam is available on a limited basis through select dealers.

How To Choose A Video Projector

Purchasing a projector can be a tricky business because there are lots of factors to consider.

Price This may be where you start, but price could limit your possible choices. The TV set projector systems range from $800 to $2,400 and the 3-tube systems range from $2,500 to $4,500.

Picture Brightness This is an extremely important criteria as many projectors virtually require a *very* dark room. Any ambient light will cause a great loss of picture quality unless the projector is capable of producing a very bright picture. Generally, the 3-tube systems like those manufactured by Advent and Sony produce a brighter picture than the magnified TV set systems.

Color Intensity and Viewing Angle Most projection systems are a convex screen which makes the picture brighter but highly directional. This means that unless you are close to the center axis of projection, the color intensity and brightness will decrease rapidly. Some projectors have better color density than others and can be viewed at wider angles.

Picture Sharpness Sharpness depends on a number of factors. Brightness and color intensity affect sharpness, and so does the quality of the picture and sound source. For instance, a good antenna or cable TV connection that brings in a strong broadcast TV station which is playing high quality videotape will look much sharper than one which is playing poor quality film or tape. Also, the internal electronics of the projector and how well it is adjusted have a lot to do with the picture sharpness.

Simplicity The one-piece and magnified TV set systems are the simplest. Some 3-tube systems combine an internal TV set with a multitube projection system which greatly simplifies the projector. The more optics and mirrors that are required, the more trouble you will have with alignment of the unit. The two-piece, multi-tube projectors need focusing when moved and may require you to design your room around the projector mechanism.

Screen Problems The most popular screen used is the Kodak Ektalite screen which is very sensitive to any kind of marks, especially fingerprints. If you touch the screen, the imprints are there permanently. This can be a real problem in a home with curious children. Screens can be re-covered, but it's costly. Newer projection systems use washable screens.

Servicing The more complex multi-tube projectors will need more servicing than the simple magnified TV set projectors. So, consider the warranties and servicing availability of a unit before you buy.

The Importance Of Reception Quality

The performance of the projector is absolutely limited by the quality of the picture and sound input source. If you live in a poor TV reception area and don't have cable TV, forget about buying a video projector unless you have or intend to buy a VCR as a program source. A projector magnifies all the garbage, ghosts and interference into gargantuan proportions. Likewise, good quality tapes projected will look much better than poor quality tapes.

The Future Of Big Screen TV

Big-screen TV is here to stay, and home VCRs give it a real reason to exist. The next step forward will be solid state liquid crystal or CCD type one-piece wall screens that will be bright and sharp and not need the bulky tubes and optics used by conventional TV projection systems. We should see these devices in about 5 years, but in the meantime, we can have a lot of fun with the Big-Screen TVs.

14

Videodisc Systems

So far all the video systems we have been discussing are videotape recording and playback systems. Another way to record is on videodiscs. The videodisc recording concept has several unique capabilities. Discs take up very little space and, in large quantities, can be manufactured at a much lower cost than magnetic tape.

Several manufacturers have been working on a number of *playback only* videodisc systems for home use. Unfortunately all the designs so far have been incompatible with each other, but with the videodisc, standardization is a must before it can become a household reality because it is completely dependent on pre-recorded programming.

The videodisc is basically a passive technology similar to a home record player in that it can only play back pre-recorded material—which it can do very well and with a great deal of flexibility, whereas the videotape recorder is an active technology which allows the user to make his or her own programs. Both technologies are very exciting and present an incredibly wide array of possibilities.

Magnavox Videodisc System

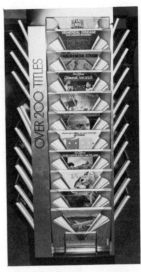

The videodisc is a home entertainment educational technology which offers many unique advantages. The videodisc unit itself is relatively inexpensive—$400-$800 retail price—and 2-hour pre-recorded discs are available at prices of $5.95-$24.95, somewhat more expensive than audio records. The videodisc connects easily to the antenna terminals of any TV set and can play back with better picture quality than a ½-inch home VCR and with better quality than you generally will receive on your TV set from TV broadcast stations or cable television. The disc also has two sound tracks that allow either bilingual sound or question and answer tracks or stereo sound. The high fidelity sound can be channeled through your home stereo system for a really impressive effect.

Types Of Disc Systems

Two types of videodisc systems exist—the OPTICAL type which employs a laser beam to recover the electronically encoded information on the disc and the CAPACITANCE type which uses a stylus and tracking arm like a conventional record player to pick up picture and audio information recorded on grooves on the disc. Neither system is compatible with the other.

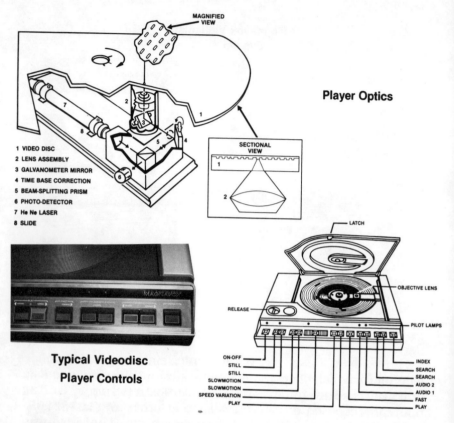

Player Optics

MAGNIFIED VIEW

1 VIDEO DISC
2 LENS ASSEMBLY
3 GALVANOMETER MIRROR
4 TIME BASE CORRECTION
5 BEAM-SPLITTING PRISM
6 PHOTO-DETECTOR
7 He Ne LASER
8 SLIDE

SECTIONAL VIEW

Typical Videodisc Player Controls

LATCH
OBJECTIVE LENS
RELEASE
PILOT LAMPS

ON-OFF
STILL
STILL
SLOWMOTION
SLOWMOTION
SPEED VARIATION
PLAY

INDEX
SEARCH
SEARCH
AUDIO 2
AUDIO 1
FAST
PLAY

Magnavox Videodisc System

The first system actually marketed was the Magnavox "Disco-vision" player introduced in December 1978 in Atlanta, Georgia. Selective test marketing continued throughout 1979 in other parts of the U.S. and several hundred videodisc program titles were also made available. These titles covered subjects such as, popular new and old movies like "Jaws," "American Graffiti," "Saturday Night Fever," "Abbott and Costello meet Frankenstein" and a variety of how-to educational and sports programming such as "Quiche Lorraine and Company" with Julia Child, "The Singing Whales" with Jacques Cousteau, "Swan Lake," "Women at Work," "Gene Littler's Golf," and "Smoking, How to Stop."

Since the Magnavox system is a joint venture with the big entertainment company MGA, it's not surprising that most of the material is comprised of Universal feature movies. As the market expands, the range of program material will also increase.

With a little imagination, one can see the enormous educational possibilities for such a system. The Magnavox system features high fidelity stereo sound, the ability to index each frame of information, rapidly access to any spot on the disc, and replay the recorded material one frame at a time. The device will play the material in slow motion, forward or reverse, changing modes instantly or with variable speed. A golf game could be minutely analyzed for specific details, and educational material could be accessed or repeated in a variety of ways. Each disc can record 54,000 frames of information, which means that entire encyclopedias could be recorded on one disc. It has been said that all the volumes in the entire Library of Congress could be recorded on 100 optical videodiscs.

Since each frame of information on the disc is individually coded and referenced, you can access to a particular single frame accurately and rapidly. The videodisc becomes an electronic book. Because each circular groove holds one entire frame of picture information and the pickup laser does not actually contact the disc, a single frame can be scanned for long periods of time without creating wear on the disc, as would be the case if a VCR would be held in the Still Frame mode.

As we mentioned, the Magnavox system produces high picture quality—330 lines of resolution vs. 240 for a ½-inch VCR. The Magnavox disc spins at 1800 rpms as a tiny .001 watt laser reads the grooves on the disc. Because there is no critical contact taking place, the disc can be handled roughly as the laser will not be affected by fingerprints, smudges or dirt. Unfortunately, the Magnavox system is very complex and sophisticated and thus is expensive relative to other disc systems. Mastering of optical videodiscs is an elaborate process and quality control has been difficult. As a result, the original disc players marketed during 1979 are somewhat experimental in nature and some problems with the units and the discs have occurred, which is to be expected from such a radical new technology.

Magnavox and MCA have entered into a joint manufacturing arrangment with Pioneer to produce industrial disc players ($3,000 each) for companies such as General Motors for use in large scale video networks. Pioneer, though, has introduced a much lower priced consumer version called the VP-1000 "LaserDisc" which is quite impressive and is compatible with the

Magnavox and the Sony optical disc systems. The VP-1000 has many sophisticated features such as a full function wireless remote control, high-speed frame by frame search in forward and reverse, slow motion, frame display, chapter display, stereo sound and the ability to utilize PULSE CODE MODULATION (PCM) high quality audio discs when used with an optional PCM adapter.

Pioneer "DiscoVision"

Pioneer "LaserDisc"

RCA Videodisc

RCA has been working for a long time on a simpler mechanical capacitance-type system which, like the Magnavox/Pioneer system, plays one hour on each side of the disc but uses a diamond stylus for pickup. The RCA system reads the information in the disc grooves on an uncoated disc which rotates at only 450 rpm. The RCA "SelectaVision" system also includes visual search and rapid access features. The visual search allows both forward and reverse scanning of a program at many times normal speed with visible picture.

Unfortunately, the initial RCA system is monaural only, but more expensive stereo models will be introduced later. Since the RCA disc is a contact-type system, the discs and the stylus will eventually wear out. However, RCA says the stylus will last "hundreds of hours" and the disc "one hundred plays." The uncoated disc is inserted into the machine by means of a plastic sleeve. The disc is removed from the machine by reinserting the plastic sleeve. The RCA disc system is very compact, weighs only about 20 lbs., uses easily replaceable off-the-shelf parts and has a price of under $500.

JVC and Panasonic Videodisc Systems

Disc Player   Random Access Control

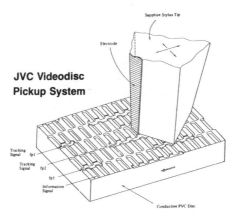

JVC Videodisc
Pickup System

JVC VHD/AHD Videodisc System

Both JVC and Panasonic offer the Video High Density/Audio High Density (VHD/AHD) videodisc system which uses a 10-inch videodisc housed in a plastic sleeve which is inserted into the player unit. The system is stereo and produces a high quality picture and excellent sound. Like the RCA system, the VHD/AHD disc system is a capacitance type system and has a 2-hour playing time capacity. The VHD/AHD disc contains no grooves, revolves at 900 rpms and supposedly can withstand over 100,000 plays. It uses a sapphire or diamond electrode which has a life of over 2,000 hours because it is a non-contact system. The stylus is guided by electronic signals over a series of "pits" engraved in the discs. Because the disc is grooveless, the stylus can move rapidly and randomly thereby allowing normal and high speed forward and reverse motion, still frame and slow motion. The player is an ingenious modular system which can be purchased as a basic unit for simple videodisc playback only or optional random access and PCM modules can be purchased also.

With the addition of the super high fidelity digital PULSE CODE MODULATION (PCM) audio adapter, the disc player will far out perform any conventional audio system including the most advanced metal tape recorders. Since the PCM system is digital, the dynamic range of the system is greatly extended (1 Hz to 20,000 Hz), and the signal can be as high as 90 db signal-to-noise ratio. Price of the basic player is about $500, the PCM decoder is $500, and the Random Access Unit about $150.

Disc Mastering

The optical videodiscs of the Magnavox/Pioneer/Sony system require very complex technology to mass produce. The discs for the RCA, JVC/Panasonic systems, on the other hand, can be pressed out rather easily from a single master rather like the audiodisc manufacturing process. All videodiscs are manufactured from polyvinylchloride (PVC), one pound of which costs about $1.50 and can make 35 discs. Discs weigh much less than film or tape, can be shipped and stored easier, and are less susceptible to damaging environmental conditions. They can be duplicated very easily and rapidly on a large scale, unlike videotape which requires long lengths of tape, an expensive plastic cassette, and necessitates real time copying. (It takes one hour to copy a one-hour videotape.)

Current videocassette technology cannot yet compete with videodiscs in terms of low cost mass duplication. The problem, though, with videodiscs is the fact that you can't make your own copies. The breakeven point for videodisc duplication is around 10,000 copies. This limits the people who can participate in videodisc program production to companies with national marketing ability and large capital. However, it's possible that Co-ops of alternative producers can reach specialized videodisc markets by consolidating capital and expertize and by using imaginative market approaches.

Videotape vs. Videodisc

Will the videodisc kill the home VCR? Very unlikely, because the videodisc has no do-it-yourself recording capability. Certainly sales of videodisc players and discs will far exceed sales of VCRs and pre-recorded videocassettes. Also, many VCR owners will also own videodisc players. Compatible formats are a problem with VCRs, but at present there is no agreement on a standard format for videodiscs either, and videodisc users are limited to whatever programming is available on that particular format.

Videodisc is not considered a mastering format, but rather a playback mass distribution format. Film and videotape will be used as the main mastering format for a long time to come. Anything can be transferred to videodisc, so really, the various mediums can work to each other's advantage.

Videodisc Software

Knowledgeable sources predict a one billion dollar videodisc industry by the mid 1980s and it's certainly possible that future college students will receive a videodisc of a particular college's offering along with an application. Neophyte home auto mechanics will learn to tune an engine by mail order disc, and supplemental sex education at home no doubt will be readily available by videodisc. Hopefully, resourceful individuals will be able to choose from subjects such as preventive health care, do-it-yourself-at home repair and gardening, how to build your own self-sufficient solar/electromagnetic/wind and water energy systems, and programs dealing with living with and within the resources of the land and the environment.

15

The Future of Home Video

Gazing into the home video crystal ball can be a difficult affair—there is so much going on it's hard to obtain a clear image. A simple place to start is with current VCRs and what changes might take place in the immediate future. 1979 has seen the most rapid evolution of VCRs as several basically identical models suddenly exploded into a vast proliferation of very different models even within a given manufacturer. Second generation programmable VCRs and portables became available in 1979 and finally provided the consumer with a complete selection of models to choose from. New lightweight and cheaper color cameras also appeared, further nudging super 8 onto the sidelines. (Kodak has dropped production of its super 8 sound cameras.)

Features to be expected from the home VCRs of the 80's include stereo sound, dolby noise reduction technology (already on some VCRs in the LP mode), better audio specs, "metal tape" VCRs, built-in or compatible VCR switching systems to provide programmable functions with Cable TV/Pay TV/mid-band channels, solenoid controls on all VCRs, automatic program locating and indexing, modular portable/programmable VCRs, LED counters, wireless remote controls, and full fledged editing capability. A number of these features have already appeared on 1979 models.

Considering inflationary pressures and the lack of strength of the U.S. dollar, it's unlikely that prices will drop. Also, as oil, raw materials and energy costs continue to rise the price of VCRs will increase, despite greater number of sales.

Color cameras will most likely show the most radical changes and as solid state Charge Coupled Device (CCD) cameras become perfected, we can look forward to a camera and miniaturized VCR all in one hand-held unit using an advanced computer type bubble memory for image and sound recording.

New Video Recording Formats—The LVR

From the "just when you think you've got it all figured out and they just went and changed everything again" department comes the LONGITUDINAL VIDEO RECORDER (LVR) sometimes also called the FIXED HEAD RECORDER (FHR). Both Toshiba and BASF are busy at work producing this new type of home VCR for 1980 which is considerably smaller, simpler, lighter weight and less expensive ($400-500) than existing ½-inch VCRs.

Toshiba LVR

Toshiba V-200 LVR

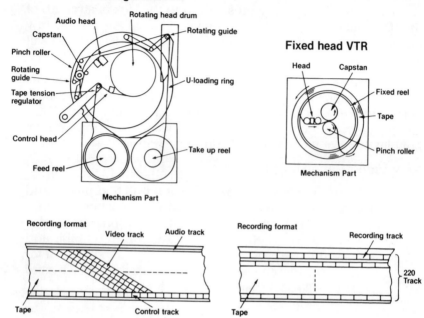

Rotating head VTR

Mechanism Part

Fixed head VTR

Mechanism Part

Recording format

Recording format

The LVR video system uses videotape, but eliminates the rotating head and substitues a fixed video head in its place. The tape travels past the head much more rapidly than in the conventional VCR system. Ordinarily this would be uneconomical because of the amount of tape used, but this problem is avoided by recording multiple tracks on the videotape and switching the head rapidly from track to track like an 8-track audio cartridge. Because an endless-loop single-reel of tape is used, no rewinding or rewind circuitry is necessary. Because of the simpler transport mechanism, the number of parts and the complexity of the mechanism can be greatly reduced.

BASF uses an 8mm size tape which is about half the size of ½-inch videotape and holds 72 tracks. BASF will also have a tiny color camera that will make the complete system one of the smallest video recording systems available.

Toshiba, who developed the world's first helical scan recording system, has also created a revolutionary new fixed-head, fixed-reel VCR. The Toshiba LVR uses a single-reel endless-loop videotape cartridge with a direct capstan drive mounted in

266

the center which gently pulls the tape over the recording and playback heads. This design allows the tape to start up at full speed, stop instantly, and then reverse at full speed, without stretching or breaking. The graphite-lubricated tape is 135 meters long and has 300 separate tracks which are accessed by the head as it moves up and down on the tape, reading one track after another. The tape moves past the head so fast (216 ips) that each track provides only 24.6 seconds of record or play time. Microprocessor controls position the head and step it to the next track when the end of the current track is reached. The head changes tracking rapidly enough so that the change is unnoticeable during a motion sequence, but a slight flash may be noticeable during a still scene. There is no inherent limit to the length of the tape, so it can be made two or four hours long.

Even more remarkable about the Toshiba is the rapid random access capability. Since no track is very far away from the video head at any time, it can select a specific spot on the tape and play it back within a few seconds. Scanning the tracks in forward and reverse is also possible as is complete remote control. Also, because of its simplicity, it uses only 1/3 the parts of a helical scan mechanism. Tape tension is much lower for longer head and tape life despite the faster tape speed. A maximum of 8.4 seconds is needed to access any point on the tape vs. about 1½ minutes rewinding or fast forward winding on a conventional home VCR. All 300 tracks can be digitally indexed and precise tape handling does not distort the tape.

The LVR's smaller size allows considerable reduction in weight and better portability. Most significantly, the Toshiba LVR single-reel cartridge allows high speed duplication of all 300 tracks at once in approximately 3 minutes for a 1-hour tape vs. 1-hour real time required for duplication of a ½-inch video cassette. This means low cost software, especially if the tapes can be produced inexpensively.

Of course, there is no compatibility among LVR systems. Nevertheless, the LVR could present a serious challenge to the videodisc in terms of economics and sophisticated capability. It will be an interesting format to watch as it evolves. Maybe you'd better wait on that videodisc purchase or even wait on that LVR purchase until "video-chip" technology appears and the entire VCR is fit on one electronic micro circuit.

Stereo TV

Obviously stereo TV is the next move in the evolution of television. Japan has had regular stereo broadcasts for years, and the FCC in the U.S. is presently studying stereo and TV standards for broadcasting and TV set manufacturers. The audio portion of television has always been sadly neglected, and as a result, many musicians have purposely avoided performing for television because of such poor sound reproduction. Although FM stereo/TV station joint "simulcasts" have occasionally occurred in the U.S., this approach is too awkward for large scale TV stereo broadcasting.

The broadcasters blame the set manufacturers for poor sound reproduction systems in the TV set and the set manufacturers blame the broadcasting system for transmitting poor quality sound. Now in an age of quality conscious audio consumers with sophisticated audio technology, video projectors and home VCRs, full spectrum stereo audio is a logical next step. TV transmission systems need to be upgraded and TV sets need to be redesigned or add-on stereo units marketed. And both these changes are already underway.

Until full TV stereo broadcasting is accomplished, probably by 1981, some improvement in audio reproduction is possible. Several manufacturers such as Magnavox are improving the sound electronics and speaker systems in their TV sets. Pioneer makes a hi-fi TV tuner, the TVX-9500 ($250) which receives all VHF and UHF channels and can be connected to the auxiliary (AUX) input of your stereo system. The sound section has the same circuitry as in high-end FM systems. Magnavox also makes a similar tuner called the TV 100 which costs $185. Neither of these devices will receive stereo sound, but they will give you improved sound which you can play through your stereo system. You can also merely connect an audio cable from your TV set's earphone jack to the auxiliary input of your stereo system for better sound. Several companies make devices which allow TV sound or VCR sound to play through your stereo system with a simulated stereo effect. (*See Chapter 3, How To Operate Your VCR—Accessories.*)

3D TV

3D TV broadcasting has begun in Australia. The system is compatible with the present TV broadcasting system. In order to view the 3D effect, though, the viewer must wear special glasses.

New Video Information Technologies

There is another area of TV information technology that we haven't yet discussed. These are the special information technologies that deliver a variety of data and programs through special telephone or cable connection to your home TV set.

QUBE

In Columbus, Ohio, the Warner Cable Company has installed a three-way cable system that performs a number of unusual tasks. Besides bringing the usual selection of TV broadcasts to its 13,000 subscribers, the QUBE system offers better reception, 30 channels (including a series of specialized channels), and a unique viewer response device that allows the viewer to talk back to the system.

QUBE CTV System

The specialized channels bring stock market and business news, consumer shopping information, a 12-hour day program channel with no sugar-coated commercials, adult movie films that can be locked out with a special key, first run movies, and a whole variety of interactive education courses programmed by local schools and universities for credit. There is also an interactive video games channel, a five-channel stereo music option, a community access channel and a home security option where sensors installed inside your house warn of fire or burglary and feed this information into the cable system computer which takes the necessary corrective steps (hopefully).

More important, though, than the special channel options is the viewer response device—an electronic box that not only selects the specific channels, but also has five viewer response buttons which permit the viewer to register opinions, answer questions, take tests, and play games. A central computer at the cable TV head-end tallies the viewer's input thereby allowing instant polling of community response. Town meetings have been held whereby the mayor has been able to elicit instant community feedback on a question and NBC used it to analyze viewer response to a speech by President Carter. A number of companies have used the system as a market research tool to gauge consumer preference to product lines or magazine covers, and help price new products. Book stores use the system to allow consumers to order new books from their homes.

The instant response option could be an effective way of sounding out people's thinking on issues of local and national concern. The computer which tallies the vote could also possibly give a demographic analysis. Politicians could present their ideas to the people and receive a response immediately instead of trying to guess how people feel. Fees for the QUBE system are based on a $10.95 montly fee with additional charges added depending on the type of programs viewed. Each viewer receives a statement at the end of the month. (Charges range from $3.50 for a first-run movie to $2–$25 for college credit courses.) So far, the QUBE system has been successful, and plans are to introduce it to other areas of the country soon. Houston, Texas, will be the next test area.

A prospective traveler from London to Sydney can figure plane fares.

One sub-index for NY French restaurants gives location choices.

Viewdata Teletext System

Teletext Systems

Another form of video information is TELETEXT, which looks like a computer readout on the TV screen. It transmits printed pages like an electronic book or, more appropriately, a newspaper, with print, color graphics and diagrams. The only thing it can't transmit is actual photographs or moving pictures. There are several large scale systems of this type operating in England for the consumer and the general public. The most impressive system is called VIEWDATA and works by connecting your telephone line to a modified TV set. It's available to three cities mainly, and was developed by the British Post Office. It transmits a 960 character page (40 characters per line) with 24 lines per page in seven colors. The signals come in from the telephone lines instead of an antenna, and a special decoding module is usually rented. To receive the service, the viewer dials a special number on his phone and leaves the receiver off the hook.

Viewdata sends the viewer information on many different subject areas, such as news, sports, weather, travel, purchasing of consumer goods, classified ads and restaurants. The viewer has access to over 80,000 pages of information and only five or six steps are needed to precisely choose a subject area from over 25,000 sub-topics. The viewer selection process is accomplished by using a unique remote control keyboard like a pocket calculator by which the viewer can interact two-way with the Viewdata central computer.

271

The basic information is provided by newspapers, so a wide variety of classified ads, theater listings, film reviews, travel bulletins, sports reports, etc., are constantly updated. As classified ads become dated they are replaced by new information. The viewer can select restaurants by type or name or geographical location, and even see a menu and prices displayed on the screen with the push of a button. An item can be ordered and paid for by entering one's credit card number into the control device. The TV set acknowledges the entry and displays the delivery date. Up-to-the-minute flight information is provided, and the viewer can make his or her own reservation.

Even more incredible is that the system can work as a calculator and figure our mathematical problems, interest rates, etc., and send a message to someone else. It can work as a telephone system for the deaf. With an add-on telecopier printer, it could deliver mail to your house electronically. A simple audiotape recorder is adequate to record and store the data that is sent over the system.

The cost for such a system is, at present, $2,000 for a modified TV set with decoder device. The decoder, however, home-made quite cheaply and is expected to drop to about $100. There is also the cost of the phone call and the per-page charge of 2–4 cents each. If you had a British modified TV set in the U.S., you could dial England and connect your TV set to the system and receive the visual data, but would have to pay a high phone bill.

Two other Teletext systems are used in England that transmit similar information over the broadcast TV channels instead of telephone lines and code the information in two unused lines at the top of the TV set. These systems are called CEEFAX and ORACLE. The basic home TV set requires a decoder to work, and 800 pages covering 100 different topics are available. These systems are much cheaper than the Viewdata system, but at present are limited to a much smaller information capacity and are not two-way interactive like Viewdata. However, they also provide a wide array of classified ads, restaurant information, sports and other useful data.

Teletext, which is the generic name for electronic information carriers is being considered for implementation in many other western European countries despite resistance by some newspapers. It's only a matter of time before a similar system develops in the U.S., assuming the FCC and American broadcasters don't oppose it. As to the future, new microprocessors will be able to store greater amounts of information less expensively, decoders will become $100 or so, and more channels will be available for such services. Teleprompter Cable Television of New York City at present, can carry 167 TV channels on a single strand of glass fiber-optic material. This means more and more information will be available over the same delivery system.

Is More Really Better?

Certainly, no one lacks access to great amounts of information given the proliferation of electronic and print media. We could argue though, that most of us don't have easy access to truly relevant and practical information. The problem is more of content than quantity. The TV set disgorges great amounts of information, but very little of it is at all really useful to the average viewer. Perhaps this can be changed with more specialized and more innovative information sources like Viewdata or QUBE. With the cost of energy and transportation becoming greater every day, it may soon become prohibitively expensive to drive around town trying to get a reference book from the library, purchase an item at the store, or spend hours at City Hall asking about a water bill. This could all be done from the home cheaper and faster with less use of raw materials and energy. You could completely bypass huge quantities of bureaucratic red tape and long waiting lines because you could get a quick answer from the TV system which might otherwise require days by conventional means.

Also, newspapers and magazines require huge quantities of trees, ink, and great amounts of energy to produce and transport. Then they pile up and have to be recycled or disposed of requiring more energy and use of natural resources. Most readers read only a small portion of a newspaper and the rest is wasted. A Teletext system makes much more sense for applications such as this, although electronics will never replace the ease of reading a paperback book on the beach.

Satellite Receiving Antenna

And Finally—Your Own TV Earth Station

In the not-too-distant future, all the wires and cable TV systems will become obsolete as the broadcasting of electronic information goes on satellites. Each home will have a small two-foot receiving dish mounted on the roof that will be able to receive an unlimited number of clear, powerful signals from broadcasting sources distributed around the world. Japan already has such a system in operation for rural communities and NHK has demonstrated three-foot receivers that would cost $375 when mass produced. Japan's satellite is a U.S. satellite. Such a system in the U.S. is strongly opposed by the network broadcasters and other groups that would like to control the information that for now must travel through wires or over existing channels. It's a situation that's similar to the opposition of U.S. utilities to decentralized energy sources such as solar, because additional alternative sources of energy, in this case, or information, threaten the traditional monopolies.

Personal earth station receivers would enable a person to tune in to the global TV information network easily from just about any geographical location. This would allow lower concentrations of people in overcrowded urban areas. A person could live in his or her remote mountain cabin, receive the New York Ballet, a French lesson from Paris, a philosophy lesson from San Francisco, a newspaper from Los Angeles, or a how-to program showing you how to improve your solar heating system. All this could be received by solar-powered private earth stations. Right now some people are building their own earth stations for several thousand dollars. Soon, Radio Shack will have personal earth stations for about $1,000 fully assembled and ready to go.

A wide range of specialized channels will, of course, be available and even two-way interactive systems will be possible from central locations. Remote communities could discuss health care problems with specialists in urban clinics and special interest groups could interact nationally or internationally from remote locations without traveling long distances. Government bureaucracies and national borders could be circumvented. The technology is here, but sadly, the politics aren't, at least not yet. Air waves don't recognize national and political borders, but people aren't so open minded yet. Nevertheless, TV does have the potential to lead the way to a more advanced planetary consciousness if used sensitively for the good of all people, not just for corporate profits and short-term national political goals.

16

VCR Program Sources

You will soon want to expand the scope of your programming beyond the myopic and saccharine offerings provided by network television. But, since home video is such a recent phenomenon, vast and diverse videotape libraries with programming relevant to the home user are just beginning to come into existance.

However, large videotape libraries do exist for the educational and industrial user because: there has been a strong demand for educational and industrial material over the years; and schools and industry have been able to afford the $120 to $180 for a 30-minute tape and the $1,500 for a ¾-inch VCR. (Most educational/industrial videotapes are 16 mm films that have been dubbed over to videotape.)

These libraries contain a variety of excellent subject content dealing with such topics as meditation, management training, video art, mathematics, speed reading, computer programming, law, psychology, medicine, etc. There are probably over 800 suppliers of prepackaged tape programs, and the number is growing every day. The best way to find out what is available is to write for catalogs. A partial list of educational program suppliers is provided at the end of this chapter.

Home Program Sources

There is also a rapidly growing industry of specifically home-oriented videocassette suppliers. Subjects of interest to home viewers generally include classic and contemporary feature movies, sports, travel and eroticism. A list of suppliers for these tapes is also provided at the end of the chapter. These programs are available primarily in ½-inch Betamax and VHS formats and generally sell for $49.95 per program. Often your local VCR distributor will have several brochures or catalogs of programs.

The Significance Of Home Video

Perhaps the most significant aspect of the home video revolution is that it represents a *decentralization of media*. A powerful, total communications medium is now coming into the hands of the people. Millions of minds have been tethered to the TV networks for so many years that people have had no choice but to ingest a daily diet of relentless, repetitive and inane jabberings. But now we have the option of viewing new kinds of programming that could enrich our lives, if we choose to exercise this option. No longer do we have to suffer the psyche debilitation that comes through constant exposure to American Broadcast Television.

The home video recorder can provide a potential escape route from all those Zippo Soap, Crust Toothpaste, inedible-sugar-coated-crispy-chemical-food-obsessed-sell-anything-to-anybody-for-a-buck Madison Avenue maniacs who seem bent on destroying any semblance of mood in television and annihilating any vestige of intelligence and health in American citizenry. If you don't have the new car, the big suburban home, the gorgeous model housewife or handsome husband, you simply "can't be happy", or so they tell you, though subtly, of course.

And according to the news programs, life is made up of bad news and constant human tragedies. It is, indeed, unfortunate that the eyes of such an influential medium are so darkened that they cannot see the joy, happiness and goodness in life. The broadcasters do the people of this society a great disservice by failing to live up to their responsibility to lead and inspire those millions to whom they speak. Sadly, those millions who listen expectantly every day and night are nothing to the broadcasters but computerized Nielsen ratings.

Perhaps a new generation of video children, inspired by the primitive but powerful video tools coming into their home, will rise to demonstrate what great possibilities television has for the expression of hope, peace, positive thinking and education all of which can lead the planet to new evolutionary peaks.

It seems evident that TV programmers and producers of commercials don't want you to *THINK* because people who think will question, and people who question are apt to want to *change* (read *improve*) things. But, change is essential to growth and evolution, for the alternative is lack of change or stagnation, and stagnation eventually kills and is certainly very boring.

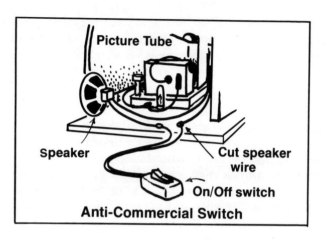

Picture Tube

Speaker

Cut speaker wire

On/Off switch

Anti-Commercial Switch

The TV broadcast structure, as it now exists in the U.S., has no interest in serving the specific needs of segments of the population. But, as the population begins to have its own TV program playback capability, be it through videotape recorders or videodisc systems, an audience will gradually develop for programming that is very diverse, creative and imaginative.

This fertile situation creates conditions under which new filmmakers, video visionaries, artists, actors and actresses, aspiring directors, producers, writers, etc., can flourish and come together to organize and create fresh new media production concepts. These independent production companies will be able to program material on any conceivable subject matter that maybe only 100 people are willing to buy, rent or lease.

The possibilities for teaching how-to subjects are unlimited. For example, the development of tapes teaching all kinds of traditional and alternative health care subjects are inevitable and a must since broadcast TV seems more intent on destroying our health than preventing illness. Tapes on child care, home repairs, starting a small business, women's studies, food preparation, art, culture, history, etc., could be very helpful in one's daily life as well as be interesting, informative and entertaining.

Although the creation of good quality videotapes for large scale distribution does require capital, technical skill, proper equipment, vision, imagination and organization, one does not need to build such large structures as NBC or CBS. It can be done very effectively on a small scale now that sophisticated video equipment is reliable, readily available, and relatively inexpensive.

Since home VCRs are now finding their way into the mainstream of the American consumer system, program listings and catalogs will naturally follow the hardware. The few distributors of movies will soon be dwarfed by large and various groups of independent producers and production companies. Consequently, the home viewer will have a very hard time making choices, but through the amazing electronic miracle of the home videotape recorder, the TV set may at last become an instrument of real education, communication, enrichment and personal enlightenment — a true manifestation of a new consciousness.

Home Program Sources

Agency for Instructional Television
Box A
Bloomington, IN 47401

Aims Instructional Media Services
626 Justin Ave.
Glendale, CA 91201

Allied Artists Video
425 Park Ave.
New York, NY 10022

American Cable Network
701 So. Airport Rd.
Traverse City, MI 49684

American Educational Films
132 Lasky Drive
Beverly Hills, CA 90212

American Poetry Archives
San Francisco State Univ.
1600 Holloway Ave.
San Francisco, CA 94132

Arts Communications
14 East 11th Street
New York, NY 10003

Blackhawk Video
1235 W. 5th St.
Davenport, IA 52808

Blue Sky Productions
Box 548
Santa Fe, NM 87501

Campus Film Distributors Corp.
Steve Campus Prod., Inc.
2 Overhill Rd.
Scarsdale, NY 10583

Cinema Concepts, Inc.
91 Main St.
Chester, CT 06412

Club Video
886 Northeast 79th St.
Miami, FL 33138

Columbia Pictures
Videocassette Services
1325 S. Arlington Hts. Rd.
Elk Grove Village, IL 60007

Dana Productions
6249 Babcock Ave.
No. Hollywood, CA 91606

DeMaio Film Service
2757 Balboa Dr.
Dubuque, IO 52001

Earth Energy Media
P.O. Box 188
Santa Barbara, CA 93102

Educational Dimensions Group
P.O. Box 126
Stamford, CT 06904

Electronic Arts Intermix, Inc.
84 Fifth Ave.
New York, NY 10011

Encyclopaedia Britannica Educational Group
425 No. Michigan Ave.
Chicago, IL 60611

Entertainment Video Releasing
1 East 57th St.
New York, NY 10022

Films Incorporated
1144 Wilmette Ave.
Wilmette, IL 60091

Fotomat Corp.
64 Danbury Rd.
Wilton, CT 06897

Golden Tape
336 Foothill Rd.
Beverly Hills, CA 90210

Great Plains Nat'l. ITV Library
P.O. Box 80669
Lincoln, NE 68501

Hollywood Film Exchange
1534 No. Highland Ave.
Hollywood, CA 90028

Home Theatre Movies
Suite 705
9255 Sunset Blvd.
Los Angeles, CA 90069

Home Cinema Service, Inc.
266 Pearl St.
Hartford, CT 06103

Home Video, Inc.
231 E. 55th St.
New York, NY 10022

Indian Univ. AV Center
Bloomington, IL 47401

Ivy Video
165 W. 46th St., Suite 414
New York, NY 10036

Lifestyle Home Video
P.O. Box 16508
Columbus, OH 43216

Magnetic Video Corp.
23434 Industrial Park Court
Farmington Hills, MI 48024

Manpower Education Inst.
127 E. 35th St.
New York, NY 10016

Maryland Center for Public Broadcasting
Owings Mills, MD 21117

Network for Continuing Medical Education
15 Columbus Circle
New York, NY 10023

Niles Video
1141 Mishawaka Ave.
South Bend, IN 46615

Nostalgia Merchant
6255 Sunset Blvd., Ste 1019
Hollywood, CA 90028

Perennial Education, Inc.
1825 Willow Rd.
Northfield, IL 60093

Phoenix Films, Inc.
470 Park Ave. South
New York, NY 10016

Portable Channel
8 Prince St.
Rochester, NY 14607

Public Television Library
475 L'Enfant Plaza, SW
Washington, DC 20024

Pyramid Films
P.O. Box 1048
Santa Monica, CA 90404

Reel Images, Inc.
456 Monroe Turnpike
Monroe, CT 06468

Sports World Cinema
P.O. Box 17022
Salt Lake City, UT 84117

Show Tapes
888 NE 79th St.
Miami, FL 33138

Texas Instruments Learning Center
P.O. Box 5012, M/S 54
Dallas, TX 75222

Thunderbird Films
P.O. Box 65157
Los Angeles, CA 90065

Time-Life Video
Time-Life Bldg.
Rockefeller Center
New York, NY 10020

Trainex Corporation
P.O. Box 116
Garden Grove, CA 92642

Trans-American Video, Inc.
1541 No. Vine St.
Hollywood, CA 90028

TVX
1643 No. Cherokee Ave.
Hollywood, CA 90028

University of California
Educational Television, EMR
San Francisco, CA 94143

VidAmerica
P.O. Box 2041
Latham, NY 12111

Videocassette Rentals
12011 Wilshire Blvd.
Los Angeles, CA 90025

Videolearning Systems, Inc.
10 Presidential Blvd.
Bala Cynwood, PA 19004

Video Tape Network
115 E. 62nd St.
New York, NY 10021

Visual Information Systems
15 Columbus Circle
New York, NY 10023

World Symposium on Humanity
P.O. Box 1925
Hollywood, CA 90028

World Television
1204 W. 27th St.
Los Angeles, CA 90007

WNET/13 Media Services
356 W. 58th St.
New York, NY 10019

Program Catalogs:
THE VIDEO SOURCE BOOK
from: National Video Clearinghouse
Box 3
Syosset, New York 11791

Educational Program Sources

Academy Films, Inc.
P.O. Box 38753
Hollywood, CA 90038

Agency for Instructional Television
Box A
Bloomington, IN 47401

AIMS Instructional Media Services, Inc.
626 Justin Avenue
Glendale, CA 91201

Alternate Media Center
NYU School of the Arts
144 Bleeker Street
New York, NY 10012

Broadside Video
Elm at Millard
Johnson City, TN 37601

Cable Network TV
12636 Beatrice Street
Los Angeles, CA 90066

California Video Resource Project
S.F. Public Library — Civic Center
San Francisco, CA 94102

Association for Educational Communications and Technology (AECT)
1201 16th Street, N.W.
Washington, D.C. 20036

Campus Film Distributors Corp.
2 Overhill Road
Scarsdale, NY 10583

CitySlick c/o Tom Klinkowstein
106 Clarendon Street
Syracuse, NY 13210

Double Helix
390A North Euclid
St. Louis, MO 63108

Educational Resources Foundation
2627 Millwood Avenue,
P.O. Drawer L
Columbia, SC 29250

283

Electronic Arts Intermix
84 Fifth Avenue
New York, NY 10011

Electronic University
Box 361
Mill Valley, CA 94941

Encyclopaedia Britannica
Educational Corporation
425 North Michigan Ave.
Chicago, IL 60611

Environmental Communi-
cations
62 Windward Avenue
Venice, CA 90291

Exec-U-Service Associates
P.O. Box 2214
Princeton, NJ 08540

Films for the Humanities,
P.O. Box 2053
Princeton, NJ 08540

Full Circle Media Archive
Box 4370
Boulder, CO 80302

Global Village Video
Resource Center
454 Broome Street
New York, NY 10012

Golden Tape
341 Foothill Road
Beverly Hills, CA 90210

Great Plains National ITV
Library
University of Nebraska
P.O. Box 80669
Lincoln, NE 68501

Index Video Exchange
P.O. Box 699
Port Townsend, WA 98368

Integrative Learning
Systems, Inc.
326 West Chevy Chase
Drive, No. 11
Glendale, CA 91204

Intercollegiate Video
Clearing House
P.O. Drawer 33000R
Miami, FL 33133

Management Video Publi-
cations, Ltd.
Box 369, Toronto-
Dominion Centre
Toronto, Ontario M5K 1K8
CANADA

Media Bus, Inc.
Maple Tree Farm
Lanesville, NY 12450

Media One
P.O. Box 1031
Belmont, CA 94002

Medical Educational
Resources Program
Indiana University School
of Medicine
1100 West Michigan Street
Indianapolis, IN 46202

Microcampus
206 Civil Engineering Bldg.
No. 72
University of Arizona
Tucson, AZ 85721

National Audiovisual
Center
GSA
Washington, D.C. 20409

Northeast Video and
Sound, Inc.
287 Kenyon Street
Stratford, CT 06497

Public Service Video
New City School
Park Square Court
400 Sibley
St. Paul, MN 55101

Portable Channel
8 Prince Street
Rochester, NY 14607

Pyramid Films
P.O. Box 1048
Santa Monica, CA 90406

Readers Digest Television
Division
200 Park Avenue
New York, NY 10017

Roundtable Films, Inc.
113 North San Vincente
Beverly Hills, CA 90211

Seton Hall University
Women and the Law
(Distribution)
School of Law
1095 Raymond Blvd.
Newark, NJ 07102

Smith-Mattingly
Productions, Ltd.
310 South Fairfax Street
Alexandria, VA 22314

Southern Educational Com-
munications Association
928 Woodrow Street
P.O. Box 5966
Columbia, SC 29250

Sports World Cinema
P.O. Box 17022
Salt Lake City, UT 84117

S/T Videocassette
Duplicating Corp.
500 Willow Tree Road
Leonia, NJ 07605

The Humanist Alternative
923 Kensington Avenue
Buffalo, NY 14215

The Satellite Video
Exchange Society
261 Powell Street
Vancouver, B.C. V6A 1G3
CANADA

Time-Life Multi-Media
Time-Life Bldg.
Rockefeller Center
New York, NY 10020

Turtle Island Media
Endeavors
Box 4094
Aspen, CO 81611

TVTV
Box 48-455
Los Angeles, CA 90048

Varjradhatu
111 Pearl Street
Boulder, CO 80302

Videoplay Merchandising
333 West Lake Street
Chicago, IL 60606

Videotakes
P.O. Box 578
Cuba, NM 87013

Video Tape Network, Inc.
115 East 62nd Street
New York, NY 10021

Washington Community
Video Center
P.O. Box 21068
Washington, D.C. 20009

William R. Ewald, Jr.
The Next Fifty Years
1730 K Street, N.W.
Washington, D.C. 20006

WNET 13 Media Services
356 West 58th Street
New York, NY 10019

GLOSSARY

AAE Automatic Assemble Editing.

AC Alternating Current. Standard 120 V 60 cycle (Hz) USA household current. Also called LINE VOLTAGE. VTRs and cameras often use the 60 Hz as a horizontal sync reference.

AEF Automatic Edit Function. An automatic assemble editing feature found on JVC and Panasonic ¾-inch portable VCRs.

AFT Automatic Fine Tuning.

AGC See Automatic Gain Control.

ALTERNATIVE TV Non-conventional TV programs and production processes.

APERTURE The lens opening, F stop or iris which determines the amount of light that enters the camera.

APLD Automatic Program Locate Device. An automatic electronic indexing system used on certain VCRs, such as the Sharp VC-6700.

ASPECT RATIO The ratio of the height to the width of a television picture, which is 3:4.

ASSEMBLE EDITING "Add Editing." A new video or audio sequence that is consecutively added to a previously edited scene.

AUDIO Sound portion.

AUDIO CUE A sound that is used to "tag" or denote an upcoming production event.

AUDIO DUB The recording of sound only, without disturbing the picture.

AUDIO HEAD A magnetic recording head that records or plays back sound.

AUDIO IN Audio Input Jack.

AUDIO LIMITER An electronic circuit which adjusts or limits the audio or video intensity to a preset level.

AUDIO MIXER A device that allows the simultaneous combining and blending of several sound inputs into one or two outputs.

AUDIO OUT Audio output jack.

AUDIO TRACK The portion of the videotape that stores the sound.

AUTOMATIC EDITING CON—TROLLER An electronic programmer used in conjunction with editing VCRs to facilitate editing.

AUTOMATIC GAIN CONTROL An automatic circuit that controls the audio or video intensity during recording.

AUTO SEARCH CONTROL An optional remote control unit used with certain industrial VCRs.

ALC Automatic *Level* Control (same as AGC).

ALC Automatic *Light* Control. A circuit in the camera which automatically compensates for changes in light intensity.

AUXILLARY Line Level (low Impedence) audio input. Cannot be used as a microphone input.

AVAILABLE LIGHT The amount of light normally present in the environment.

AZIMUTH The angle of a particular recording head.

B-LOAD A type of cassette loading design used in Betamax and Beta VCRs.

BACK LIGHT The light that is present behind the image to be photographed. Can be used to create depth or it can cause severe silhouetting.

BACKSPACING The process of rewinding the tape slightly in preparation for an edit.

B&W Black and White.

BARN DOORS Adjustable shades on the top and sides of lights which allow the light beam to be widened or narrowed.

BETACORD Sanyo home VCR

BETAFORMAT Toshiba home VCR.

BETASCAN A rapid or variable-speed forward and reverse tape shuttle process used by Beta VCRs.

BETA-2 Sony 2-hour ½-inch videocassette recorder.

BETAVISION Sears home VCR.

BLACK Horizontal and vertical sync information without picture information.

BNC A professional type bayonet video connector.

BOOM A long arm or device used to suspend a microphone or camera over the action.

BROADCAST TV A type of programming and bureaucracy that produces TV programs specifically for over-the-air broadcasting.

BURN A permanent image which persists in the same position on the target of the camera tube.

CABLE TV Television signals transmitted primarily by cable instead of antennas.

CAMERA CHAIN *See Film Chain.*

CAMERA CONTROL UNIT (CCU) An external electronics package required to operate the camera.

CANNON CONNECTOR An audio plug, also called XLR plug.

CCD Charge Coupled Device

CAPSTAN A roller and rotating shaft in the VTR that is motor-driven and determines the speed at which the tape is moved through the VTR.

CAPSTAN SERVO a precise speed control system used in VCRs.

CARBON BACKED A type of videotape with a carbon backing.

CARDIOD A type of microphone that has a heart-shaped pickup pattern.

CATV Cable TV.

COLOR TEMPERATURE A measure of the temperament of light as measured in Degrees Kelvin. (OK).

CCTV Closed Circuit Television. Any self-contained, non-broadcast TV system.

CHANNEL A specific band or frequency assigned to a radio or TV station.

CHROMA (CROMINANCE) The hue or saturation (intensity) of color.

CU Close up.

CUE A warning or indication of an event that is about to take place.

CUE CHANNEL An audio track on the videotape that contains cueing information.

CUT Stop action or make an edit.

CHROMIUM DIOXIDE A magnetically-sensitive coating on videotape.

CLEAN EDIT A perfect undistorted transition from one scene to another.

C-MOUNT Standard screw-in 16mm lens-mount found on most video cameras.

COAXIAL CABLE COAX. The standard single-ground, single-conductor cable which is used for most video connections. Technically referred to as 75 ohm Type RG-59U cable.

COLOR DISSECTOR TUBE A camera tube capable of separating an image into red, blue and green color values.

COLOR LOCK A circuit that stabilizes the color hues during playback.

COLOR PHASE The timing relationship of the color signal. The correct color phase will produce the correct color hues.

COLOR STRIPE FILTER A color filter placed on the front of a camera tube to permit recording of a color image.

COLORIZER Device that produces electronically-generated color.

COMPOSITE SYNC The complete sync containing both horizontal and vertical sync signals.

CONDENSER MICROPHONE A high-quality microphone that uses condenser plates to produce sound. Condenser mikes contain built-in amplification and require batteries.

CONTRAST RATIO The degree of difference or ratio between the light and dark areas of the scene.

CONTROL TRACK The portion of the tape containing the speed control pulses.

CONTROL TRACK HEAD The head which records or plays back the control track pulses.

CONTROL TRACK PULSES Speed control pulses created by the VTR.

COMPATIBILITY The ability of one piece of equipment to interface with another (interchange-ability).

COSMIC INTERFERENCE Influences generated from sources not normally perceived by the senses.

CRT Cathode Ray Tube. The vaccum tube used in all TV sets.

CROP The cutting off of picture elements by the camera framing.

CROSSTALK The undesirable interference created by one track on another.

—D—

db *See decibel.*

DC Direct Current. Electrical current that maintains a steady flow and does not alternate.

DECIBEL A subjective measure of sound volume or strength.

DEFINITION The degree of detail or sharpness in a TV picture.

DEPTH OF FIELD The area of the picture between the closest and farthest objects that are in focus — varies with the F stop.

DEW VCR indicator that signals excessive amounts of moisture in the environment and shuts off the VCR.

DIE-CAST CHASSSIS A VCR construction design which utilizes a single-piece annealed aluminum chassis on which are mounted the critical VCR components.

DIFFUSION SCREEN A wire mesh screen placed in front of a light to reduce and soften the intensity of the light.

DIRECT DRIVE A motor drive that is mounted inside a cylinder which eliminates the usual rubber belt drives. This system produces a more stable picture.

DIRECTIONAL A narrow pickup pattern used by microphones.

DISSOLVE The gradual fading in of one picture while the other fades out.

DOLLY The movement of a camera toward or away from an object. Also the wheeled apparatus on which the camera is mounted.

DOUBLE AZIMUTH A playback technique used by the Sony SL-5800 to produce a stable and clear still frame picture.

DRAMATIC A video production of a theatrical nature.

DROPOUT A loss of picture signal during tape playback—displays as a black or white streak in the monitor.

DROPOUT COMPENSATOR (DOC). An electronic circuit that replaces a missing line of video information (dropout).

DUBBING The duplication of a videotape or the addition of new audio information to the tape.

DYNAMIC MICROPHONE A pressure sensitive microphone.

—E—

ECU Extreme Close Up.

EDITING The process of putting into a predetermined sequence the various segments of master tapes.

EDIT PREVIEW An editing feature found on sophisticated automatic editing systems which allows the operator to preview his edit before it is actually made.

EDIT REHEARSAL The second generation edited tape which has become the "new" master containing all the edited scenes in the proper sequence.

EFP Electronic Field Production.

EJ Electronic Journalism.

ELECTRONIC EDITING The process whereby a videotape is edited.

ELECTRONIC VIEWFINDER A small 1.5-inch to 5-inch TV monitor which allows the camera operator to view the scene his camera is shooting.

ELECTRET CONDENSER MICROPHONE A very sensitive microphone that requires a power supply in the microphone and needs a battery.

ELECTROSTATIC FOCUS A newer type of camera tube that is able to focus the electron beam without using heavy deflection coils.

ENG Electronic Newsgathering.

ERASE HEAD A magnetic head that erases electronic information on the tape.

ESSENTIAL AREA That area of a graphic which the camera will see. *See Aspect Ratio.*

ESTABLISHING SHOT Initial camera scene, usually a long, wide shot that allows the viewer to orient himself to the location of the program.

E TO E Electronics to Electronics; a method of analyzing the output of a VTR relative to its input.

ETV Education Television.

EXTENDED LENGTH TAPES The tape is made thinner, thus permitting more tape to be wound on a reel.

EXTERNAL MICROPHONE A separate microphone that is not built into the camera.

—F—

FADE A gradual change in the picture or sound intensity.

FADE TO BLACK The picture is faded out until the screen is dark.

FERRITE A brittle, high frequency response material that is used to make video heads.

FIELD One half of a complete TV scanning cycle, or 261½ scanning lines; one half of a 525-line TV frame.

FILL LIGHTS Supplementary illumination used to eliminate shadows.

FILM CHAIN An optical system whereby an image from a film or slide projector is transferred to a video camera for use in a television system.

FIRST GENERATION The original recording of master tape.

FLAGGING Skew induced distortion produced at the top of the playback picture.

FLUID HEAD TRIPOD A tripod head that moves very smoothly.

FOCAL LENGTH The distance between the center of a lens and where the image is in focus, usually the image plane or the camera tube's target plate.

FOLLOW FOCUS The continual adjustment of a lens to keep the subject in focus when the subject and/or the lens are moving.

FOOTCANDLE FT-c; generally measured in LUMENS per square foot. The amount of illumination from 1 international candle falling on a 1-square-foot surface at a distance of 1 foot.

FORMAT A limited grouping of similar VTRs, such as in ½-inch and ¾-inch or small-format and large-format.

FRAME A complete TV picture of 525 horizontal lines which is composed of 2 scanned fields of 262½ lines each. One complete TV frame is scanned in 1/30th of a second.

FRAME RATE The speed at which the frames are scanned— 30 frames a second for video.

FREQUENCY The number of times a signal vibrates per second.

FREQUENCY RESPONSE The ability of an electronic device to reproduce a wide range of frequencies.

F-STOP A calibration on the lens that indicates the width of the opening of the lens iris.

"F" TYPE CONNECTOR A metal screw-like connector used for connecting a VCR to an Antenna or CTV system and to a TV set.

FLYING ERASE HEAD An extra video head which erases video information during the editing process.

—G—

GAIN The level of signal amplification.

GEL CELL A lead gelled acid battery.

GENERATION The number of copies away from the original.

GENLOCK The locking up of the sync generators of one or several sources to a main sync source; i.e., a VTR locked up to an SEG.

GLITCH Any picture distortion.

GRAY SCALE The various shades of gray in a TV picture which corresponds to color.

GUARDBANDS The separations between the video tracks on the tape.

—H—

HARDWARE Equipment.

HEAD An electromagnetic device that records or retrieves information from magnetic tape.

HELICAL SCAN A helix-like method of recording video information on tape in which the signal is recorded diagonally in adjacent strips. Also called SLANT TRACK recording.

HERTZ (Hz) Cycles per second.

HIGH DENSITY Videotape that packs more magnetic particles per square inch on the tape.

HIGH IMPEDANCE (HI-Z) 800-10,000 ohms. *See Impedance.*

HORIZONTAL RESOLUTION The number of vertical lines that can be perceived by a video camera in a horizontal direction on a test chart.

HPF Hot Pressed Ferrite.

—I—

IC Integrated Circuit.

IMAGE ENHANCER Any electronic device that sharpens the picture.

IMAGE PLANE The point at which the image is focused — generally at the camera tube target plate.

IMAGE RETENTION "Lag," the tendency of the Vidicon tube to retain the image.

IMPEDANCE The resistance of a component to the flow of electrons—rated in ohms (Ω). Generally expressed as high impedance (hi-Z) or low impedance (low-Z).

IN-CAMERA EDITING The technique of editing as you shoot.

INPUT SELECTOR The VCR control found on VHS machines that selects the proper recording input, i.e. Camera, VTR, TV Tuner.

INSERT EDIT The additon of new video and/or audio information into any point of a pre-existing video program.

INTERNAL INTELLIGENCE The inherent energy-bonding pattern present in all matter.

IPS Inches Per Second — Tape speed or writing speed.

IRIS The adjustable opening on the lens which controls the amount of light entering the camera.

—J—

JACK A plug or connector.

JOY STICK A lever that controls the position of a special effect on a screen, or the motion of tape on a VTR during the editing process.

JVC Japanese Victor Corporation.

—K—

KELVIN (K) The unit of measurement which denotes the temperature of light-expressed in °K.

KEYING The matteing of one picture over another.

KEY LIGHT The light used for primary illumination of a scene.

KILOHERZ (KHz) Thousand cycles.

KINESCOPE "Kine," the process or recording a TV picture by photographing a TV set with a film camera.

—L—

LAG See Image Retention.

LAP DISSOLVE See Dissolve.

LAVALIER Small microphone worn around the neck.

LED Light Emitting Diode.

LENS SPEED The ability of the lens to collect light. A "fast" lens collects more light than a "slow" one.

LEVEL The average intensity of an audio or video source.

LIGHT LAG The tendency of a camera tube to retain its image causing a ghost-like effect.

LIGHT LEVEL The intensity of the light as measured in foot-candles.

LINE IN An audio input for other VTRs or an audio mixer.

LINE LEVEL 600 ohms; a low impedance signal.

LINE OUT Audio output.

LIVE The process of transmitting a program the instant it is taking place.

LOCK OUT LOGIC An electronic circuit which prevents the improper sequencing of controls.

LONG LENS A telephoto lens.

LONG SHOT A shot from a great distance.

LOW IMPEDANCE 30 to 600ohms—See Impedance.

LOW LIGHT Subdued illumination.

"LP" Long Play.

LUMEN See Footcandle.

LUMINANCE The photometric brightness or radiance of a light source.

LUX An old-fashioned measurement of light. One Ft-c =10.76 lux.

—M—

MACRO LENS A lens that is capable of close-up focusing.

MASTER TAPE FOOTAGE The original tapes.

MATCHING TRANSFORMER An electromagnetic device which equalizes the impedance of 2 different input sources.

MEDIUM SHOT The camera view between a close up and a long shot.

MEGAHERTZ (MHz) Million Hertz.

MEMORY ACCESS See Auto-Search Control.

MIL A unit of measurement used for denoting videotape width, 1 MIL = .001 inch.

MINI-PLUG A small audio plug, sometimes called a Sony plug.

MISTRACKING The picture distortion caused by improper tape-to-head or tape-path contact.

MIXED FIELD TRINICON A type of Vidicon tube used by Sony.

MIXER A device that combines and blends 2 or more audio or video sources.

M-LOAD A type of cassette tape loading mechanism used in VHS VCRs.

MOIRE Herringbone interference patterns in a TV picture.

MONITOR A TV set without receiving circuitry that is used primarily to display video signals.

MONITOR/RECEIVER A dual function standard TV receiver and monitor.

MONOCHROME Black and white.

MOVIEOLA Mechanical device used to edit film.

—N—

NEWVICON TUBE A Panasonic camera tube which has very good sharpness and low light characteristics.

NI-CAD Nickel Cadmium battery.

NOISE Random undesirable picture or sound interference.

NTSC National TV System Committee — USA color TV standard.

—O—

OERSTEADS OF COERCIVITY The measurement of the ability of videotape to store information.

OMNI-DIRECTIONAL A microphone pickup pattern that is sensitive to sounds coming from all directions.

OMNIVISION Panasonic ½-inch VCR.

OPEN-REEL A recording device which uses 2 exposed reels.

OSCILLOSCOPE An electronic device that measures electronic signals. It is used for alignment of video equipment.

OXIDE The magnetic particles that are bonded on the tape.

—P—

PAL Phase Alternation Line — The British-German color TV standard.

PAN The movement of the camera horizontally.

PAUSE A VCR control which momentarily stops the tape.

PEAKS The highest level of signal strength.

PHASE The relative timing of one signal to another.

PHONE PLUG An audio plug with ¼-inch wide connector shaft.

PHONO PLUG RCA audio plug.

PICKUP PATTERN The pattern of sound sensitivity characteristic of a specific microphone.

PORTAPAK A portable video system.

POST PRODUCTION The editing phase of TV program production.

PRE-PRODUCTION Preparation activity that occurs prior to actual shooting.

PRE-ROLL The process of backing-up tapes and VTRs in preparation for an edit.

PROGRAMMABLE VCRs VCRs that allow presetting for automatic recording.

PROGRAM SELECTOR A control on VCRs which selects the VCR output to the TV set.

—Q—

QUADRUPLEX A video recording system that uses 4 video heads and scans the tape at a 90° angle.

QUARTZ LIGHTING Very bright and efficient lighting.

—R—

REEL-TO-REEL *See Open Reel.*

REGISTRATION The overlapping of the red, blue, and green signals to form a correctively colored image.

REMOTE Any program originating outside the studio.

RESOLUTION The amount of resolvable detail in a picture.

RETROFOCUS A lens with close-up focusing ability.

RF Radio Frequency; the range of frequencies used to transmit electric waves.

RF AMPLIFIER An amplifier used for amplyfying RF signals.

RF CONVERTER A device that allows video and audio signals from a VTR to play back on a standard TV set.

RF SPLITTER An inexpensive junction box which divides one RF input into two or more RF outputs.

RG-59U Coaxial video cable.

ROTARY ERASE HEAD *See Flying Erase Head.*

RPM Revolutions Per Minute.

—S—

SATICON A more expensive broadcast-type camera tube.

SCANNING The horizontal and vertical movement of the electron beam in the camera or TV tube.

SEARCH A VCR function which causes it to locate or stop at a particular point on a tape.

SECAM *Sequential Couleur a Memoire;* The French color TV system.

SECOND GENERATION *See Generation.*

SEG Special Effects Generator.

SHOOTING RATIO The amount of tape recorded relative to the amount of tape actually used.

SHOTGUN MIC A highly sensitive microphone which allows good sound pickup from a great distance.

SIGNAL Information transposed into electrical impulses.

SIGNAL LEVEL METER An indicator used on certain color cameras to show the correct degree of video signal relative to the amount of light.

SIGNAL-TO-NOISE RATIO The amount of visible "snow or noise" in a given picture relative to the actual picture signal. The *higher* the signal-to-noise ratio, the better the picture.

SKEW The tape tension.

SKIP FIELD RECORDING A recording process whereby only one field is reproduced twice instead of reproducing both fields and interlacing them.

SLANT TRACK *See Helical Scan.*

SMALL-FORMAT The small width videotape equipment such as ¼-inch, ½-inch, ¾-inch and 1-inch.

SOFTWARE Program material.

SOLENOID An electromagnetic circuit control system.

SOLID STATE Electronic circuitry that contains no vacuum tubes.

"SP" Standard Play.

SPECIAL EFFECTS GENERATOR (SEG). A video-mixing device that allows switching between several cameras and a variety of special effects such as dissolves, fades, inserts, wipes, etc.

SPEED SWITCH A VCR control that selects one of 2 different speeds.

STAND BY An indicator found on BETA VCRs which signals that the tape is being loading.

STRAIGHT DUBBING. The process of simply copying a tape in real time without editing.

STRIPE FILTER A single color camera tube where sequential stripes on the face of the tube are used to derive the red, blue, and green and luminance signals.

SUPER-SCAN Toshiba high-speed fast forward tape mode.

SWITCHER A video switching and mixing device.

SYNC Synchronization; the timing pulses that drive the TV scanning system.

SYNC GENERATOR An electronic circuit which produces the sync pulses.

—T—

TAPE CONFIGURATION Tape packaging.

TAPE PATH The path of the videotape past the heads.

TARGET The image forming area of the camera tube.

TEARING A picture condition when the image is displaced horizontally, usually caused by horizontal sync problems.

TELECINE *See Film Chain.*

THIRD GENERATION 2 copies removed from the original tape.

TIGHT SHOT Close-up.

TIME BASE CORRECTOR A device that electronically corrects the mechanical and electronic errors created by a VTR.

TIME BASE STABILITY The degree of error or lack of error in sync pulse timing during VTR playback— generally caused by VTR mechanical irregularities.

TRACKING The position of the video head over the recorded signal on the videotape.

TRACKS The area on a tape which contains the video or audio information.

TRANSFER A dub or a copy.

TRINICON TUBE A Sony color tube which contains 3 color filters.

TRUCK The lateral movement of the camera dolly.

—U—

UHF Ultra High Frequency; a connector used for video cables.

U-LOAD A type of cassette loading mechanism used in U-Matic VCRs.

U-MATIC Sony trademark name which refers to the ¾-inch videocassette format VTRs.

UNI-DIRECTIONAL A selective microphone pickup pattern.

UNIVICON-2 Low light sensitive Vidicon tube used by Toshiba.

—V—

VARIABLE FOCAL LENGTH LENS *See Zoom Lens.*

V-CORD II Sanyo 2-hour ½-inch videocassette recorder.

VCR Videocassette Recorder.

VERTICAL INTERVAL SWITCHING New picture information is edited in during the blanked out period of the TV scanning process thus producing an invisible switch to the new picture.

VHS Very High Frequency.

VIDEO Picture information; television equipment; also the concept of television used as a decentralized personal medium of visual expression.

VIDEOCASSETTE One reel of videotape and one empty reel in a closed plastic container.

VIDEODISC Video information recorded on a large round disc.

VIDEO DISTRIBUTION AMPLIFIER An amplifier that strengthens video signals.

VIDEO GAIN The amplitude of the video signal.

VIDEO IN A video input.

VIDEO OUT A video output.

VIDEO SWITCHER *See Switcher.*

VIDEOTAPE RECORDER An electromechanical device that records pictures and sound on magnetic tape.

VHS Video Home System.

VIDICON TUBE An inexpensive and versatile electronic pickup tube used in TV cameras.

VIDSTAR A VCR manufactured and distributed by JVC.

VIGNETTING An effect produced by a lens when it fails to cover completely the camera tube image area.

VOICE OVER (VO). A spoken message or narrative added to the picture.

VU METER Volume Unit meter; measures audio levels.

VTR Video Tape Recorder.

—W—

WATT A unit of electrical power.

WHITE BALANCE The video camera's ability to produce white correctly.

WHITE SET The adjustment of a color camera to correct white reference.

WIDE ANGLE LENS A lens with a very wide angle of view.

WIPE A special effect whereby one image "pushes" another image off the screen.

WRITING SPEED The resultant difference between the speed of the video heads and the speed of the videotape.

X1 One-hour play/record mode on Beta VCRs.

X2 Two-hour play/record mode on Beta VCRs.

—Y—

Y The symbol for the luminance portion of a color signal.

—Z—

ZOOM LENS A lens that is capable of varying its focal length and serving as several lenses at once.

Popular Video Books

Ancona, Barry, ed. THE VIDEO HANDBOOK (SECOND EDITION). N.Y.: Media Horizons, Inc. 1974.

A more generalized and commercial (watch out for the ads!) synthesis of video equipment, production, distribution and reference materials. Offers basic and practical information for the layperson.

Bretz, Rudy. HANDBOOK FOR PRODUCING EDUCATIONAL & PUBLIC-ACCESS PROGRAMS FOR CABLE TELEVISION. Englewood Cliffs, N.J.: Educational Technology Publications. 1976.

Concerned with the nature and development of the Cable TV Industry, this is a pertinent reference for those seeking to distribute video programming through such systems.

Burrows, Thomas and Donald Wood. TELEVISION PRODUCTION: DISCIPLINES & TECHNIQUES. Dubuque, Iowa: W. C. Brown Publishers. 1978.

Designed as a teaching text and includes all introductory aspects of TV production. Though not specifically aimed at the home video user, but rather at institutionalized recording situations, this is comprehensive and easily understandable.

Kirk, David. AUDIO & VIDEO RECORDING. London: Faber & Faber. 1975.

A somewhat outdated guide to audio and video equipment, with a nice focus on audio: how components function, what they are designed to do, audio mixing, monitoring, editing, effects and transcription.

Kybett, Henry. VIDEO TAPE RECORDERS. Indianapolis: Howard Sams. 1978.

Explains, in simple language and diagrams, the helical VTR system: how it works, its principles, circuitry and mechanics. No production techniques.

Lachenbruch, David. VIDEO-CASSETTE RECORDERS: THE COMPLETE HOME GUIDE. N.Y.: Everest House. 1979.

An up-to-date, all-around guide aimed at helping the new videophile select, buy and maintain his/her VCR. No discussion of techniques or production. Helpful for buying and setting up your new VCR, but the rest is up to you.

Marsh, Ken. INDEPENDENT VIDEO. San Francisco: Straight Arrow Books. 1974.

Although chapters on video equipment, production and aesthetics are included, a great emphasis is placed on the intricate electronic technology behind the video revolution.

Mattingly, Grayson and Welby Smith. INTRODUCING THE SINGLE-CAMERA VTR SYSTEM. N.Y.: Charles Scribner's Sons. 1973.

Aim is to help VTR user comprehend and apply basic skills and knowledge, and exercises are included. For half-inch b&w VTRs with some information concerning portapacks.

Murray, Michael. THE VIDEOTAPE BOOK. N.Y.: Bantam Books. 1975.

Concrete examples—by people who have done video work—make this a particularly comforting guide to using your VCR camera. This is for portapack systems, but there is little information on actual equipment.

Robinson, Richard. THE VIDEO PRIMER. New York: Quick Fox Publications. 1974 (Revised 1978).

A classic how-to introductory text to small format video. This book is used extensively by media workshops. It's a bit wordy, but provides a good detailed overview of video equipment operation and production techniques.

Top Value Television. THE PRIME TIME SURVEY. San Francisco: Top Value TV, Inc. 1974.

A production narrative by the experimenters who wrestled some prominence for independent videorecording with insightful videotape portraits of the Democratic and Republican Conventions in 1972. Theirs is an activist approach to changing TV, and what they've learned is useful for anyone questioning the possibility of amateur fame.

Weiner, Peter. MAKING THE MEDIA REVOLUTION. N.Y.: Macmillan. 1973.

Easy reading, a wealth of illustrations and comprehensive coverage of the various facets of videotape recording make this an excellent manual for a beginner video user. The exploding nature of video technology, however, renders it somewhat outdated.

Westmoreland, Bob. TELEPRODUCTION SHORTCUTS. Norman, Oklahoma: Univ. of Oklahoma Press. 1974.

Simplified procedures and techniques, aimed specifically at videotape recorders, are offered for the educator who must produce professional-quality programming with a minimum of equipment and less-than-ideal conditions.

Willener, Alfred et. al. VIDEOLOGY & UTOPIA. London: Routledge and Kegan. 1976.

The socio-technical potentials in videotaping are seen as a new "Third Culture," in which independent production will constitute the "Post TV Age." The theoretical discussion is supplemented with video techniques, but this is not for the absent-minded reader.

Williams, Richard. TELEVISION PRODUCTION: A VOCATIONAL APPROACH. Salt Lake City: Vision, Inc. 1976.

A production manual which is easy-to-read, aimed at beginning videophiles and is geared for small studio working conditions.

Videofreex. THE SPAGHETTI CITY VIDEO MANUAL. N.Y.: Praeger Publishers. 1973.

This focuses on video theory, systems, and the basic and not-so-basic maintenance shortcuts for troubleshooters who want to become more self-sufficient with their half-inch video hardware. The "spaghetti" refers to wires and cables, the problems with which have caused more than one headache.

Zettl, Herbert. TELEVISION PRODUCTION HANDBOOK. Belmont, CA: Wadsworth Publishing Co. 1968.

The do's and don'ts of television production techniques are outlined here with illustrations in what many critics still consider to be a fundamental manual. As far as aesthetics are concerned, Zettl's SIGHT SOUND MOTION (Belmont: Wadsworth, 1973) is worth investigating.

DIRECTORIES, AIDES

FOCAL ENCYCLOPEDIA OF FILM & TELEVISION TECHNIQUES. N.Y.: Hastings. 1969.

Incorporates history, operation, editing and troubleshooting of video equipment. The 10,000 references, indexed thoughtfully in the back, assume an elementary knowledge of video by the reader.

Gadney, Allen. CONTESTS, FESTIVALS & GRANTS. L.A.: Festival Publications. 1978.

A massive listing of 1800 International film, video, photography TV-Radio broadcasting, writing, poetry, playwriting and journalism contests, festivals and grants, this directory is perhaps the best single source for such information. This very well cross-indexed reference work contains the addresses, dates, deadlines, entry requirements, judging criteria and relevant statistics for each festival and contest. *Available from VIDEO-INFO PUBLICATIONS, P.O. Box 1507, Santa Barbara, CA 93102 for $15.95 (shipping and postage included, Calif. residents add 6% tax).*

Huffman, Kathy, ed. SOUTHERN CALIFORNIA VIDEO RESOURCES DIRECTORY 1979. L.A.: Some Serious Business, Inc. 1979.

The first section lists independant producers; the second, institutions which support video work; the third, businesses and individuals which supply technical skills, editing services, sales and rentals. This is designed for Southern California and is most useful for individuals living in that area.

Legge, Nancy, ed. ACCESS: FILM & VIDEO EQUIPMENT, A DIRECTORY. N.Y.: Publishing Center for Cultural Resources. 1978.

Divided into 6 US regions, and listed alphabetically by state and institution, this is a fruitful list of facilities from which video equipment can be borrowed or rented. Media artists who are seeking production and post-production equipment/facilities should undoubtedly consult this work.

Melton, Hollis, ed. A GUIDE TO INDEPENDENT FILM & VIDEO. N.Y.: Anthology Film Archives. 1976.

A foundation from which the videophile can gather info-sources concerning the hows, wheres and whats of video production, distribution and funding. Arranged in 5 headings: Video-Making, Distribution, Exhibition, Study and Funding, and includes addresses and services of each entry.

Penny, Steve. HOW TO GET GRANTS TO MAKE FILMS. Santa Barbara: Film Grants Research. 1978.

A well-explained introduction to the art of "grantsmanship," this book shows how to go about the process of selecting appropriate film and video grant sources and submitting proper grant applications. The common pitfalls made by beginning grant writers are discussed and much valuable first hand experience is offered by the author along with key addresses and contact information. *Available from VIDEO-INFO PUBLICATIONS, P.O. Box 1507, Santa Barbara, CA 93102 for $14.95 (shipping and postage included, Calif. residents add 6% tax).*

VIDEO AND TELEVISION MAGAZINES:

EDUCATIONAL AND INDUS-
TRIAL TELEVISION
Also VIDEO TRADE NEWS
and VIDEOPLAY REPORT
C.S. Tepfer Publishing Co
607 Main St.
Ridgefield, CT 06877

TELEVISION INTERNATIONAL
P.O. Box 2430
Hollywood, CA 90025

VIDEOCASSETTE AND CATV
NEWSLETTER
Martin Roberts Associates
P.O. Box 5254
Beverly Hills, CA 90210

*PANORAMA MAGAZINE
Box 950
Wayne, PA 19087

*VIDEO MAGAZINE
Reese Publishing Co.
235 Park Ave. South
New York, NY 10003

*THE VIDEOPHILE
2003 Apalachee Parkway
Tallahassee, FL 32301

*VIDEO REVIEW
CES Publishing Co.
325 East 75th St
New York, NY 10021

*of interest to home video enthusiasts

Address of Manufacturers:

ADVENT CORPORATION, 195 Albany St., Cambridge, MA   02139

AKAI AMERICA LTD., 2139 East Del Amo Blvd. Compton, CA 90220

GBC CLOSED CIRCUIT CORP., 74 Fifth Ave., New York, NY 10011

GENERAL ELECTRIC CO., Portsmouth, VA 23705

GTE SYLVANIA, 700 Ellicott St., Batavia, NY 14020

HITACHI SALES CORP. OF AMERICA, 401 Artesia Blvd., Compton, CA 90220

JVC INDUSTRIES INC., 50-35 65th Road, Maspeth, NY 11378

KLOSS VIDEO CORP., 145 Sidney St., Cambridge, MA 02139

MAGNAVOX VIDEO SYSTEMS, 1700 Magnavox Way, Fort Wayne, IN 46804

NORTRONICS CO. INC., 8101 Tenth Ave., Minneapolis, MN 55427

PANASONIC VIDEO SYSTEMS, Matsushita Electric Corp. of America, One Panasonic Way, Secaucus, NJ 07094

QUASAR ELECTRONICS CORP., 9401 West Grand Ave., Franklin Pk., IL 60131

RCA CORP., 600 North Sherman Dr., Indianapolis, IND 46201

SANYO ELECTRIC INC., 1200 West Artesia Blvd., Compton, CA 90220

SEARS, ROEBUCK AND CO., Sears Tower, Dept. 702, 40th Fl., Chicago, IL 60684

SHARP ELECTRONICS CORP., 10 Keystone Place, Paramus, NJ 07652

SONY CORPORATION OF AMERICA, 9 West 57th St., New York, NY 10019

TOSHIBA AMERICA INC., 240 Park Ave., New York, NY   10017

ZENITH CORP., 1100 Seymour St., Franklin Park, IL 60131

Video Accessories Catalogs:

COMPREHENSIVE VIDEO SUPPLY CORPORATION, 148 Veterans Dr., Northvale, NJ 07647

TOTAL VIDEO SUPPLY CORP., 9060 Claremont Mesa Blvd., San Diego, CA 93123

WIDL VIDEO, 5245 West Diversey, Chicago, IL 60639

To Learn More...

If this book aroused some enthusiasm in you to learn more about video, you might want to purchase **The Video Guide,** another excellent book by Charles Bensinger. Now in its up-dated "Second Edition," **The Video Guide** is designed for the serious-minded media student and professionally oriented video person and deals primarily with industrial and broadcast video equipment.

The Video Guide

Second Edition

by CHARLES BENSINGER

Here's what they say —

"A plethora of extremely valuable information can be found in this book."
—**Media & Methods Magazine**

"... is required reading for ITV coordinators, producers, students and others ..."
—**Televisions Magazine**

"Invaluable for use today ... Provides a wealth of detail on equipment operation and application. This is not aimed at technicians, but rather at actual systems users."
—**Mass Media Booknotes**